AARON JAY KERNIS

AMERICAN

Composers

A list of books in the series appears at the end of this book.

Aaron Jay Kernis

Leta E. Miller

UNIVERSITY OF ILLINOIS PRESS
Urbana, Chicago, and Springfield

Publication of this book was supported by a grant from the Henry and Edna Binkele Classical Music Fund.

Supplementary materials, including audio recordings of selected works, can be found on the book's Web site: http://www.press.uillinois.edu/books/miller/kernis/.

Manufactured in the United States of America
1 2 3 4 5 C P 5 4 3 2 1
♾ This book is printed on acid-free paper.

Library of Congress Cataloging-in-Publication Data
Miller, Leta E author.
Aaron Jay Kernis / Leta E. Miller.
pages cm. — (American composers)
Includes bibliographical references and index.
ISBN 978-0-252-03853-2 (cloth : alk. paper)
ISBN 978-0-252-08013-5 (pbk. : alk. paper)
ISBN 978-0-252-09644-0 (ebook)
1. Kernis, Aaron Jay. 2. Composers—United States—Biography.
I. Title.
ML410.K386M55 2914
780.92—dc23 [B] 2013050774

CONTENTS

ACKNOWLEDGMENTS

THIS BOOK WOULD NOT HAVE BEEN POSSIBLE without the enthusiastic cooperation of Aaron Jay Kernis, who not only opened his archive of documents to me but also gave unstintingly of his time for interviews and innumerable email messages. He was frank and forthcoming and, although he read every word I wrote (in some cases several times), he allowed me complete independence in interpreting his works and in covering the successes and challenges in his artistic life.

I owe a great debt of gratitude as well to Kernis's wife Evelyne Luest, to his manager Elizabeth Dworkin, and to those who graciously granted me interviews: Marin Alsop, Michael Barone, Jean-Luc Choplin, Andrew Cornall, Eva Gruesser, Linda Hoeschler, Welz Kauffman, Anna Kruger, Rebecca Miller, James Rushton, Marc Satterwhite, Gerard Schwarz, and Hugh Wolff.

The staff at G. Schirmer were extremely helpful, generously providing me with perusal scores without charge and allowing me to search through their large archive of documents. In particular, I thank Katy Tucker and David Flachs. Similarly, staff members at the New York Philharmonic, the St. Paul Chamber Orchestra, and the Minnesota Orchestra were very supportive in providing photographs, programs, and other materials needed for my research. Katherine Adamov kindly made available copies of the twenty ISCM films, which are now housed at the library of the University of California, Santa Cruz, in Special Collections.

Others whose generosity aided this project include Laura Kuhn of the John Cage Trust, Vivian Perlis at the Yale Oral History Project, Uziel Adini of Gratz College, and pianist Emanuele Arciuli. Several people agreed to read part or all of the text and offered extremely helpful comments; I thank in particular Peter Cole, Elizabeth Dworkin, and the two anonymous readers engaged by the University of Illinois Press.

I was assisted in this project by grants from the University of California, Santa Cruz, Arts Division and Committee on Research, and by graduate students Giacomo Fiore and Jessica Loranger.

AARON JAY KERNIS

I Introduction

"I'M SO PLEASED YOU'RE WRITING ABOUT ME," said Aaron Jay Kernis when I approached him about this book. "My only hesitation is that I feel I should be twenty years older." Indeed, readers may pose the same question: what justifies a book about a composer who is only fifty-four years old?

On the most basic level is Kernis's impressive productivity: the large number of substantial works for forces ranging from solo piano to full orchestra. His current Schirmer catalog lists more than one hundred compositions: a dozen orchestral works (including three large symphonies); another dozen concerti with large orchestra or wind ensemble; a group of works for soloist with chamber orchestra; nearly two dozen compositions for two to six players and the same number of pieces for chorus; fourteen pieces for solo voice accompanied by piano or chamber groups; and a dozen compositions for keyboard. No writing to date has attempted to survey, much less assess, this large body of work. (A catalog of the works discussed in this book appears in the appendix. Selected audio examples, as well as a list of recordings and YouTube excerpts, are included on the book's Web site, http://www.press.uillinois.edu/books/miller/kernis/).

Quantity, however, is but one measure of achievement. In Kernis's case, quality has been repeatedly affirmed by a steady stream of awards and commissions, by the enthusiastic reception from renowned performers, and by the strong response

Aaron Jay Kernis. (Photo by Richard Bowditch. Used by permission.)

his music elicits from audiences. He has already won three major prizes coveted by contemporary composers: the Pulitzer (1998), awarded to U.S. composers; the Grawemeyer (2002), whose compass embraces composers from around the world; and the Nemmers (2012), which honors "classical music composers of outstanding achievement in a body of work and a unique creativity."[1] Other awards include the Rome Prize, a Guggenheim Fellowship, and an NEA fellowship (all in 1984), the Stoeger Prize in Chamber Music (1993), and numerous BMI and ASCAP awards and citations. In 2011 he was elected to the American Academy of Arts and Letters. Commissions have provided continuing support: Kernis has received them from the Koussevitzky and Fromm Foundations; the Dartington, Aspen, and Ravinia Festivals; the Santa Fe Chamber Music Society; the Birmingham Contemporary Music Group; the Orpheus Chamber Orchestra; the American Composers Orchestra; American Public Radio; the BBC Proms; and the Disney Company, to name only a few. Major orchestras have commissioned substantial works or presented their premieres: the New York Philharmonic and the Baltimore Symphony (*New Era Dance*, 1992), the Philadelphia Orchestra (*Color Wheel*, 2001), the San Francisco Symphony (*Colored Field*, 1994), the Minnesota

Orchestra (*Lament and Prayer*, 1995), the Seattle Symphony (*Symphony of Meditations* [Symphony no. 3], 2009), and the St. Paul Chamber Orchestra (*Symphony in Waves*, 1989; Double Concerto, 1996). His works have been played, commissioned, and recorded by esteemed performers such as Pamela Frank, Joshua Bell, James Ehnes, Renée Fleming, Jorja Fleezanis, Truls Mørk, and the Lark Quartet, and they have been programmed by prominent conductors devoted to the music of the United States, including Marin Alsop, Hugh Wolff, and Gerard Schwarz.

A comprehensive and broadly based examination of the composer's stylistic development is thus long overdue. Information about Kernis's music must currently be culled from newspaper and magazine articles, liner notes, and a variety of short interviews, which necessarily address a limited repertoire or time span. In contrast, this book surveys Kernis's work over the course of more than thirty years, detailing both continuities and changes in his musical language. It is based on published documents, personal interviews, and materials in Kernis's extensive collection of programs, reviews, and correspondence. The composer has read the manuscript, clarifying factual details and offering compositional insights but never attempting to censor the contents.[2]

During the period covered in this text, Kernis's compositional path has shown decided—and sometimes quite deliberate—turning points. Early works based on strict structural foundations gave way to less rigid conceptual plans, then to an increased focus on classical influences, and finally to his most recent approach, which is highly intuitive. At the same time, his musical development shows distinctive elements of continuity—the markers that define a composer's personal voice.

The turning points serve to delineate creative periods. Compositions from Kernis's pre-college and college years (through 1983) tend to be process-oriented; he imposed on himself severe rhythmic or melodic constraints sometimes akin to minimalist aesthetics. From 1984 through the beginning of the 1990s, he began to free himself from such restrictions. Developing greater confidence in his intuition, he allowed broader conceptual stimuli to guide his creative process, thereby discovering a more personal means of expression. This transformation led him unexpectedly toward Classical forms such as the symphony and string quartet—genres steeped in historical tradition. His *Symphony in Waves* (1989) arose from this new embrace of tradition, as did his first string quartet (1990), in which Kernis integrated his increasingly individualistic voice with forms solidified in the late eighteenth century: sonata-allegro, theme and variations, scherzo, and rondo.

The period from 1991 to 1996 includes two contrasting strands. The most profound works from these years—dark (or at least introspective) compositions punctuated by occasional rays of hope—reflect Kernis's political conscience.

The catalyst for these intense works was his distress over global conflicts: the first Gulf War (Second Symphony, 1991), the war in Bosnia (*Still Movement with Hymn*, 1993), his visit to World War II concentration camps (*Colored Field*, 1994), and the fiftieth anniversary of the Holocaust (*Lament and Prayer*, 1995). Also dating from this period is *Goblin Market* (1995) for narrator and chamber orchestra, whose surrealistic text by the nineteenth-century poet Christina Rossetti describes the near-death experience of a young woman who succumbs to the temptations of demons but who ultimately is saved by the love and bravery of her sister. These emotionally wrenching compositions are balanced by works exuding humor and levity and often owing a debt to popular music and jazz: *New Era Dance* (1992), *100 Greatest Dance Hits* (1993), and the uproarious *Superstar Etude no. 1* (1992).

From 1996 through 2001 a more hopeful spirit began to come to the fore. Here we find Kernis's compositional process motivated by material-driven forms, the building of large structures on traditional bases. Among the most important pieces from this period are the Double Concerto for Violin and Guitar (1996), the second string quartet (1997, which won the Pulitzer Prize), *Valentines* (2000, for Renée Fleming and the Minnesota Orchestra), *Garden of Light* (1999, a Disney commission to celebrate the millennium with the New York Philharmonic), and *Color Wheel* (2001, written for the opening of the Kimmel Center in Philadelphia).

The influences of family find expression in the works from 2002 and beyond: the optimism occasioned by the birth of Kernis's children in February 2003 contrasted with sorrow over the death of his parents in 2004. Judaic influences, which form a consistent strand throughout his oeuvre—and which became particularly prominent in the dark political works of the early 1990s—reappear in this period in the reflective, yet ultimately transcendent poetry of the eleventh-century Sephardic mystic Solomon Ibn Gabirol, which forms the basis for Kernis's Third Symphony. This work, premiered by the Seattle Symphony in 2009, is a composition of Mahlerian proportions: nearly seventy minutes long, it calls for a large chorus and a huge orchestra.

A more universalist approach appears to be guiding Kernis's works since 2011. Gone, for the time being at least, are the references to popular musics and even to Judaic themes. It is too soon, at the time of this writing, to determine whether this trend will continue, but one representative example illustrates the possibilities that might lie ahead: *Pieces of Winter Sky* (2012), Kernis notes, "takes more chances coloristically and formally than any piece since *Colored Field*." The work was one of the finalists for the 2012 Pulitzer Prize.

Although Judaic references and cantorial melodic expression have formed a common trope in Kernis's work (making an appearance as early as his 1981 *Death Fugue*), other consistencies appear as well: his devotion to lyric melodies, often taking the form of scalar themes with leaps at their endpoints and frequently developed through additive processes; his use of rounded formal structures that are, at the same time, marked by a firm resistance to exact repetition; his attraction to ostinato patterns that develop and evolve; his careful placement of points of cadential arrival marking internal sections; his love of lush mediant progressions; his sensitivity to timbre, manifest in inventive orchestration; his devotion to integrating popular (and, most recently, non-Western) musics into classical forms; his grounding in tonality, which is nonetheless contrasted with a dissonant harmonic language; his attraction to lengthy and emotionally reflective poetry, which he often rearranges to create his own narrative; his virtuosic demands on performers—both technical and emotional; and his reliance on visual or literary images as stimuli for himself and his audiences, often reflected in programmatic titles.

A number of reviewers over the years have questioned Kernis's embrace of stylistic diversity. Some critics looking for a consistent voice have been puzzled by his apparent eclecticism. As early as 1996 Bernard Holland raised such concerns in a review in the *New York Times*. "Somewhere behind the Kernis pieces played here must lie a single personality," Holland wrote; but he then praised such breadth of expression: "That pop, rock-and-roll and white-hot late Romanticism can share one mind with such mysterious grace speaks for the breadth of Mr. Kernis's experience and imagination."[3] Nine years later Holland was still marveling about this diversity, now linking it specifically to an "American" worldview: "What marks the American-ness of Mr. Kernis is his manyness. In a society of mixing and clashing cultures, his music leaps athletically from style to style: one moment bitterly avant-garde, the next insouciantly pop; here reticence, there garrulous displays of virtuosity."[4]

What the present book hopes to show are the consistencies that run through Kernis's output, one of which, in fact, is the very eclecticism that has impressed many of his reviewers. Popular and classical inspirations appear not only in different works but also in different sections of the same work, where they do not so much clash as complement one another, linked by the composer's personal language and underlying aesthetic principles. "Many of my young works were a crazy mixture of several things," Kernis told Carlo Boccadoro in 1998. "I had this idea, which still interests me . . . that music should contain everything at the same time. Tonality, atonality, [and] pop-music influences went hand-in-hand with a complex structural planning of overall form, so that in a single work you could find minimalist patterns that turn suddenly into funk, romantic melodies that froze into static sonic strata, very dissonant passages orchestrated in a very pyrotechnical way."[5] Kernis never abandoned this commitment to synthesis, even when he freed himself from the detailed structural planning of his early years. His most recent works continue to integrate diverse elements (the Third Symphony stands as one of the most inclusive, in fact), but over the years he has perfected the art of smoothing the borders and refining the linkages. This variety might even be the secret of his success, mused Benjamin Ivry in a review in the *Christian Science Monitor* in 2002.[6]

Asked in 1999 to characterize his music, Kernis immediately offered the adjectives "colorful" and "dramatic" and emphasized the role of melody and expressivity. "I have a great love for . . . expansive melody, long lines that may not necessarily repeat for quite a while," he said. Indeed, during the composition process, he often sings to himself, an outgrowth of his longtime engagement (as both singer and composer) with vocal music.[7]

The dramatic expression of Kernis's compositions stands in contrast to his unobtrusive demeanor. He speaks slowly, quietly, and thoughtfully. Yet behind the calm exterior lies a powerful musical voice that has created some of the most forceful music of the late twentieth and early twenty-first centuries. Each work, he says, is a transformation, and his task lies in taking his audiences on a journey: "I think of myself as a communicator. Music is my medium, the language I speak in."[8]

2 Learning the Craft

Early Years and Training (1960–1983)

AARON JAY KERNIS WAS BORN on January 15, 1960, in Philadelphia. For the next eight years his family lived in the Olney area in the northern part of the city. His father Frank (1923–2004) was a mail carrier, a job that brought him great pleasure. Kernis recalls, "He loved to talk to people along his route; he loved the outdoors; he loved to walk."[1] Frank Kernis also loved jazz, particularly Sarah Vaughan, Count Basie, and Ray Charles. The family often went to summer jazz concerts (and an occasional Philadelphia Orchestra concert) at Robin Hood Dell. Frank was a quiet man, and Aaron remembers him as being "mostly in the background" while he was growing up. "He had a strange, enigmatic sense of humor, and sang to himself often in his customary cracked voice. He was quiet in his support of me over the years, but believed in what I was doing, whether he understood it or not."

Mildred Kernis (1926–2004), on the other hand, was very involved with her son's schoolwork and started him on his first music lessons. She worked as a business secretary in a small office. Beginning in the 1970s, she became a bank teller and finally the branch's financial services manager. Frank Sinatra and George Gershwin exemplified her musical taste.

The family owned some classical records, but it was Aaron who eventually pushed his parents in that direction. During high school, he dragged his mother

Kernis's parents, Frank (1923–2004) and Mildred (1926–2004) at the time of their wedding in 1949. (Photographer unknown.)

to the Philadelphia Orchestra's Friday matinees. Soon his parents were taking him to evening performances as well. Those he recalls as most memorable were Mahler's Third Symphony, the U.S. premiere of Shostakovich's Fifteenth Symphony, and Bartók's Concerto for Orchestra. (His response to the Mahler: "I felt I had seen God.") Frank and Mildred, in contrast, dozed off during the concerts, and he recalls that "half the audience walked out" during the Bartók.[2]

In late 1968 the Kernis family moved to Long Beach, California, in search of better weather.[3] Frank was tired of slipping on the ice. Aaron might not have been too sorry to leave Philadelphia, either. Third grade in Olney with Barbara Donovan apparently had frustrating moments for an artistic child who loved to read and who marched to his own drummer. "Aaron must remember to sit correctly with both feet on the floor," Donovan wrote in the very brief comments on his first report period, and he "must read library books only in his spare time." Furthermore, she stated, "his handwriting should be more slanted."[4] (He apparently conquered the handwriting problem; his musical scores, even in high school, are extremely neat. See figure 1.)

In California the Kernises found a lovely apartment near the Gardenia Freeway,[5] but the relocation didn't last long. By 1970 they had returned to Pennsylvania, this time settling in Cornwells Heights, an unincorporated community in Bensalem Township about fifteen miles northeast of their previous home. The motivation for the return was Aaron's dissatisfaction with the Long Beach public school system (despite his placement in an accelerated program).

Although the stay in California was brief, two experiences created long-lasting impact. The first was a radio broadcast by the Los Angeles Philharmonic; works by Dvořák and Villa-Lobos stayed in his memory for years. So did the singing of a cantor at a large Conservative synagogue. Kernis was particularly moved by his emotional, unaccompanied performance. The cantor's musical worship reinforced Jewish experiences from Philadelphia, where Kernis had attended classes at the School of Observation and Practice run by Gratz College. The program offered cultural and religious activities to Jewish grade-school children throughout the city.[6] Kernis recalls celebrating the holidays there, learning a bit of Hebrew, and singing Jewish songs, all of which intensified his connection to his cultural heritage.[7]

Additional evidence of the influence of Jewish culture during the year in Long Beach is a seven-page fictional essay from February 1969 titled "Israel Adventure, by Aaron Kernis, age 9." It is the tale of young Moshe, who moves to Israel for three months with his family. On his first morning there, he turns on the radio but, of course, finds everyone speaking Hebrew. So he locates a station playing Israeli folk music and begins jumping on the bed in rhythm. Later in the story he dances to Israeli music. The essay, which is meticulously typed with no spelling or punctuation errors (Mom's help is apparent), was likely encouraged by fourth-grade teacher Jean Snyder, who wrote in her end-of-term report that the class "enjoyed the stories and plays" Aaron created—a foreshadowing of his lifelong devotion to narrative.[8] He also read a great deal of poetry in this period, and wrote his own. These childhood interests in literature and dance come to the fore repeatedly in his later artistic creations.

Despite Aaron's developing interest in his Jewish roots, the Kernis family was not particularly observant. Frank and Mildred did not take part in the traditional Sabbath evening home rituals of candle-lighting and Kiddush, and they attended services mainly on holidays. Nevertheless, they instilled in him an awareness of, and pride in, his heritage. "My mother made a particular point of saying, 'Know who you are and where you came from,'" he notes. As Kernis approached the age of bar mitzvah, friction arose within his extended family. Relatives lobbied for the intensive preparation the ceremony would have required, but Aaron was troubled by the prospect of memorized recitation. "I refused to intone the prayers and the Torah portion by rote," he says. In the end, the bar mitzvah ceremony never took place.

Before the move to California, Mildred had arranged for some voice lessons for Aaron. (To this day he is puzzled by her motivation, since there were no other musicians in the family.) And in Long Beach he learned the basics of the flute and the clarinet. But only after the family's return to Pennsylvania did his involvement with music begin in earnest. He attended two different middle schools (the family moved to a new house in 1972).[9] Concert programs from March and May 1972 list him as singing in the junior high school choir at Cecelia Snyder Middle School, and one from December 1972 records his playing violin in the orchestra at Neil A. Armstrong Middle School. During the seventh grade, Mary Jane Scholl, a freelance music teacher, started Kernis on the violin. She also introduced him to some basic concepts of music theory and elementary composition—writing simple counterpoints (melodies to bass lines and vice versa) and four-part chorales—which eventually led him into free composition and his first instrumental pieces. Kernis subsequently took some private violin lessons but never became very proficient. "I wasn't much of a success as a violinist," he told Joshua Kosman in 1999. "The problem was that I sounded so dreadful I couldn't stand to hear myself play. And none of my teachers ever helped me figure out how to get a good sound."[10] Nevertheless, he did achieve enough technical competence to act as the leader of the second violins in a concert of Baroque music at Bensalem High School in November 1974 and as concertmaster of the school's moderate-sized orchestra during the 1976–77 academic year.[11]

Kernis also began to teach himself piano "by sight-reading all the music [he] could get [his] hands on."[12] He convinced his parents to purchase a three-octave electronic organ, then a Farfisa electronic keyboard (preferred by a number of rock musicians during the 1960s), and finally—in what was a significant expense for the family—a large Baldwin upright piano, which they bought at Wanamaker's Department Store. He still owns that instrument today. "My interest in music became so intense that I started to read book after book on the subject," he noted in a 1977 biographical sketch.[13] He was particularly drawn to texts about orchestration and contemporary music, areas of inquiry he augmented with a new-found devotion to record collecting.

During high school Kernis studied jazz keyboard harmony at Temple University. He also took private piano lessons there, but after acting as his own teacher for so many years, he had developed enough bad habits that both he and the teacher were frustrated. He regularly sang in middle school and high school vocal ensembles as well as in large regional choral groups that drew students from many schools in the area. Kernis found a supportive mentor in Bensalem High School choral director Donald Thullen, who made him accompanist for the choir, appointed him assistant director of the madrigal singers, and encouraged his interest in composition. He even composed a work for chorus and orchestra, using texts by Langston Hughes and others. Similarly supportive was band director Charles Smith. Kernis learned to play percussion in order to join the band, and he performed on piano in Smith's jazz ensemble.

During junior high school Kernis had also participated in musical theater, playing Pappy Yokum in *Lil' Abner* and Benny Southstreet in *Guys and Dolls*. This interest continued at Bensalem High, where he acted as assistant music director for theater productions. He and his friend Dan Krysty also formed a little garage band. Kernis recalls, "We would both write songs. We would sit in his basement and do multi-track recordings. That's where I first heard Frank Zappa—in Dan's room." Kernis played glockenspiel or "out-of-tune piano," and Krysty "would honk away on the saxophone. It was all good clean fun, and stuff that no one would ever want to hear," he joked years later.[14] His record collection became quite eclectic (among the highlights were Crumb, Cage, Reich, Xenakis, Penderecki, Zappa, jazz, and punk rock), as did his concert preferences, which now included frequent attendance at jazz performances. Among the most influential concerts he attended was one at the University of Pennsylvania by the ensemble Steve Reich and Musicians. "They played the entire repertoire of their breakthrough Deutsche Grammophon box set in the same year it was released," Kernis recalls. He became hooked on minimalism.

In the summer of 1974 Kernis spotted an ad by the Philadelphia Musical Academy (PMA) calling for the submission of original scores by young people. Several pieces were to be chosen for a public reading by the institution's New Music Ensemble.[15] He spent the summer composing Suite for Chamber Ensemble, scored for violin, viola, cello, bass, bassoon, piano, and two percussionists. It was accepted along with the works of five other high school students.[16] In a free performance on Saturday, November 9, Greek composer Theodore Antoniou conducted the work's first section, "Conflicts," which portrays a boxing match. The cello and bassoon are the two opponents; the bass and piano (according to the program notes) are their managers. The other instruments are spectators (see figure 1). The four sections of part 1 combine tonal and atonal elements, a foreshadowing of Kernis's later harmonic language. The main fight between the solo opponents takes place in section 4, "starting with the 'real' music (atonal) and the 'surreal' music (tonal): the former standing for what is actually happening, and the latter comprising what is going on in the opponent's minds."[17] The piece drew from an array of influences, Kernis later said, using "all sorts of extended techniques—rapping on the violins, and some notation that I'd stolen

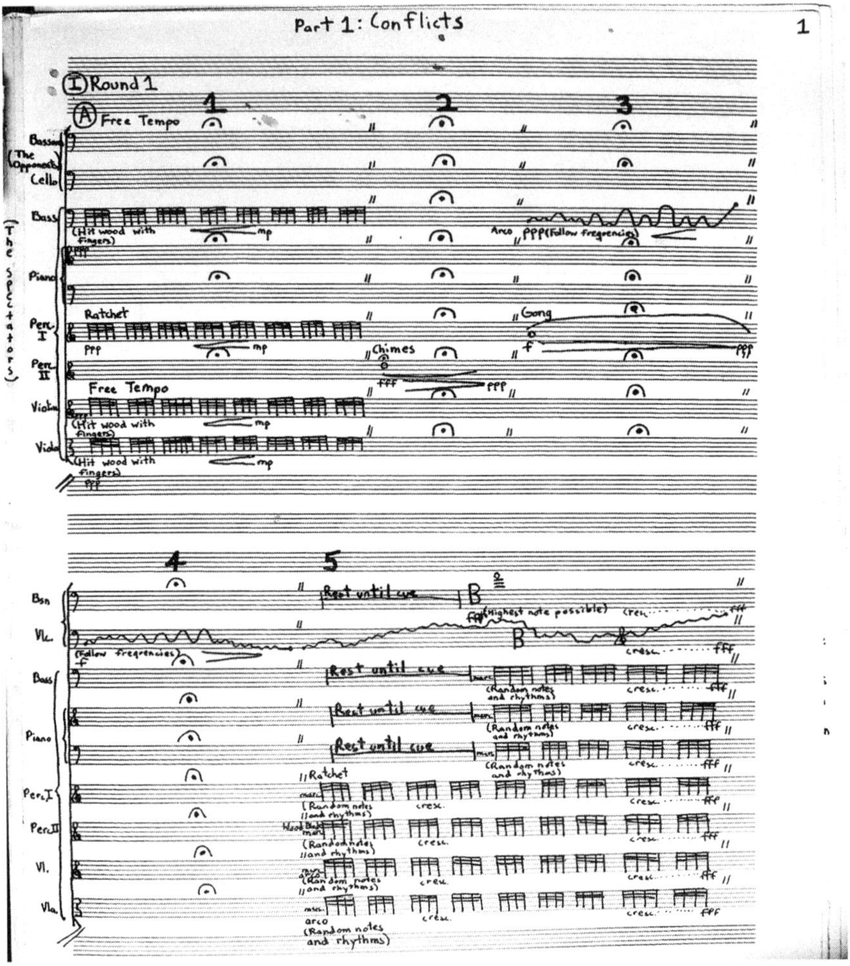

Figure 1. Suite for Chamber Ensemble, I, "Conflicts" (unpublished student work from 1974; reproduced courtesy of Aaron Jay Kernis).

from Penderecki. . . . I'd throw in some . . . rather good Baroque counterpoint all of a sudden and some very extreme gestures which I still remember as being very funny."[18]

After the PMA event Kernis began composition lessons with Antoniou that were sporadic but that nevertheless set him on a disciplined course of study. The experience also solidified his determination to pursue a career in composition.

Two months after the PMA open reading, Kernis wrote a paper for his high school English class titled "The Life of the Composer." He opened with the recognition that a composing career constitutes a "hard struggle" between "personal satisfaction" and financial strain, and then quoted the words of pianist Rosina Lhévinne as found in the introductory chapter of Alan Rich's *Careers and Opportunities in Music*: "He who aspires to a career in music must face one question of paramount importance, and that is whether music is so essential to his spiritual and artistic nourishment that it simply has to be his life's work. . . . Only if the answer to this searching question is an unquestionable Yes should he seriously plan to enter music as a profession."[19] Such dedication, Kernis explained in the essay, can sustain a composer "even though he may be knocked down by his problems" and can provide the strength to persevere "until his means of writing and playing music become more accessible to the public." The essay, though clearly a youthful work, nevertheless shows a surprisingly realistic assessment of the difficulties of a career in composition. The comment about writing music "accessible to the public" is also telling: Kernis's primary aim was then, and continues to be, meaningful communication with his listeners.

Following closely on the heels of the PMA event came a scholarship to the Pennsylvania Governor's School of the Arts, a six-week summer program at Bucknell University. During his attendance there in 1975, Kernis again interacted with Antoniou. After the summer program he began private lessons at Temple University with Joseph Franklin, director of the avant-garde ensemble Relâche. Franklin remembers Kernis's dedication: in order to get to his lessons each week Aaron and his mother rode two buses and then took the elevated train twenty miles. A composition lesson became an all-day affair.

Antoniou introduced Kernis to principles of twelve-tone composition and good voice leading (using Ernst Křenek's *Studies in Counterpoint* and the second volume of Paul Hindemith's *Craft of Musical Composition*). Franklin, on the other hand, tried to ground him in "the inner workings of traditional harmony and counterpoint."[20] For Kernis, however, their most important influence was the window they opened into new developments in composition: Antoniou's avant-garde "extended instrumental techniques and open, aleatoric" forms, and Franklin's "musical mobiles."[21] Franklin recalls with a good deal of modesty the lessons he provided. "For two years Aaron visited me once each week, bringing his dense but elegantly designed musical ideas in for my analysis and opinion. It was hard for me to really guide him as a composer since I discovered immediately that he had much more natural talent than me."[22]

Kernis's single-minded commitment to music inevitably exacted a toll elsewhere: he received consistent *A*s in English but somewhat lower marks in other academic subjects. The situation was clearly time-limited rather than ability-limited. Using standard IQ testing procedures of the time, the "Brief Psychological Report" issued by school officials pegged his "mental age" on April 9, 1976, at 20 years 6 months (four years older than his chronological age and in the top 2.3 percent of the population). More important, the testers noted that he initiated activities and responded quickly and that his "problem solving behavior" was both persistent and eager.

Franklin ultimately judged himself inadequate as a teacher. Years later he wrote: "After a while it was clear to me that Aaron needed to move on, he needed someone with a larger musical vocabulary than I had to decipher all the notes he was committing to paper. One day I told him to leave, find someone else outside of Philadelphia. He was stunned at my directness, I think, but eager to accept the challenge."[23]

Kernis graduated from Bensalem High in June 1977. At the ceremony, a senior vocal ensemble, accompanied by piano, performed his arrangement of David Gates's song "If," originally released in 1971. Three months later, Kernis enrolled at the San Francisco Conservatory of Music. There, in his second semester, he found a new mentor: John Adams.[24]

College: The San Francisco Conservatory and the Manhattan School

By the time Kernis left for college in the fall of 1977, he had already won awards in composition from the National Federation of Music Clubs (NFMC) for "Two Sonnets" (for mezzo-soprano and piano) and the choral works "Little Tree" and "Madrigal," and from BMI for the ensemble work *Geometrics*, whose movement titles are shapes (see figure 2).[25] He was the youngest of the thirteen BMI award winners in 1977 from a pool of more than five hundred entrants. Kernis also submitted *Geometrics* to the NFMC, where it prompted judge Stanley Austin, a faculty member at the College of New Jersey, to write two full pages of comments. "At times I get the feeling you have tongue in cheek," he wrote, anticipating the humor that would appear in many of Kernis's later works. Austin complimented the piece's "colorful, at times experimental orchestration" (a foreshadowing of numerous similar comments in future years) and concluded with a piece of personal advice: "I expect you to grow rapidly because this is excellent work. Never take comment from anyone as negating your own convictions. Beethoven stuck

Figure 2. *Geometrics* (student work from 1976–77; reproduced courtesy of Aaron Jay Kernis).

by his beliefs and look what happened." Kernis, as we will see, never wavered from that advice.

During his college years Kernis received additional recognition as a student composer: a first prize from the NFMC for his Fantasy for Flute and Piano and another from the Pennsylvania Federation of Music Clubs ($15) for Four Miniatures for Two Alto Saxophones; the runner-up and finalist places in composition contests sponsored by the Tucson Flute Club (1978) and the Lancaster (Pennsylvania) Orchestra (1981); and another BMI award in 1983 for Music for Trio (Cycle IV).

Although Kernis loved San Francisco and many aspects of the conservatory's program, this second move to California proved even shorter than the first. After one year he transferred to the Manhattan School. The problem was not Adams, whose music and teaching inspired him and who was personally supportive. Nor was it specific courses; he now reflects that counterpoint with Elinor Armer and Schenkerian analysis with Joan Gallegos were the most valuable classes he took during his entire college career. They helped him hone his awareness of structure and counterpoint. He also values his piano studies with Scott Foglesong, who worked with him to develop color and line in his phrasing. Rather, Kernis's dissatisfaction with the conservatory arose from his need for more structured guidance (he found the West Coast too "laid back" and "could sense a better match in the potential for creative intensity in the East") and from his disinclination to work with Andrew Imbrie, who would have become his composition teacher had he continued in the program. Kernis visited Imbrie at his home one day and played various original works for him. Imbrie complained that the music was too static. Kernis sensed that Imbrie was both uninterested in and unsympathetic to minimalism—a style that was increasingly absorbing Kernis's attention as he looked for ways to make use of repetition and slow-paced harmonic change. Looking back on this experience, he now feels that his reaction to Imbrie probably reflected a growing confidence to follow his inner voice "without compromise."

At the Manhattan School Kernis first studied with Charles Wuorinen, whose complex structuralism, stimulated by serialist principles and mathematical theories, could not have been further removed from the minimalist-inspired, eclectic, and tonally inspired aesthetic of Adams. "I was terrified of Wuorinen," Kernis recalls. "He was asking me questions about music I couldn't answer yet, [questions] that frustrated and challenged me."[26] Despite his terror, Kernis now considers that year as one of the most important in his development. "Wuorinen didn't really like the kind of music that I wanted to compose," he recalls; yet "he helped me clear several problems concerning form." And he spurred Kernis to explore new and different solutions to those problems. He "really made me jump," Kernis says.

In their discussions of minimalism, Wuorinen remarked that he "wished that repetitive music had dramatic change." That idea resonated with Kernis's own inclinations; in fact, he had found it one of the most attractive aspects of Adams's music. "It was with great excitement that I came to know those early works of Adams's," Kernis remarked in 1992, works in which Adams "was . . . pushing past Minimalism's inherent boundaries, molding its steady state, no-beginning-no-end quality into music with sensual surfaces and dramatic shapes that reflected romantic emotionalism."[27] The model of these early Adams pieces continued to guide Kernis's approach to using elements of repetition for years to come. As we will see, he soon began implementing strict structural processes, but these restrictions actually helped him realize the developmental aesthetic that Wuorinen advocated. Under his guidance Kernis composed *Six Fragments of Gertrude Stein* (for soprano and flute), which he now considers his opus 1. It features a mixture of pitch-centric and atonal languages—a compositional strategy to which he has returned over the years.

For the remaining two years at the Manhattan School Kernis worked with Elias Tanenbaum, who gave him a great deal of freedom to explore his own artistic inclinations. Among the works he completed were *Stein Times Seven* (1980), which was recognized with "special distinction" by the NFMC, *Meditation (In Memory of John Lennon)* (spring 1981), and Music for Violin and Orchestra (his senior thesis). Although Kernis eventually rejected the last of these pieces, he later incorporated its six-minute first movement into his first major orchestral work, *"dream of the morning sky."*

Stein Times Seven, for five-part chorus, soloists, and piano, exemplifies both the process-oriented, minimalist-influenced style Kernis was exploring during his college years and his commitment to introducing elements of change into the most rigid procedural strictures. It also contains a number of personal stylistic traits that have stayed with him to the present day, notably, mediant progressions, linear melodic lines, varied repetition, and tonal centricity within a dissonant harmonic context.

As table 1 shows, each movement of this work is tonally centered, although Kernis's language does not follow traditional principles of functional harmony.

The opening choral movement is based on simple expansion outward from the central C♯ as well as consistently accelerating rhythmic motion. The finale is fugal. Neither movement, notes Kernis, would have been possible without his counterpoint classes in San Francisco.

The five solo movements explore various types of ostinato structures in the piano. The third is the most restricted: the piano's two-chord, single-measure pattern appears fifty-six times without change. The vocal line, on the other hand, is free,

TABLE 1. *Stein Times Seven*, movement list

Movement no.	Scoring	Tonal center/basic scale
1	5-part *a cappella* chorus	C♯ minor
2	Soprano and piano	A♭ major
3	Tenor and piano	B♭ lydian
4	Soprano and piano	E major, but ending in G
5	Baritone and piano	E♭ major
6	Alto and piano	C♯ minor
7	5-part *a cappella* chorus	d minor to F major

beginning in a restricted range and gradually expanding in terms of both absolute pitches and increased rhythmic activity. Its phrases lengthen in the middle of the movement and then shorten again toward the end. In the fifth movement Kernis restricted the piano part to two mediant-related chords: E♭9 and G♭9. The piano's rhythm increases in complexity in the middle, then returns to simplicity at the end.

In the fourth movement the pianist plays with the right hand only, articulating an unbroken rhythm of ten sixteenth-notes per measure (figure 3). The even-numbered notes are identical, thus forming, in effect, an interrupted drone. Two basic ostinato patterns form the core material of the movement, featuring as drone tones E and D♯, respectively (table 2).

The second and sixth movements each build in density, the sixth ending at its point of greatest complexity, the second reaching its densest moments in the middle. The form of the sixth movement, shown in table 3, demonstrates the rigor of Kernis's method but also his preference for irregularity, often, in vocal works, driven by the structure of the text. The ostinato in all cases is two measures long.

The second movement shows a similar additive procedure and irregularity. In the beginning section (mm. 1–21), the right hand plays steady eighth-notes in various compound meters, starting with a single pitch, A♭, and then expanding to chord tones or adjacent pitches: A♭–C, then G–A♭–C, then G–A♭–C–E♭, then F–G–A♭–C–E♭. This additive expansion coordinates directly with Stein's text: "Little by little two go if two go three go if three go four go." The number of notes in the right-hand part corresponds to the numbers in the text. In the central section of the movement (mm. 22–50), the ostinato moves first to f minor and eventually to D♭ major—two mediant progressions. The last eleven measures retrace in reverse the pattern of the first twenty-one, ending, as the movement began, with the single A♭. In all of these movements, the voice part provides a freedom that counterbalances the rigors of the accompaniment.

Figure 3. *Stein Times Seven* (1980), mvt. 4, beginning. (Copyright © 1980 by Associated Music Publishers, Inc. International Copyright Secured. All Rights Reserved. Used by Permission.)

TABLE 2. *Stein Times Seven*, summary of movement 4

Musical section	Ostinato pattern number	Drone pitch	Number of pattern repetitions
A	1	E	10
	1, plus an added note on the downbeat of the first and fourth patterns	E	6
B	2	D♯	10
A'	1, but with an added note on the last beat of each measure	E	9
B'	2, but with an added note on the last beat of each measure	D♯	2
	2, but with G♯ and D♯ changed to G♮ and D♮	D♮	11

TABLE 3. *Stein Times Seven*, summary of movement 6

Musical section	Piano ostinato pattern: number of contrapuntal voice parts	Number of pattern repetitions	Number of measures
1	3 parts (S, A, and B ranges)	5	10
2	4 parts: same ostinato with added part in the T range	3	6
3	5 parts: same ostinato with added part on top	3	6
4	6 parts: same ostinato with added part in the alto range	4	8

Meditation (In Memory of John Lennon) is the earliest of many laments Kernis would write in the years to follow. The stimulus in this case was the tragic assassination of the Beatles singer by Mark David Chapman at about 11 P.M. on December 8, 1980. That night Kernis and his friends wandered with thousands of others in the area where the shooting occurred—the Dakota Building at 72nd Street and Central Park West—overcome by the senseless violence, stirred by the candlelight vigils, and moved by people singing Lennon's "Imagine": "Imagine there's no heaven . . . / No hell below us / Above us only sky / Imagine all the people / Living for today . . . / Nothing to kill or die for . . . / Living life in peace."

A few months later Kernis composed a memorial for Lennon using "Imagine" as the inspiration for a ten-minute elegy for cello and piano. The piece unites minimalist techniques with numerical procedures and includes aural recollections of the song's melody and harmony, so transformed, however, that the original piece is never quoted exactly. Throughout the elegy the pianist plays unvarying half notes—a series of repeated chords, occasionally embellished by shorter notes in the right hand (see figure 4). The cello's vocally inspired part is primarily slow and legato, although occasionally it includes pizzicati to create timbral variety.

In its opening section Lennon's song moves from tonic to subdominant to dominant. Kernis adopted this commonplace progression but stretched it out over nearly five minutes. At the outset, the pianist repeats an E major chord, over which the cello twice articulates the notes of the triad (E–B–G♯) and then plays the rising major third that characterized Lennon's melody (B–D♯). Meanwhile, the pianist's right hand captures, in slow motion, one of the most memorable moments in the vocal line (figure 4, line 3: C♯–D♯–F♯), but, in contrast to his model, Kernis presents these notes in a dissonant relationship to their accompaniment. After

Figure 4. *Meditation* (*In Memory of John Lennon*; 1981), beginning. (Copyright © 1981 by Associated Music Publishers, Inc. International Copyright Secured. All Rights Reserved. Used by Permission.)

three and a half minutes of E major, the piano accompaniment changes to the subdominant and then, after another minute, to the dominant.

Five and a half minutes into the meditation, Kernis makes reference to the most striking harmonic moment of Lennon's song: a mediant progression followed by a half-step rise (in Kernis's version, E–G♯7–A). In Lennon's original the progression appeared at the end of the text line "You may say I'm a dreamer." Indeed, mediant progressions have a particularly dreamy, Romantic quality, characterized by one (or sometimes two) common tones with chromatic movement in the other parts. Although they are traditionally associated with Chopin and Schubert, mediants appear as early as the sixteenth century; many madrigalists of that period used them to illustrate dramatic moments in the text. This progression clearly spoke to Kernis in an emotionally charged way. He used it frequently in later works, and it often serves to gently divert the music to a new tonal direction.

Meditation is constructed using strict numerical processes. The motive E–B–G♯ that opens the cello line appears repeatedly throughout the piece, but with its note-lengths gradually shortened and then lengthened. At the outset, each cello note lasts for twenty half-note beats (see figure 4). After a three-measure interlude the motive recurs with each note held for sixteen beats; then, eleven bars later, it reappears with twelve beats per note. When the harmony changes to A major, the motive returns (as A–E–C♯) with the cello notes shortened to ten beats. Following a brief intervening free section containing cello pizzicati, the harmony changes to B major. The cello notes (now transposed to B–F♯-D♯) are now eight beats long, and at the end of this part (again in E) they are further reduced to four. From there to the end of the piece, Kernis reverses the procedure, expanding the note-lengths to eight, ten, twelve, sixteen, and finally twenty beats, as at the outset.

Kernis was influenced to use this type of process in part by the works of John Cage, particularly pieces such as *Metamorphosis* and *Sonatas and Interludes*, which employ the mathematical (often micro-macro) processes Cage developed in the 1930s and 1940s for his early percussion music. Although Kernis (as well as Cage) soon abandoned such processes, they stood him in good stead as organizing principles in these early works while he was mastering his craft.

The apparent simplicity of *Meditation* is deceptive. As with so much of Kernis's music, the work is actually difficult to perform convincingly. Many pianists, he notes, try to use rubato and have trouble making the lines "warm, legato, controlled, with a subtle groove." The piece not only anticipates the many lamentations that would follow but also highlights Kernis's propensity to write slow legato passages that require relentless concentration, control, and intense yet (in this case) restrained passion.

Graduate Work: Yale

In the fall of 1981 Kernis entered the master's program in composition at Yale University, where he was encouraged to study with a variety of teachers. He worked first with Bernard Rands and then with Gilbert Amy, Morton Subotnick, and Jacob Druckman. Later he became Druckman's assistant. "I helped him correct score drafts [and parts], and acted as an assistant during rehearsals," he recalled. "It helped me very much to understand the science of orchestration, the exact weight that every instrument can have in the orchestral texture."[28] Kernis spent two years at Yale and completed all the music coursework but never received the degree because of his failure to fulfill the foreign language requirement. (He had had difficulty with foreign languages throughout his public school years.)

During the summer before entering Yale, Kernis composed *Death Fugue* for bass-baritone, string bass, and percussion. The piece is his second work prompted by brutal and senseless death and his first to draw on his Jewish heritage. The text is by the Romanian poet Paul Celan (born Paul Antschel in 1920), whose parents died in Nazi concentration camps. Celan was himself imprisoned in a labor camp and committed suicide in 1970. His *Todesfuge*, which began to take shape in 1944, graphically reflects the Nazi repression, specifically referencing situations in which Jewish prisoners were forced to perform German dance music for their captors. The first stanza (translated by Joachim Neugroschel) reads in part,

> Black milk of dawn we drink it at dusk
> we drink it at noon and at daybreak we drink it at night
> we drink and we drink
> we are digging a grave in the air there's room for us all
> A man lives in the house he plays with the serpents he writes . . .
> he whistles for his Jews he has them dig a grave in the earth
> he commands us to play for the dance.[29]

Celan's poem—a fugue in the pathological sense of the word—closely resembles musical minimalism: the first seven lines of stanza 1 recur in various configurations in succeeding stanzas, sometimes rearranged; components may be separated and recombined; and at times the poet embellishes them with new text. In that sense the poem attracted Kernis not only by the poignancy of its subject but also by its structure and rhythm.

Kernis's musical setting, on the other hand, is not at all minimalist. In fact, if anything, it shows a return to the atonality he had explored during his year with Wuorinen. The dark, intense, eleven-minute setting opens in stasis with a two-minute instrumental introduction: low, static rolls on the timpani, strikes on cymbals and gong, and deep slides in the string bass's lowest octave. The singer begins on a low repeated E and remains in that range for ten bars. As the work progresses, the repetitions in the text evoke an increasingly agitated musical setting. Typically, Kernis does not couple text repetition with musical repetition. Instead, the tessitura rises and the music becomes increasingly desperate. In the final stanza the singer holds a long high E two octaves above his opening pitch. Later he moves up to a high F. Both pitches set the word "death," which has now become a sought-after goal, an escape from the horrors of the prisoners' earthly torture.

During his two years at Yale, Kernis also continued a series of works he had begun when he first entered college. These compositions bear the subtitle "Cycle" (given in parentheses after their main titles) and were composed using process-oriented rhythmical structures that functioned as self-imposed boundaries to control his imagination. "At the time I was convinced that too much freedom was damaging to writing music," he said years later. "I didn't want to fall into *pastiche* and therefore I needed some quite serious rules to filter all the different musical ideas that I had in mind."[30] His pre-compositional processes were often mathematical, sometimes minimalist or serialized. In other cases they involved setting up texts to form a logical progression or drawing inspiration from visual stimuli to suggest a structure that would yield large-scale coherence. Whatever the controlling parameters, Kernis sought to achieve both recollection and transformation over the course of each work. The cycle pieces don't aim for exact recapitulation, but their endings make reference to elements that appeared in the beginning. Kernis later abandoned the strict compositional controls that mark these pieces, but the use of an altered return at the end of a work created a cogent, comprehensible, yet dynamic logic that he found effective for years to come.

A case in point is Music for Trio (Cycle IV) for flute, cello, and piano, which Kernis now sees as a turning point in his compositional evolution. He wrote it between his two years at Yale. The trio is based on a small amount of material, but the development of that material shows his increasingly assured grounding in the harmonic elaboration of scales and small motives. In short, Music for Trio draws on minimalist principles but is, at the same time, directional.

In this case, the pre-compositional processes revolved around the number three. Time signatures are mostly multiples of three (primarily 3/4, 6/4, and 9/4).

There are three continuous movements and three main tonal centers: D at the beginning, B♭ at the start of the second section, and F♯ in the third—that is, symmetrically positioned major thirds. The work is built on a scale of nine notes consisting of three groups of three with identical intervallic content (a major second followed by a minor second):

D–E–F / **F♯**–G♯–A / **B♭**–C–C♯

The trio's first movement features long notes that gradually fracture into rapidly repeating thirty-seconds, while a legato melody slowly emerges above them. A transitional section using an arpeggiated ostinato B♭ major triad in the pianist's left hand leads into a minimalist second movement. The B♭ triad becomes simply two notes in succession, D–F, then C–F, then C–D–F, and so on. Meanwhile a new melody arises in the alto flute, at first echoing the same pitches but then becoming increasingly independent of them before moving to the cello. During another transition the music devolves into repeated notes, leading into the final movement, which is characterized by flurries of sixteenths. It begins in a very high range (the flutist now changes to piccolo) and gradually descends. As the end approaches, elements of the beginning recur but are combined with material introduced later in the piece. For instance, the bursts of repeated notes heard in the first movement now reappear simultaneously with the third movement's flurries. Then the long notes of the beginning reenter, as do elements of the B♭ triad. The ending includes remembrances of the opening movement, now transformed through our twenty-minute journey. Yet the work ends not on D, where it began but, rather, on an A/F sonority.

As would be the case in many of his future works, Music for Trio has a larger metaphysical, almost programmatic undercurrent. Kernis wrote in his program notes that during the piece the trio becomes a duo: particular pitches or melodic ideas are shared between two of the three instruments. These sections drive toward others in which all three instruments "become unified as one. This merging of the spirit and the idea," he wrote, "is where the true essence of the work lies."[31]

Music for Trio was in some ways an ending point for the composer. "When I was done with that approach," Kernis says, "I moved on" to increased freedom. That directional change, in which he developed greater self-confidence and trust in his intuition, was enhanced by a major event of 1983: his encounter with the New York Philharmonic and its music director Zubin Mehta.

3 Kernis Meets the New York Philharmonic

ON JUNE 7, 1983, A HIGHLY PUBLIC—and widely publicized—event catapulted the twenty-three-year-old Kernis into the national spotlight. At 8:00 that evening, in Avery Fisher Hall at Lincoln Center, in front of an audience of nearly a thousand, the New York Philharmonic spent an hour reading through and rehearsing Kernis's *"dream of the morning sky"* (Cycle V), conducted (and critiqued) by music director Zubin Mehta.

Nearly every biographical sketch of Kernis cites this event, with varying degrees of accuracy. Major national publications ran stories about it at the time as well: the *New York Times* and *Daily News*, the *Philadelphia Inquirer*, the *Village Voice*, the *New Yorker*, *Time*, *Newsweek*, the *New Criterion*, and *Musical America*, among others. Most critics gave little more than generalized descriptions of Kernis's score. One called it "intoxicatingly beautiful"; a second found its finale "soaring and rhapsodic"; a third (more mixed) called it "rich and imaginative" but "a little spoiled at the last by the rhetorical insistence of the pantheistic text."[1] All of the reviewers, however, recounted what Tim Page characterized as the "sometimes heated dialogue" between conductor and composer. Sympathies clearly lay with the young composer. Reviewers lauded him for defending his compositional choices and for what Alan Rich called, with considerable exaggeration, his "energetic sass." In contrast, many of them shot poison arrows at Mehta. The music was "seriously under-rehearsed," wrote Patrick Smith in *Musical America*, forgetting, perhaps, that the event was an open rehearsal, not intended as a polished presentation; and, he added, it was "brusquely treated by the music director." Most damning was the lengthy article by Samuel Lipman, covering the festival that included this event. Lipman harshly criticized many of the concerts, while at the same time praising the festival's intent. Mehta, said Lipman,

> assumed a patronizing attitude toward Kernis, lecturing him (in front of the audience) on his inadequate technique in orchestration. . . . Though Mehta felt free to make jokes to the audience, he showed no familiarity with the music, finding little to comment on as he riffled through the pages of the score. . . . Given his evident lack of interest in the task he was publicly performing, one could only wonder why he had chosen to do it in the first place.[2]

Fortunately, there's no need to reconstruct this crucial event from news reports or faded memories, for the Philharmonic recorded the open rehearsal in full and Kernis was kind enough to allow me to listen in. The audio recording shows Mehta as frequently humorous, generally at ease, occasionally condescending, at times defensive, and above all, resolutely assured in his critiques, which mostly dealt with tempos and balance. Kernis managed to maintain his composure under what Joan La Barbara called a "torrent of compositional advice tossed at him rather audaciously from the maestro on the podium."[3] Soft-spoken as always,

Kernis with conductor Zubin Mehta and soprano Gwendolyn Bradley at the Horizons '83 performance, June 7, 1983. (Photo by Bert Bial. Courtesy of the New York Philharmonic.)

Kernis firmly corrected tempos, dynamics, and balance issues he found amiss. The audience, for its part, clearly enjoyed the verbal jousting, even, at times, applauding Kernis for coming to his own defense.

This open reading was part of an ambitious festival called "Horizons '83: Since 1968, a New Romanticism?" Two weeks of activities featured the Philharmonic in six full-length concerts plus the open rehearsal, presenting music by twenty-six living composers under the direction of seven conductors.[4] Ancillary events included four symposia and "Meet the Composer" sessions. Mehta himself conducted two events: two-thirds of the open rehearsal and the concert the following night.

The festival's artistic director was Jacob Druckman (Kernis's teacher at Yale), a Pulitzer Prize–winning composer who was at the time the Philharmonic's composer-in-residence through a grant program sponsored by Exxon, the Rockefeller Foundation, and the National Endowment for the Arts.[5]

Critic Linda Sanders, editor of Horizons '83's commemorative booklet, explained that the festival's organizers defined Romanticism not by musical style but by "attitude, goal, vision." Druckman explored this same issue in his introductory essay.[6] Noting that the past two centuries had witnessed "an increasing celebration of the individual as solitary iconoclast," he pointed to "the almost total abandonment of the notion of a common language . . ., an ever increasing diversity and a constant acceleration of aesthetic change." At the same time Druckman detected, over the course of many centuries, a constancy rooted in change: namely, regular pendulum swings between Apollonian and Dionysian ideals, which he characterized as "a steady underlying rhythm . . . in the progress of the arts." In its most recent manifestation, he explained, the postwar generation, stimulated by a Webernian ideal, "constituted the apogee of the tidal shift toward the Apollonian . . ., an elevation of rationalism to unprecedented heights." But then, as in the past, the tide began to turn, signaling a re-emergence of Dionysian "sensuality, mystery, nostalgia, ecstasy, transcendence" that made its first appearance in the aesthetic goals of East European avant-garde composers during the 1960s (in particular, Penderecki, Lutoslawski, Ligeti, and Berio). The "Dionysian" music of the period 1968–83, which Druckman characterized as "leading us into a mysterious and fragrant garden of dreams," became the focus of the Philharmonic's festival.

Druckman's concept for the open rehearsal was to present a behind-the-scenes demonstration of how a new work is shaped through the interaction of composer, conductor, and players. Kernis, for his part, was astonished that Druckman recommended his piece, and he raced to complete it. Morton Subotnick, his teacher that semester, helped him finalize the score. Kernis also faced considerable expense in having the parts copied. Fortunately, two women at Yale—development officer Anne-Marie Soulliere and soprano Phyllis Curtin—came to the rescue by locating a patron to cover the cost.

Kernis's piece opened the rehearsal on June 7, followed by a reading of a work-in-progress by George Crumb (conducted by Arthur Weisberg) and a rehearsal of Nicholas Thorne's *Symphony from Silence*. The Philharmonic had practiced the Kernis and Thorne pieces twice—for two hours on May 28 with Druckman conducting, and for two and a half hours on the morning of the open rehearsal, under Mehta.[7] The conductor explained that his original intention "was to let you, the audience, participate in . . . the first meeting that we have on stage with a young composer's work," but after seeing the complexities of the two scores, he "didn't dare" attempt the task for the first time in public—a confession the audience greeted with sympathetic laughter.

After Druckman introduced the program, Kernis gave the audience a succinct two-minute summary of his work's aesthetics. "*Dream of the morning sky*," he said, moves from the amorphous to the concrete on both a musical and a metaphysical plane. The first movement centers on clouds and "large spaces," the second on "small points" that gradually transform into long lines, and the third on a "unified melodic line." The transformation during the course of the work, he noted, is captured in the soprano solo in the finale, set to a text by the Pulitzer Prize–winning Kiowa-Cherokee poet N. Scott Momaday, whose poem, explained Kernis, "talks about . . . the true humanity that's present in all of us."

Mehta conducted the opening movement in its entirety and, in response to the audience's appreciative applause, offered a somewhat sardonic riposte. "You ain't heard nothing yet!" he said, prompting a good deal of laughter and ushering in his critique: certain accents in the woodwinds were inaudible; violin harmonics could never sound *forte*; a notated crescendo from *piano* to *mezzo-piano* was ineffective.

After five minutes of banter, Mehta moved directly to the second movement, the most difficult of the three. He began by confessing to Kernis that he was "a little confused as to the canons" on which the movement is built—not a surprising comment, because the canonic structure (which in this case is rhythmic, rather than melodic) is barely perceptible to the ear. As we will see, the movement's first section consists of six overlapping pointillistic rhythmic patterns—each about seven measures in length—whose notes are scattered among the various instruments. These patterns gradually pile atop one another, allowing Kernis to build an increasingly intricate fabric of disparate points. To complicate the structure further, each new pattern introduces a new melodic interval. Apparently, as soon as Mehta mentioned the canons, he regretted doing so, because he only allowed

Kernis to say three words before jumping to the middle of the movement. As he did repeatedly during the evening, Mehta broke any perceived tension with some winning humor. ("There is no orchestra in the world that you give these Bartók pizzicatos to that they won't exaggerate. . . . The cello becomes a bow and arrow.") But he also couldn't resist further instruction:

MEHTA [to Kernis, re m. 137]: Just a moment. You *have* marked it *piano* and they're playing it *piano*. If you want it "*piano cantabile*," it has to be mentioned. . . .

KERNIS [gently]: I did write "*cantabile*." It's very small. . . . [audience laughter]

MEHTA [somewhat aggressively]: I don't have it in my score. Where is it?

KERNIS: It's very tiny. It's right there [more laughter, followed by applause]. It's marked larger in their parts. It's a little c-a-n-t. Very tiny.

After another few minutes, disagreement arose over a spot where Mehta slowed down despite a notated *accelerando*. "I did the *ritardando* because these notes are so high," he explained. "It's completely in the stratosphere."

During the ensuing discussion, Mehta revisited his concerns about the canonic structure: "Does it come out because you know you've written it and you hear it," he asked, "or does it really come out?" "What I want," replied Kernis, "is not that every single individual note of the canon comes out, but that the large—" Mehta interrupted and diverted the discussion to other matters.

During the concluding part of the movement (m. 171), Kernis stopped the rehearsal himself to remark that the tempo was too slow.

KERNIS: I marked it 88 to 92 and . . .

MEHTA: Give me 88.

KERNIS [continuing his previous sentence]: . . . I like it on the fast side . . .

MEHTA [with some force]: Give me 88 please.

[Kernis, a bit disconcerted, counts 1–2–3–4 at his desired tempo.]

Mehta, to his credit, resumed his good humor, but he couldn't resist correcting the composer when Kernis asked the brass to play more *legato*. "More *portato*. Longish. You don't want them to play *legato*." Kernis agreed. He also acquiesced to Mehta's suggestion that he eliminate doublings in the brass at mm. 192ff. to allow the woodwinds to come through. But when Mehta asked, in reference to the melody at mm. 204ff., "Is that not too raucous for you?" Kernis replied, "Oh no!" to which the conductor responded, "It's rather disturbing, you know. It's so strident."

The third movement, featuring Metropolitan Opera soprano Gwendolyn Bradley, went much more smoothly until Mehta again stopped to critique the balance.

MEHTA: You don't find this all too thick?

KERNIS: It's very hard to tell from up here, but I found, at rehearsal . . .

MEHTA [interrupting]: I have *always* to judge from up here. It's too thick.
KERNIS [quietly but firmly]: It's too *loud*, too loud [scattered applause].

The reading to the end of the piece continued without further interruption and the audience greeted the conclusion with enthusiastic applause, shouts of "bravo," and even a few whistles.

The inclusion of "*dream of the morning sky*" on the Horizons '83 program was a strong indication of things to come. The work, in fact, represents a major turning point in Kernis's creative life, embodying at once the process-oriented, rigorously planned methodology we have seen in his earlier works and the freer, more intuitive, and (yes) Romantic instincts that had always been present beneath the surface and would soon dominate his musical creativity. The work was prescient in other ways as well—in Kernis's love of metaphysical texts, his exploration of scalar-based melodies, his propensity to use programmatic titles (often associated with nature), his love of third-related chord progressions, his ability to build large-scale forms with moments of dramatic climax, and his uncanny sensitivity to orchestration.

"*dream of the morning sky*" had its origins in Music for Violin and Orchestra, Kernis's senior thesis at the Manhattan School. He explained to Ev Grimes in an interview in 1986, "The first half of [the thesis piece] was like a twelve-part rhythmic canon, all E major." The second part, on the other hand, "was like a [musical] trip around the world. . . . It was really awful." Kernis revived and reorchestrated the first section and used it as the middle movement of "*dream*," adding a new conclusion and then surrounding it with two newly composed movements.

The work's challenging central movement is in three balanced sections, each just over forty measures long. Section 1 introduces six complex rhythmic patterns, each seven measures in length, and each comprising groups of one to six notes interspersed with rests of asymmetrical lengths. Figure 5a shows the *a* pattern,

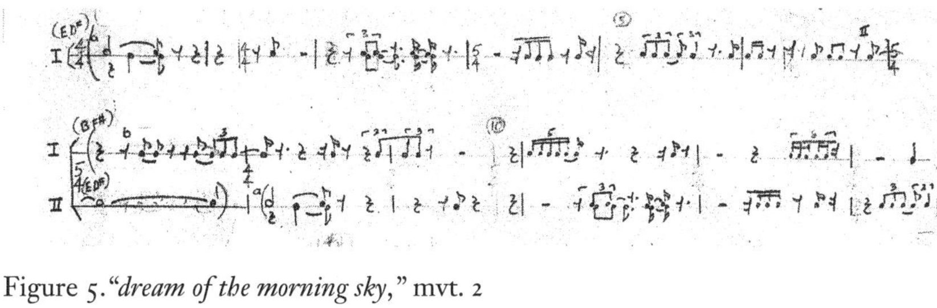

Figure 5. "*dream of the morning sky*," mvt. 2

a. Beginning of Kernis's rhythmic plan. This excerpt shows pattern *a* (mm. 1–7, then repeated starting in m. 8) overlapping with the beginning of pattern *b* (starting in m. 7). (Figure reproduced courtesy of Aaron Jay Kernis.)

Figure 5. "*dream of the morning sky*," mvt. 2

b. Beginning of the movement, showing the realization of the first six measures of pattern *a* in full orchestration. Note that the only pitches at this point are E and D♯. (Copyright © 1982 by Associated Music Publishers, Inc. International Copyright Secured. All Rights Reserved. Used by Permission.)

introduced in mm. 1–7, followed by its repetition beginning in m. 8. The repetition overlaps with the *b* pattern (which starts in m. 7). These patterns would be difficult to hear, much less recall, if they were assigned to a single instrument, but they are even more thoroughly disguised by being scattered among the various instruments of the orchestra in what at first seems to be a bare Webernian texture. Figure 5b shows how the first six measures of pattern *a* are realized in the full orchestral texture. As this figure also shows, the pitch content of the *a* pattern consists only of two notes: E and D♯. The *b* pattern in contrast, uses only B and F♯.

As table 4 shows, each successive subsection overlays new rhythmic patterns (which always consist of small groups of notes interspersed with rests), as well as new pairs of pitches. The *a* pattern is played six times in this section, the *b* pattern five times, the *c* pattern four times, and so on. With the notes of each pattern distributed throughout the orchestra, the individual rhythmic patterns become less and less distinct from one another. The pitch content, on the other hand, is clear. Each rhythmic pattern uses two pitch classes, and in total there are only seven, consisting of the notes of the E major scale.

In the middle section of the movement, points gradually turn into lines. Another set of six canons begins in m. 44, first appearing in the violins. In contrast to the first six patterns, these new ones consist primarily of long notes without

TABLE 4. Structure of the opening third of "*dream of the morning sky*," movement 2. The numbers after each letter show the repetition (a1 = first rendition of the *a* pattern; a2 = second rendition of the *a* pattern, etc.).

Beginning measure of the new pattern	1	7	14	21	28	35
Rhythmic patterns	**a1**	**b1**	**c1**	**d1**	**e1**	**f1**
(Pitch content)	(E, D♯)	(B, F♯)	(D♯, F♯)	(A, C♯)	(G♯, D♯)	(E, F♯)
		a2	**b2**	**c2**	**d2**	**e2**
		(E, D♯)	(E, D♯)	(E, D♯)	(E, D♯)	(E, D♯)
			a3	**b3**	**c3**	**d3**
			(B, F♯)	(B, F♯)	(B, F♯)	(B, F♯)
				a4	**b4**	**c4**
				(D♯, F♯)	(D♯, F♯)	(D♯, F♯)
					a5	**b5**
					(A, C♯)	(A, C♯)
						a6
						(G♯, D♯)

Ex. 1. "*dream of the morning sky*," mvt. 2, rehearsal letter V (selected instruments only). Note the introduction of the first of the new legato motives in Violin I, while the pointillistic motives of the first part of the movement continue in other instruments. (Measure numbers in the score run continuously from movement 1; this excerpt presents mm. 43–46 of the second movement.)

intervening rests. (The first of these new patterns is shown in example 1, Violin I.) Each pattern forms a legato line and, in contrast to the first section, is played by a single instrument or section of the orchestra. The new *A* pattern, for example, appears in the first violins, then in the violas, then in the second violins, and so on. As the *A* pattern migrates, five additional patterns, each legato in character, enter

Ex. 1. (*Continued*)

one by one. These long-breathed lines stand out distinctly from the pointillistic texture of the first set of motives, which continue from the previous section until each of them has been stated seven times (the interplay of the two types of patterns is shown in example 1). The result of this process, as demonstrated by the chart shown in figure 6, is the gradual replacement of the first set of six motives (*a–f*), which are pointillistic rhythms, by the second set (*A–F*), which are linear melodies. By m. 79 the original texture has been almost completely replaced by an intricate Romantic counterpoint. In terms of pitch content, each of the new motives in this section embraces all seven notes of the E major scale, which thus emerges more and more distinctly.

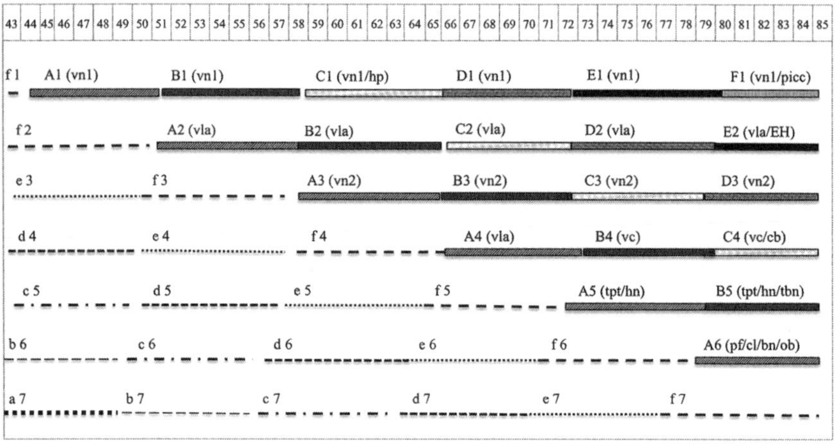

Figure 6. "*dream of the morning sky*," mvt. 2, mm. 43–85, diagram of the motivic structure. *A–F* represent linear motives in specific instruments introduced in this section. Lower-case letters *a–f* represent pointillistic motives introduced during the previous 43 measures (as shown in table 4 and fig. 5b above).

The final section of the movement, added to the material Kernis drew from his thesis, begins with a lush mediant progression (E major to G major) and then abandons the canonic structure entirely. It reaches a tremendous crescendo (the section Mehta found raucous) and suddenly drops off into a single pitch: an A hummed by the soprano that begins the finale.

Thus, like Music for Trio, the middle movement of "*dream of the morning sky*" revolves around the manipulation of a restricted set of elements—in this case, first a set of rhythmic motives, and then a set of melodic lines. Unlike Music for Trio, though, the work's outer two movements arise from a freer, more intuitive compositional idiom culminating in the lyric song of the finale. Kernis would never return to the approach of Trio and other early works, but he willingly admits that he needed such restrictions at the time. Before freeing himself from such parameters, he had to solidify his craft.

At the same time, Kernis did not necessarily intend that his listeners hear the skeletal basis of his process. Let us return, for a moment, to his unfinished explanation to Mehta: "What I want is not that every single individual note of the canon comes out, but that the large . . ." Clearly, his intended conclusion to the sentence was that the large-scale transformation from points to lines constituted the message he wished to convey. Throughout Western music history composers have routinely prioritized the broad sweep of a work over the revelation of compositional procedure. When Bach writes a canon in which one voice is the inversion or retrograde of the other, or when Ockeghem composes a work with two simultaneous canons in four simultaneous meters, does the listener immediately identify the compositional process? More important, does it matter? The composer, in order to discipline his or her creativity, needs to set up limitations, whether they be tonal progressions, contrapuntal rules, serial processes, minimalist boundaries, or some individualized methods of organization. Even John Cage, who attempted to disavow his own compositional choices—or perhaps *especially* John Cage—had to devise pre-compositional procedures to guide the creation of a work of art. Without such restrictions, there are simply too many choices. The composer, as Stravinsky reminds us, needs limits in order to find freedom. "The more art is controlled, limited, worked over, the more it is free," he wrote. "I shall go even farther: my freedom will be so much the greater and more meaningful the more narrowly I limit my field of action and the more I surround myself with obstacles. Whatever diminishes constraint diminishes strength."[8] Kernis's canonic structure in the middle movement of "*dream of the morning sky*" functioned precisely in this manner. It was a pre-compositional restriction that allowed him to create a larger aesthetic progression, namely, a transformation from disjunction to linearity, from disarray to coherence, from rhythm to song.

The finale of "*dream of the morning sky*" is a lyrical paean to nature and life. Momaday's text consists of a series of short lines, each beginning with "I" and each drawing a metaphor with the natural world:

> I am a feather on the bright sky
> I am the blue horse that runs in the plain
> I am the fish that rolls, shining, in the water
> I am the shadow that follows a child.

It ends with an affirmation of life:

> I am alive, I am alive
> I stand in good relation to the earth
> I stand in good relation to the gods
> I stand in good relation to all that is beautiful.[9]

The poem, says Kernis, was "very much a statement of purpose on my part, a reaffirmation on locating a sense of beauty in music after many arid years."

His setting begins with a single A—first hummed, then transformed into the vowel I—and then opens up into an ascending melody, rising as the text itself reaches up from the poet's personal center to the world beyond. The shape of this melody, a rising scale with a leap at the end, is one that Kernis would reuse many times. The scalar ascent links his harmonic language to traditional tonality; the leap creates a sense of ecstasy. By the end of the movement, however, the scale disappears, to be replaced by octave leaps on the concluding words "I am alive," first articulating the tonal center of A and then stretching beyond it to a ninth, perhaps symbolically suggesting the poet's reach beyond the possible to grasp the "farthest star."

After the Festival

The Horizons festival brought Kernis to a new height of optimism about his future career. But after the immediate outburst of critical response there followed a deafening silence. "All I have to do," he had thought, was "sit at home for a while and . . . start getting calls."[10] But no calls came. Having completed his coursework at Yale, he moved to New York, where he scraped together a living by playing the piano, accompanying and making arrangements for the Harlem Boys Choir, and proofreading scores for other composers. "The old fears started to fall very heavily on me that I wasn't going to be able to write anything that was as good as this piece. . . . I was terrified."

At the same time, *"dream of the morning sky"* did facilitate a very important association with a publisher. In fall 1983 James Rushton, who worked for Chester Music in London, came to New York to set up a U.S. branch of the Wilhelm Hansen publishing group (Chester's parent company). One of Rushton's jobs was to seek out new works for publication. Kernis played a tape of the open rehearsal for him, and Rushton sensed in the music "a freedom of style, exuberance, and great lyricism." He convinced Hansen to sign Kernis to the Northlight Music label. In 1988 Music Sales, the umbrella company of G. Schirmer, bought out the Hansen group. Schirmer became, and remains, Kernis's publisher.[11]

Despite Kernis's melancholy, he did manage to compose two substantial works for vocal soloists and chamber orchestra in the months following the festival. *Morningsongs* is a fifteen-minute piece for baritone and ten instruments begun as a work for voice and piano in 1982 and subsequently expanded for chamber ensemble. Kernis completed it in the summer of 1983. *America(n) (Day) Dreams*, for mezzo-soprano and eleven instrumentalists, was presented for the first time in March 1984.

The poetry used in *Morningsongs* is by Jon Anderson (1940–2007),[12] and it reflects Kernis's gloominess in this period. As he wrote in his program notes, it's "a work about loss . . . of one's security, family or friends . . ., of a sense of purpose or direction in one's life . . ., of love." The three poems all deal with the morning in a spirit of discontent. The first, "Paris," focuses on loneliness ("I will be homeless again"); the second, "The Blue Animals," recounts broken love ("as I was turning / to call out again for you, / I saw there was no harm / at all, though you were gone"); and the third, "Walking Barefoot," dwells on life's choices and sorrows. The text of the last movement captures Anderson's laconic style:

> In the morning,
> I'm not used to it . . .
> and the dew
> burns; I had thought
> to give up every kind of pain.
>
> There is the other life
> without passion or memory.
> It goes alongside.
>
> It is the turtle's shadow.
> It is the snail's shadow.
>
> In each of my steps the grass darkens,
> filled with discontent.

Morningsongs consists of three slow movements. Despite the sadness of the texts, however, the music has nothing of the dark character of *Death Fugue*. Instead it projects a sense of resignation.

Kernis composed the five-minute "Blue Animals" before the other two movements, setting the text for voice and piano to be performed by the bass-baritone Robert Osborne, who at the time was Kernis's fellow graduate student at Yale. He later donated the song to baritone William Parker's AIDS Quilt Songbook project. "The Blue Animals" opens and closes with a duet for two clarinets, reflecting the image of a pair of animals in the text. Thirds and fifths predominate, imbuing the music with a lyric, tonal character.

"Paris," the opening movement, builds on Kernis's interest in minimalism. By superimposing two harmonic major thirds in the accompaniment, F/A and E/G♯, he created a dense chord featuring semitones (E/F and G♯/A) that remains constant throughout the three-minute movement. In only one place does another pitch temporarily intervene. The inspiration in this case was the music of Morton Feldman, manifest in Kernis's fondness for small cells of pitches used in rotational fashion.

The third movement is the highlight of the set. Here Kernis extends Anderson's short text by dividing it into three sections separated by lengthy instrumental interludes. (Sections 2 and 3 of the poem quoted above constitute the middle section.) The first of the interludes introduces a timbre indicative of orchestration choices Kernis would use in later works. While the strings play in harmonics along with the piccolo (*pianississimo*), the harp and glockenspiel (later replaced by crotales) interject intermittent groups of two or three quick descending notes like glimmering stars or showers of falling light. This accompaniment continues as the voice re-enters, and it remains until the end of the vocalist's second section. The piece then concludes with a short dénouement. Osborne sang the premiere of *Morningsongs* at Tanglewood on August 21, 1983, conducted by Kernis's former teacher Theodore Antoniou.

America(n) (Day) Dreams has a far different character: its five movements and epilogue are varied in tempo and style, upbeat, occasionally ironic, and often funny. The text, by Utah poet May Swenson (1913–89), attracted Kernis by its "diversity, humor, gentle irony, and sense of word-play."[13] Her colorful poetry has a rhythmic quality that Kernis found congenial, and he was attracted by the imagery, which often lies on the border between fantasy and reality. The second movement, for example, describes two white whales who appear in the Waldorf-Astoria's restaurant, flying over customers, biting waiters, stealing strawberries, and then ascending to the sixth floor, where they turn "candy-pink" between the bed sheets—after which they appear on Park Avenue drawing a blue VW "on a swaying chain of bubbles." The singer acts as a narrator in this movement, anticipating two later works in which Kernis would call for spoken text over an instrumental ensemble (*Le quattro stagioni dalla cucina futurismo* and *Goblin Market*).

The third movement, for unaccompanied voice in semi-recitative style, sets a nonsense text about a dream that in itself reflects Kernis's fascination with minimalist patterns and developmental repetition: "I had a dream in which I had a dream, and in my dream I told you, 'Listen, I will tell you my dream.' And I began to tell you. And you told me, 'I haven't time to listen while you tell your dream.' Then in my dream I dreamed I began to forget my dream. . . . And you tell me: 'You dreamed I wouldn't listen to a dream that you forgot?' . . . And now I begin to forget that I forgot what I began to tell you in my dream."

The fifth movement concerns Apollo 17—the eleventh and final manned moon mission—and includes both sexual and political overtones:

A nipple, our parachute
covers the capsule: an
aureole, on a darker aureole

like the convex spiral of

a mollusk, on a great breast:
the skin removed: agitated

glandular pattern revealed:
the SPLASH, seen from above,
from the helicopter:

Apollo 17 comes home
to the Pacific: the moon
strewn with our trash:

module platforms, crashed LMs,
metal flags and plaques, dead
sensor devices like inside-out

umbrellas, a golf ball. A small
steel alloy astronaut doll
bites the black dust.

Part of Kernis's attraction to this text was the association of word "aureole" with his teacher, Jacob Druckman. *Aureole* is the title of Druckman's most popular orchestral work of this period—a fourteen-minute piece first performed by the New York Philharmonic in 1979, only a few years before the Horizons Festival. The work is characterized by colorful orchestration, forming a model for Kernis in this early period. In Kernis's piece, the singer engages in a kind of sprechstimme—at first articulating text and pitches in a whisper, then rising in volume and converting to actual speech. Part of the way through, the conductor lays down the baton and becomes an actor who engages in dialogue with the singer over the trash left on the moon, while the instrumentalists freely repeat various pitch patterns during a series of five-second-long units. The movement ends with the harp alone playing stark quarter notes "like a mechanical toy winding down."[14] On its last note, all lights are extinguished to usher in the finale.

The epilogue, "The Pure Suite of Happiness," suggests a bar lounge. A spotlight appears on the pianist (who plays for the first time). The singer is lightly amplified. In contrast to the rest of the piece, the music is consonant and tonal, evoking the Sinatra style that Kernis's mother loved. Here, however, it serves as the final irony of Swenson's imaginative poetry and Kernis's varied harmonic language.

America(n) (Day) Dreams summarized, in some sense, the diversity of experiences and compositional approaches Kernis had thus far explored. In particular, he aimed to apply Swenson's blurring of the line between fantasy and reality to his own (and his audience's) self-perception—to focus on daydreams of past, present, and future. Kernis evoked his own past by reviewing pedagogical influences. He dedicated each movement to a teacher or source of inspiration: Bernard Rands, Morton Subotnick, Vincent Plush, Elias Tanenbaum, Jacob Druckman, and Milton Babbitt (particularly the contrast between his highly intellectual concert music and his love of popular song). The ensemble Music Elements presented the premiere in March 1984.

During this period of discontent, Kernis applied for five grants and prizes: a Guggenheim Fellowship, the Rome Prize, an NEA grant, and composition awards from ASCAP and BMI. He submitted "*dream of the morning sky*," Music for Trio, and *Morningsongs* in the hope of receiving one or two awards. To his astonishment, by the spring of 1984, he had received all five. A new chapter in his life was about to begin.

4 Coming to Grips with History (1984–1991)

FOR KERNIS, THE PERIOD 1984–1991 was one of wandering physically, emotionally, and artistically. He lived in Europe, various parts of the United States, and Canada. He experienced periods of intense loneliness but also the pleasure of a significant romantic attachment. And, after freeing himself musically from strict self-imposed controls, he confronted head-on the challenges of history, coming to grips with the forms and modes of expression pioneered by his predecessors while adapting these traditions to his personal language. His success in confronting these personal and professional challenges manifested itself in commissions for his first symphony (the *Symphony in Waves*, 1989) and his first string quartet (*musica celestis*, 1990) and in the establishment of important associations that would serve him well far into the future with the St. Paul Chamber Orchestra, the Lark Quartet, and pianist Evelyne Luest, who would become his wife in 1996.

After he received the five awards in the spring of 1984, Kernis managed to postpone the $21,000 Guggenheim Fellowship for a year so that he could accept the Rome Prize. The American Academy in Rome endows annual residencies for fifteen scholars of Italian art history and fifteen emerging artists in art, architecture, literature, and music. Kernis was one of two composers honored with a residency that year; the other was Paul Moravec. In September 1984, then, he set off for Italy.

Kernis at first found it difficult to adjust to European life. "The social demands were constant," he recalls, "and immersion in a new language provoked insecurity."[1] On the other hand, the stimulation of interacting with creative artists in a variety of fields presented an opportunity that would broaden his aesthetic, cultural, and political perspectives. He immediately began work on an orchestral piece designed as a follow-on to "*dream of the morning sky.*" His plan, which he later abandoned, was to write a trilogy depicting morning, afternoon, and evening, representing birth, youth, and maturity. He completed the second part of the trilogy, titled *Mirror of Heat and Light (Cycle V, Part 2)*, in the fall of 1984 and devised plans for the third, based on Milton Avery's painting *Tangerine Moon and Wine Dark Sea*. *Mirror of Heat and Light* presents an aural representation of the afternoon sun, which becomes unbearably hot—in essence, "deafening in terms of light." There is even "a hint of nuclear holocaust. . . . It's not a very positive piece," Kernis told Ev Grimes in 1986.[2] Whereas "*dream*" moves from semi-coherent fragmentation to melodic clarity and lush harmony, *Mirror* consists of "relatively short sections and phrases, and is often aggressive in tone."[3] The work was indeed a mirror, not only in its depiction of the blinding afternoon sun but also in its reflection of Kernis's unsettled state. As he wrote in his program notes, the piece depicts "the emotional upheaval and intensity one experiences during the chaotic transition from youth to maturity."[4] In February 1985 he returned to New York for its premiere by the Youth Symphony Orchestra conducted by David Alan Miller. *Mirror of Heat and Light* won the $2,000 Bearns Prize from Columbia University (Kernis's piece tied with one by William E. Coble), but he was never happy with it. He has now withdrawn it.

Despite his ultimate dissatisfaction with this work, Kernis now comments that *Mirror of Heat and Light* was an important stepping stone in his career not only in building on the visual images of light, heat, and fire that had stimulated him in the past but also in anticipating, in some ways, the Second Symphony, which would shake the contemporary music scene in 1991 with its brutal outburst of anger and pessimism.

During the spring of 1985 Kernis traveled periodically within Europe while beginning work on a piece for viola and piano, *Passacaglia-Variations*. Although he claimed that he had always detested variation pieces, it was neither the first time he had written a passacaglia nor the first time he had made reference to Baroque genres. In 1981, while still at Yale, he had written a suite for guitar containing both a passacaglia and a toccata. Two years later he arranged those movements for organ. At the same time, he felt uncomfortable with the variation structure, seeing all but the best of such works as a means for a composer to "show off his tricks."[5] The passacaglia he began in early 1985, then, represented for him an attempt to make peace with variation forms in general and with repeating ground basses in particular. Perhaps because he was struggling with his own hesitations about the form, the composition was slow to materialize. He did not finish it until December 16.

In retrospect, Kernis realized that forcing himself to work within the variation structure helped him move away from the mathematical procedures he had previously found necessary and find a less deterministic method of developing his material. As the work's title implies, the eighteen-minute piece is built on a repeating bass line—in this case an ascending B♭ natural minor scale—but its starting pitch, rhythm, and intervallic structure do not stay constant, as they would in a Baroque passacaglia. After an introduction for the viola alone featuring delicate harmonics and mysterious murmuring flurries of soft sixteenth-note triplets, the pianist introduces the ground bass in the left hand. Simultaneously, the right hand articulates a Mahlerian melody—tonal, consonant, and mournful—which the viola imitates. As the bass line repeats, the overlying melody becomes increasingly dissonant and independent. The basic scale itself eventually changes as well: its original D♭ and G♭ are replaced by their natural counterparts. Later it is transposed, beginning on F♯ (a mediant relation to the opening tonal center). As with many variation works, the piece then becomes freer: the passacaglia scale is filled in by intervening pitches; it is transformed from accompaniment to primary melodic material; it is combined with a reminiscence of the introductory harmonics in the viola; and at one point it is transposed to B♮, each of its notes separated by measures of rest and elaborated by arpeggiations featuring dissonant clusters (figure 7; the notes of the rising scale begin the figurative patterns in mm. 150, 152, 154, 156, 157, 159, and 161). The end reverts to the near-immobility of the opening, ultimately settling on a peaceful cadence on the original B♭.

In summary, the variation form provided Kernis with a broad framework for organizing a composition, but he found room to maneuver within that framework in order to indulge his invention. The result is a coherent structure overlaid by imaginative spontaneity. Having made peace with the variation principle in this way, he would return to the form again and again, creating some of his most memorable works: the slow movement of his first string quartet, the orchestral piece *Color Wheel*, and the recent *Perpetual Chaconne*, to name a few.

Figure 7. *Passacaglia-Variations* for viola and piano (1985), mm. 148–61. (Copyright © 1985 by Associated Music Publishers, Inc. International Copyright Secured. All Rights Reserved. Used by Permission.)

In the summer of 1985 Kernis left Rome to attend the Dartington International Summer School of Music near Totnes in South Devon, England. There he took a composition seminar with Harrison Birtwistle. At the end of this residency, the institute awarded him a commission for a new work that eventually became *Invisible Mosaic I.* After a short time in London, Kernis moved in September to Amsterdam, where he enjoyed a lovely apartment not far from the Prinsengracht, the city's longest canal. At first he found the environment beautiful and made good progress on the *Passacaglia-Variations.* But after he failed to establish meaningful liaisons personally or within the musical world, his feeling of isolation increased dramatically as the grey of winter set in, and he began to experience what appeared to be a series of anxiety attacks.

In March 1986 Kernis returned (temporarily) to New York, but the next few years were marked by a physical transience that seemed to reflect his professional and personal meanderings. He lived in three different apartments in downtown New York and spent extended periods in artist colonies throughout the country, including a residency at the MacDowell Colony in 1988. A stint in Toronto in 1989 prompted by a romantic relationship with Canadian writer Catherine Bush was followed by a period in Provincetown, Massachusetts.

Not surprisingly, the music Kernis wrote after he returned to the United States was at first inspired by his European experiences. Perhaps the most vivid of these was a visit to the mosaics of Ravenna, which stimulated in him a type of hallucination "brought on by their densely colored, fragmented surfaces." As he describes it:

> Initially I was overwhelmed, seeing only whirling, broken-up fields of color devoid of form or figuration. It was like being thrown into a room with a million flashing, multi-colored lights which completely overtook the senses. Only later was I able to piece together what I had seen into continuous shapes that had formal design and spiritual intent. I now see this visual experience as being symbolic of many of my emotional states of that time.[6]

Kernis's physiological response to the artworks found voice in three compositions he titled *Invisible Mosaic,* composed in 1986–88. They call for ensembles of increasing size. *Invisible Mosaic I* (begun in Amsterdam and completed at the Djerassi Resident Artists Program in northern California in November 1987) is a half-hour-long quartet for clarinet, violin, cello, and piano and is "the most troubled and tragic of the three."[7] *Invisible Mosaic II* (about sixteen minutes) calls for a chamber orchestra of seventeen players; *Invisible Mosaic III* (about seventeen minutes) is for full orchestra.[8]

Kernis transformed his visual experience into a musical structure: each work moves from a "broken-up field of color devoid of form" to a "continuous shape."[9] In musical terms, "fragmented ideas and gestures" become "long, sweeping melodic lines." In all three works, the ending brings "some kind of resolution," he notes, "be it emotional or harmonic." In this sense the three mosaic pieces can be seen as direct outgrowths of the central movement of "*dream of the morning sky*," now liberated from the strict controls that governed that movement. At the same time, Kernis began to realize how important those controls had been for him: they enhanced his sensitivity to proportion, which remains a vital consideration in his compositional process to the present day.

Invisible Mosaic II shows other similarities to "*dream*" as well. Not only does it move from confusion to clarity, but it also features rising scalar melodic lines, virtuosic instrumental writing, extremely high solo passages on the violin (such as the one Mehta criticized in the middle movement of "*dream*"), and a truly raucous opening. Notable as well is Kernis's increasing skill in orchestration, as seen in a *leggiero* section featuring woodwinds, vibraphone, marimba, and celesta (at rehearsal number 2 in the score); the foregrounding of a guiro (rehearsal 12); strings reinforced by bass drum, tom-tom, and piano (rehearsal 25); a furious, frantic descent into a single stroke on the gong that resonates for ten to twelve seconds (rehearsal 36); seamless timbral modulation from horn to flute (rehearsal 41–42); and most notably, a two-minute-long section featuring flutter tonguing in the woodwinds (rehearsal 48–50). The piece is extremely challenging. Conductor Gerard Schwarz recalls that in preparation for the U.S. premiere by Music Today at Merkin Hall, he scheduled a full day of sectionals to work through its technical intricacies.[10]

In *Invisible Mosaic III* Kernis returned to "a complete and convinced use of tonality."[11] It is in many ways a transitional piece, setting the scene for his interest in classical forms that would emerge in the *Symphony in Waves* and, most dramatically, in the first string quartet. *Invisible Mosaic III* is also eclectic: it contains overt acknowledgments of Debussy and Berlioz, as well as of minimalism and jazz.

The work's opening section presents a kaleidoscope of motives: fast chromatic descending scales in the winds, not unlike those that opened *Invisible Mosaic II*, and simultaneously a slower rising scalar theme in the tuba; a syncopated pizzicato motive in the cellos; repeated note figures in the brass coupled with ostinati in the strings and a jazzy motive in the woodwinds; a delicate staccato section; a joyful dance; and a contrasting lyric legato melody. These motives recur in alternation or in collage, evoking the swirling colors of the mosaics. A short transition that pays homage to Debussy's *Jeux* (Kernis even writes "merci à Monsieur Debussy" in the score) leads into a scherzo and trio, quite Classical in format. Introducing this scherzo is the most unusual percussion effect in the piece: one player shatters "a small pane of glass, preferably with a small hammer." It "makes a fantastic sound," says conductor Hugh Wolff, "but OSHA [the federal government's Occupational Safety and Health Administration] tends to get upset. Then you have to have people wear goggles and hard hats."[12] Near the end of the scherzo Kernis inserted a mini-fugue starting with the double basses and contrabassoon, followed by imitative entries in the higher instruments, much like the last movement of Bach's fourth Brandenburg concerto. The trio (rehearsal letter I) is slower, lyrical, and yet at the same time a bit drunken in feel (influenced, Kernis says, by Berlioz's Queen Mab scherzo). As in the eighteenth-century third-movement form, the scherzo then reappears, but as usual with Kernis, it's revised and rearranged. The tonal expression begins to emerge near the end with a strong cadential arrival on D♯ (m. 349). In its enharmonic spelling, this note becomes the harmonic goal of the entire work. The culminating coda—the last minute and a half of the piece—solidifies its preeminence. The brass instruments carry the scalar theme in long notes, presenting it in an additive fashion reminiscent of the procedures Kernis had used in *Stein Times Seven*, and rising eventually to the dominant: G–A♭; G–A♭–B♭; G–A♭–B♭–E♭; G–A♭–B♭–E♭–F; G–A♭–B♭–E♭–F–G; G–A♭–B♭–E♭–F–G–B♭. Meanwhile, ascending scalar motives appear in shorter note values (at several speeds at once) in the strings, woodwinds, chimes, and crotales, beginning with scale fragments, then expanding into full scales until all forces coalesce on E♭ for a Beethovenian-type closure with triadic emphasis on the tonic. Perhaps it was here that Kernis's synesthetic association linking various keys with colors began. There's a reason, he thinks, that E♭ was one of Mozart's favorite keys: it is, in his opinion, one of the richest and most sonorous tonalities.

Thus *Invisible Mosaic III* at once revisited compositional procedures Kernis had explored during the previous decade—minimalism, additive procedures, scalar melodies, broad A B A' structures—but also charted new territory. In this work he unabashedly indulged his debt to tonality, allowing triads and strong cadential arrival to emerge from a highly dissonant context. Kernis himself described the work's harmonic language as "a journey from a language of chromaticism to an embrace of consonance."[13] It was a rather audacious path to follow, one that was not encouraged in most academic compositional circles, where tonality's demise was taken as a credo that had begun with Schoenberg. But it was also an expressive language that had attracted him for years. His own inclinations led him to welcome Western music history's tonal heritage, and he now had the confidence to boldly combine that heritage with his own voice. Stanley Austin's advice from 1977 comes to mind: "Stick by your beliefs." In Kernis's case, those beliefs mandated a wide inclusivity, accepting and combining diverse traditions from tonality to serialism to minimalism. The originality of the resulting language comes from the unique combination of elements rather than from the forging of a new system.

Also dating from 1987 are three contrasting pieces: the half-hour-long *Love Scenes* for soprano and cello, a lullaby for piano, and *Phantom Polka* for accordion. Kernis composed *Love Scenes* for soprano Dawn Upshaw and cellist André Emelianoff, using poetry by the Polish author Anna Świrszczyńska (Anna Swir), who had served in the Polish resistance movement during World War II. The year after her death in 1984, Czesław Miłosz published a translation of her poetry in a collection titled *Happy as a Dog's Tail*, from which Kernis selected eleven poems and arranged them in semi-operatic fashion to create his own narrative—a process he repeatedly would find successful in future years. The work started out as a small commission, but what emerged, says James Rushton, was almost symphonic in scope.[14]

The narrative Kernis created is divided into three parts separated by two interludes and surrounded by a prologue and an epilogue. Miłosz identifies the central theme of Swir's poetry as flesh: "Flesh in love ecstasy, flesh in pain, flesh in terror, flesh afraid of loneliness, exuberant, running, lazy, flesh of a woman giving birth, resting, snoring, doing her morning calisthenics, feeling the flow of time or reducing time to one instant."[15] Kernis arranged his chosen texts to create a descriptive progression moving from love tinged with sorrow and death ("I am filled with love, / as a great tree with the wind, / as a sponge with the ocean, / as a great life with suffering, / as time with death") to violence ("We will throttle each other / me and my bloody fate / till one of us / drops dead"). The movements range from twenty-two seconds to more than four minutes and word-painting illustrates the text throughout, often expressed in the general tenor of the movement but also, at times, in the literal portrayal of individual words. To cite two specific examples of the latter, rapid thirty-second-note runs in the prologue portray wind, and long melismas in the first interlude illustrate freedom. On a broader level, the theme of number 6, "Our love is rough as the tongue of a wild cat," prompted double-stop glissandos and very high fast notes in the cello; in number 8 a long double-stop slide and high skittering on the fingerboard accompany the text "Our embrace lasted too long. / . . . I hear the bones grind, I see / our two skeletons." Then, as the soprano sings "Tonight I am going to sleep alone," the cello drops out entirely, leaving the singer exposed in monophony. Most dramatic, however, is the very end, when the soprano leaps down to a long held B♮ followed by B♭ on the words "drops dead," while the cello repeats an A that becomes a dyad (A–B♭) reiterated eleven times (for the eleven movements, perhaps?) with the lower note gradually rising microtonally until it almost reaches the pitch of the upper one. "Remain poised as if prepared to continue," Kernis instructs the performers at the end of the set.

Microtones and pitch bending make an appearance in the penultimate movement, which also has a violent text: "We will kill our love / We will strangle it as one strangles a baby." Then as the singer "shoots love in the heart," the cellist responds with Bartók snap pizzicatos. (Mehta's comparison of them to bows and arrows comes to mind.)

The texts of "Gentle World" and "A Night of Love" are far more peaceful. The first opens with the soprano humming then opening to "Ah," as in the finale of "*dream of the morning sky.*" Without text she becomes a companion instrument to the cello, and the two function for a while in a pseudo-canon. During this section, phrases gradually lengthen in a free application of the additive procedures Kernis had toyed with in earlier works. "A Night of Love," in contrast, is a humorous parody of nineteenth-century opera. In the center is a cadenza for the two instruments (mostly in thirds) marked "brilliante" and recalling the one in *Lucia di Lammermoor*, complete with its references to madness.

The piano lullaby—the second work from 1987—is quiet, but like the *Meditation* for John Lennon, its apparent peacefulness is in fact a lamentation disguising an underlying tension. Kernis composed the piece in response to a devastating gas leak in Bhopal, India, in 1984 that caused thousands of deaths and injuries. He originally intended it to be part of a set of "poisoned nocturnes," but instead he incorporated it, three years later, into the children's suite *Before Sleep and Dreams*.

The accordion polka, in contrast, is simply fun. Kernis wrote it for Guy Klusevsek, one of the founding members of Joseph Franklin's Relâche ensemble. The contrast to *Love Scenes* aptly illustrates Kernis's need—which we will see again in his "war" period—to lighten the burden of producing long, serious works with humorous diversions. Some reviewers have detected multiple personalities in these contrasts, but for Kernis it is simply a matter of finding emotional relief.

The ISCM film

In 1988 the International Society for Contemporary Music (ISCM) joined forces with Polish television to produce a series of twenty films featuring twenty living composers from twenty countries. Leading the project was composer-pianist Zygmunt Krauze (b. 1938), who had served, among other residencies, as a visiting composer at Yale in 1982. In that same year, Pierre Boulez invited Krauze to be an adviser at the Institut de Recherche et Coordination Acoustique/Musique (IRCAM) in Paris. He became vice president and, afterwards, president of ISCM.

The premise of the film project was rather unusual: ten older and ten younger composers were selected (table 5), and each filming segment involved two of them: generally, one established figure and one emerging one. Kernis was paired with Louis Andriessen.

The organizers aimed for broad representation. Although the majority of invitees came from western Europe, the group also included representatives from Asia, Central and South America, eastern Europe, and Australia. (The original proposal projected the participation of composers from Uruguay, Cuba, and the Philippines as well.)[16] Exactly half of the younger composers were women.

The producers then created twenty half-hour programs from the ten filming sessions. Each focused on a single individual and included performances of excerpts

TABLE 5. Composers featured in the ISCM films, listed in chronological order according to year of birth. (Horizontal rows do not correspond to pairings within the films. Kernis, for example, was paired with Andriessen.)

Composers born before 1949	Country	Composers born in 1950 or later	Country
Iannis Xenakis (1922–2001)	France (Greece)	Lam Manyee (b. 1950)	Hong Kong
Klaus Huber (b. 1924)	Switzerland	Chen Yi (b. 1953)	China
Luciano Berio (b. 1925–2003)	Italy	Anders Hillborg (b. 1954)	Sweden
Krzysztof Penderecki (b. 1933)	Poland	Máté Hollós (b. 1954)	Hungary
Paul Gutama Soegijo (b. 1934)	Indonesia	Judith Weir (b. 1954)	United Kingdom
Robert Aitken (b. 1939)	Canada	Martin Smolka (b. 1959)	Czech Republic
Louis Andriessen (b. 1939)	Netherlands	Ana Lara (b. 1959)	Mexico
Barry Conyngham (b. 1944)	Australia	Aaron Kernis (b. 1960)	United States
Clarence Barlow (b. 1945)	Germany	Alejandro Iglesias Rossi (b. 1960)	Argentina
Jukka Tiensu (b. 1948)	Finland	Karen Tanaka (b. 1961)	Japan

of his or her works by Muzyka Centrum, Krakow, interspersed with three segments of dialogue. In the first, the composers answered a given set of queries, posed by Krauze rather in the style of a quiz show: fast-paced questions, short answers ranging from one word to a few sentences, and no follow-up. For example:

•Imagine you are in the desert alone in a complete silence. What would you like to hear?
Kernis and Lara: the wind
Andriessen and Tanaka: water
Wier: people
Berio: the sound of an umbrella protecting me from the sun
Penderecki: Mozart
• What is music for you?
Kernis: A confirmation of my soul . . . of my being
Xenakis: A way of traversing life
Penderecki: Communication
Andriessen: A way of talking to people, and an expression of how things move

Although this exercise might at first seem rather superficial, the necessity of giving spontaneous responses to complex queries in brief sound bites actually forced the composers to identify the essence of their aesthetic principles. In response to a question about music's function in society, for example, Kernis replied, "Self-expression." Others gave similarly metaphysical responses. "Catharsis," replied Andriessen. "To coordinate the mind and the body," suggested Berio. The final question related to Krauze's assumption that there was often a lack of "joy, per se" in contemporary music. In response, many composers cited the devastating political complexion of the twentieth century. "Look at our own century; how much joy do we see around us?" replied Judith Weir. "The world is sick," said Andriessen. In contrast, Kernis looked inward: "I think there is too much concentration on idea rather than the expression of the soul," he said, echoing Druckman's comments at the Horizons Festival about the mid-twentieth-century domination of the Apollonian aesthetic.

Producer Katharine Adamov enlisted John Cage's participation in the project as well. Using the composers' answers to Krauze's questions, Cage created twenty of his famous mesostics: poems in which the central letters line up vertically to form an important phrase. Cage reads these poems in the middle of each film, always beginning with a quote from the composer that epitomizes his or her philosophy and then freely combining words or phrases from their answers in the manner of an indeterminate musical composition. For Kernis, "Music is a confirmation of my being" can be read vertically down the center of Cage's text:[17]

a confirMation of
aboUt
direction aS
I was
aspeCt
own dIrection
iS
rAther than the expression
aspeCt
tO
developmeNt
selF
thIngs music
fiRst
following My own
A human
To
Incredible
Of thought
New
On
oF the
too Much
mY
Body of
anothEr
Is
a humaN
expression I was followinG.

Cage also introduced each film with a brief speech highlighting the internationalization of contemporary music.

International is the wrong word
Music is now global
The world is village
The concert is heard everywhere
Population has increased and increases
Technology continues to change
We have more kinds of music
More composers than ever before
The future is only known
When it is already part of the past.

In the film featuring Kernis the musicians perform "The Blue Animals" from *Morningsongs* and two excerpts from *Invisible Mosaic II.* In one selection Kernis plays the piano; in another he conducts. Krauze comments on the contrast between the two pieces, but Kernis instead draws attention to their similarities, citing their "spiritual essence"—the "incredibly emotional, but beautiful feeling" they try to capture. Each film ends with Krauze in dialogue with Rolf Liebermann, assessing the featured composer's style, aesthetics, and influence. In Kernis's case, Krauze marvels that a composer living in the middle of Manhattan could write music evocative of the nineteenth century. Liebermann counters that Kernis really belongs to Vienna, particularly to Mahler's Vienna. He has "the courage, if I might say, to try to find the melody again . . . the forgotten melody which is not allowed, which Pierre Boulez never would permit, . . . just expressing what he feels; and it is very beautiful."

A First Symphony and a First String Quartet

This trip to Poland would have additional, far-reaching consequences for Kernis. At Krauze's urging, he visited the former Nazi death camps of Auschwitz and Birkenau, and then, on his return to the United States, he began to read Holocaust literature, including Lucy Dawidowicz's *The War Against the Jews*. The Holocaust would later serve as a stimulus for several war works of the 1992–95 period, and the visit to Birkenau would directly stimulate his concerto for English horn, the piece that would ultimately win the Grawemeyer Award.

Meanwhile, however, Kernis devoted himself to writing his first symphony, commissioned by the St. Paul Chamber Orchestra (SPCO) in 1988.[18] The impetus came from John Adams, who at the time served as creative chair and frequent conductor of the orchestra.[19] (In this period, the musical leadership of the SPCO was divided among three conductors: Adams, Hugh Wolff, and Christopher Hogwood.)[20] The idea of writing a symphony was anachronistic for Kernis. "It seemed such an outdated and irrelevant form," he said. He would soon decide otherwise, however, becoming "increasingly excited by the communicative potential, by the highly varied ideas and emotions, latent in traditional forms."[21] In retrospect, his embrace of the symphony and string quartet seems a logical extension of his turn toward tonality. Instead of rejecting tradition, as had so many ultra-modernists, Kernis decided to cultivate it.

As usual, the inspiration for the piece was extramusical, in this case, waves in their various manifestations—water, sound, and light; swells and troughs; flickers and roars. Although Kernis gave a title to this and most of his other instrumental works, the *Symphony in Waves* is not programmatic. The wave analogy is simply a suggestion, a means by which Kernis revealed his inspiration and at the same time gave license to his listeners to formulate their own visual images—which, of course, did not prevent most of the reviewers from trying to assign specific types of waves to the various movements. Kernis does not discourage this type of association. In fact, he encourages it, explaining:

> I tend not to be shy and to say, "Yes, I had this experience. I saw this color. I was present in this landscape." I had my internal emotional picture world influenced by something that became a starting place for a piece. But when a listener comes up to me and says, "Oh, I saw that color when I heard the music; I imagined that place"—their own version, their own story, their own experience—that's priceless.

The *Symphony in Waves* turned out to be longer and more difficult than the orchestra had projected and therefore required more rehearsal time than was available. So when Adams conducted the premiere, on November 3 and 4, 1989, the orchestra played only the first two of its five movements. Reviewers lauded the work, as well as the decision to favor a better prepared but shorter presentation, but the missing movements captured the headlines ("Composer Departs with Half a 'Wave,'" reported the *Star Tribune*.)[22] The premiere of the full work didn't take place until two years later, when Gerard Schwarz conducted the New York Chamber Symphony on November 9 and 10, 1991.

Following the full premiere, *New York Times* critic Bernard Holland called the *Symphony in Waves* the "most arresting new orchestral piece" of the year[23] and praised Kernis for his "fearless originality and powerful voice." At the same time, he also worried about the piece's difficulty: the strings play very high in their range, absolute rhythmic precision is mandatory, and soloists must execute slow, wide leaps and "remain poised and in tune." Despite its technical challenges, however, this symphony not only has had a respectable performance history but also has been recorded twice.

The five movements of the *Symphony in Waves* form an arch: opening and closing fast movements (ten and seven minutes long, respectively), short, lively second and fourth movements (a four-minute scherzo and a two-minute intermezzo), and in the center a fifteen-minute slow movement. The opening of the first movement seems to take off directly from the end of *Invisible Mosaic III*. It begins in tonal clarity: overlapping arpeggiated triads, first C major, then A♭, then E (again the Romantic mediant relationships), from which rises a lyrical, legato theme in the cello. After two minutes, the texture thins out to only the double basses, who play rising scale fragments—three, four, five, and six notes—gradually joined by the higher instruments, similar to the fast rising scales in the strings that appear at the end of *Invisible Mosaic III*. Likewise, the end of the symphony's fifth movement features ascending scale fragments in the trumpets and horns. In fact, this movement builds directly on a work called *Jacob's Ladders* for large mixed chamber ensemble that Kernis composed for Jacob Druckman's sixtieth birthday.

If the first movement and the end of the symphony look back at Kernis's previous music, however, the inner movements look forward to his compositions of the 1990s—both the lamentations that would arise from his distress over world conflicts and the lighter, humorous pieces that provided him emotional relief. The scherzo, for example, ends with a series of repeated dissonant chords in the piano that rise in volume from very soft to *fortississimo*. Kernis wrote in the score: "Play it like Jerry Lee Lewis!" (Kernis would playfully imitate Lewis's heavy-handed pounding on the keys in his *Superstar Etude no. 1* of 1992.) This movement illustrates as well his ever-expanding imagination in terms of orchestration. Some examples are the chirping motives at the beginning in harmonics in the violins, here divided into six parts and playing in extremely intricate rhythmic interplay; simultaneous trills in three horns, producing an almost vocal effect; and rapid-fire dialogue among cello, piano, and bass clarinet. The fourth-movement intermezzo opens with the violins alone, divided in three parts in close canonic imitation at a distance of an eighth note. The shimmering effect created by these soft legato lines continues for nearly half of the movement. When a disjunct staccato motive enters (still using only the violins), the imitation becomes even tighter, occurring at a distance of a sixteenth note. Holland's comment about the need for absolute rhythmic precision springs to mind.

The dramatic highlight of the symphony is the central "Still Movement," which is still not in the sense of "quiet" (it is, in fact, often powerfully loud) but, rather, in its extended periods of harmonic and textural stasis. The movement opens with huge chords. At first they are consonant (starting in A minor), but dissonance quickly intrudes in the form of a minor second. The attack of each chord is reinforced in the percussion by alternate strokes on a bell plate and chimes. The intense immobility of these gradually changing big chords continues for more than two minutes. After a transition, Kernis eliminates everyone but the first violin section, which plays an excruciatingly slow two-minute-long melody that rises in a gradual wave three times. This unison passage would challenge even the most expert ensemble in terms of pitch matching and coordination, but the effect, when done well, is electrifying.

Other solo passages occur later in the movement, most notably, a two-minute-long flute solo that unfolds over held chords in the string section. Then a percussionist plays a lengthy roll on the tam-tam that rises from *pppp* to a deafening *fff*, an effect Kernis would later take up at the end of his Second Symphony. Here, however, it ushers in a reprise of the static chords of the movement's opening. At the end, the dynamic decreases to nothingness.

The passionate outcry of this movement, coupled with Kernis's call for near-motionlessness, brings to mind the early *Death Fugue*, now, however, in more confident and experienced hands. We will see this unhurried tension reemerge later in the *Lament and Prayer* and *Still Movement with Hymn*, where Kernis again indulges his love for temporal spaciousness. He has no fear of drawing out the drama of slow movements for extended periods, which places demands on the performers but also speaks with breathtaking drama to audiences.

The year after Kernis completed the *Symphony in Waves*, the Lark String Quartet won the prestigious Naumburg Foundation chamber music prize.[24] The foundation had been giving awards to solo artists since 1925, but the chamber music prize was not initiated until 1965 and only established as an annual award in 1971. Each year the foundation chooses a maximum of two groups, whom they not only sponsor in New York appearances but also authorize—in cooperation with the National Endowment for the Arts—to commission a new work. After an extended search for a composer whose music moved them ("Everything we heard was either too abstract or too familiar," recalls first violinist Eva Gruesser), the group discovered the music of Kernis through a recommendation from Michael Barrett, cofounder of the New York Festival of Song. Gruesser was impressed by what she heard in concert and contacted Kernis, who sent her a tape of the *Symphony in Waves*. "We knew he'd write something substantive," says violist Anna Kruger, "and that we'd not be wasting our time learning his piece." Learning the piece in fact turned out to be far more time-consuming than the members of this virtuoso ensemble had anticipated. But they found the result rewarding. "We expected to be taken on a journey," says Kruger. "Boy, were we right!"[25]

Titled String Quartet (*musica celestis*), this work represents in some ways a culmination of Kernis's turn toward historical styles, which had first emerged in the *Passacaglia-Variations* he had begun in Rome. It is, in fact, very difficult to write a string quartet without coming to terms with the form's illustrious beginnings in the late eighteenth and early nineteenth centuries, in particular the quartets of Beethoven, which inspired—and intimidated—his successors. Kernis's flirtation with Baroque forms in the passacaglia and then his re-embrace of tonal roots in *Invisible Mosaic III* and the *Symphony in Waves* led in a direct line to his exploration of Classical forms in this quartet.

Especially momentous for Kernis was making peace with sonata-allegro form. This standard vessel into which composers from Mozart to Schoenberg (and beyond) had poured their musical ideas was frowned on in many contemporary composition circles—especially in the academy. It was something "you just did not do in school," Kernis recalls. He was haunted by conflicting emotions: "Was it a reactionary thing? Was it a radical thing? It was something I knew I needed to do, but at the same time the idea felt so uncomfortable." Even now, after so many composers have welcomed a postmodern resurgence of tonality, Kernis continues to sense a resistance among many students to "developmental forms that are not purely process forms." What ultimately fascinated him about sonata form—and opened the way for him to adopt it as one more element in his compositional toolbox—was not so much its rhetorical structure (the posing of a conflict in the exposition, the intensification of that conflict in the development, and the ultimate resolution in the recapitulation) as the "expansive landscape" he saw in the works of Mozart, Haydn, and Beethoven. In particular, he became fascinated with the wide range of affects and thematic expression that could coexist successfully within a single movement. Furthermore, he realized that the form offered a coherent scaffolding that admitted endless variation. Re-examining Beethoven's piano sonatas, Kernis marveled at the way each movement in sonata form differed from the others not only in its component harmonic and melodic materials but also in the suppleness and elasticity of the form itself. "Every one is different; Beethoven never repeats himself," he notes, reflecting his own aversion to exact repetition.

Overall, Kernis's quartet is a compendium of Classical period structures. The first movement is an extended sonata form, the second is a slow theme with variations, the third is a scherzo and trio, and the finale is a rondo.

Having determined to write a sonata-form opening movement, Kernis sought a personal interpretation of it. Indulging his love of melody, he developed a version of the form with multiple themes in each of the traditional "key areas," as opposed to the typical (but by no means universal) pattern of two contrasting themes. (Twentieth-century composers using sonata form have often retained the element of two contrasting themes even while abandoning the traditional dichotomy of tonic and dominant keys.) Keeping in the foreground a sense of the movement's proportions, harmonic relationships, and large-scale formal design, Kernis let his intuition guide him in working out the details. The result is a clear sonata form imbued with complex melodic interrelationships and elements of rondo. The first theme group introduces two motives: a gentle, yet ebullient A theme and a crisp, dry B motive (see figure 8). The expansive legato opening melody features three

A theme

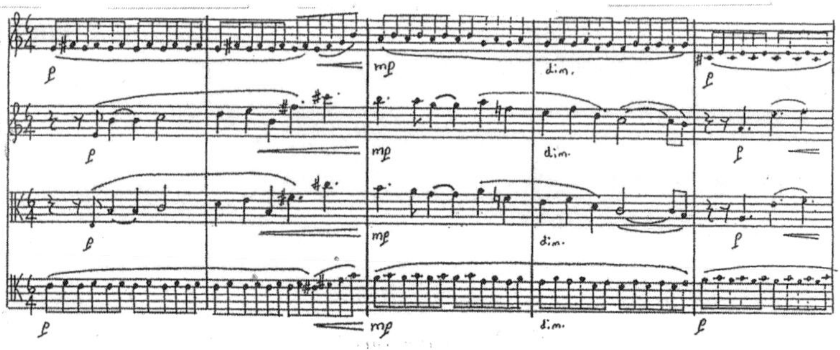

B theme

C theme

Figure 8. *String Quartet "musica celestis"* (1990), themes and ending.

End of movement 1

Figure 8. (*Continued*)

upward leaps of a fifth. Underlying the melody is an accompaniment of undulating eighth notes. In contrast, the B theme is staccato and restless, its meter shifting and its character agitated. The second theme group recalls elements of A (now with sparse interjections) and then offers a crisp, decisive C theme consisting of three-note groups (figure 8). A short recollection of A leads into a legato closing theme. Kernis presents these themes in his long exposition (164 measures) in a pseudo-rondo form: A B A'—A" C A"' Codetta. The somewhat shorter development section (108 measures) concentrates primarily on the A motive, introducing, on occasion, a pastoral mood. But the development also includes "bursts of fifths."[26] Here Kernis transforms the striving melodic interval introduced in the A theme into repeated double-stop open fifths in all the instruments. The effect is a series of frantic, tense, and unsettled interruptions, highly dissonant in character because the fifths appear in a polytonal relationship (for example, C–G, F–C, A–E, and C♯–G♯ simultaneously in m. 212). A retransition leads into a recapitulation, altered in detail but containing all of the exposition's elements. The movement ends with a coda dominated by theme A but also including fifths in harmonics and rising fast scales reminiscent of those at the end of *Invisible Mosaic III* and in the first movement of the *Symphony in Waves* (figure 8).

The second movement is itself titled "musica celestis" and was inspired, Kernis wrote in his program notes, "by the medieval conception of that phrase which refers to the singing of the angels in heaven in praise of God without end. . . . I don't particularly believe in angels," he wrote, "but found this to be a potent image that has been reinforced by listening to a good deal of medieval music, especially the soaring work of Hildegard von Bingen (1098–1179)." The inspiration of Hildegard was more spiritual and emotional than musical; the movement contains no direct references to medieval chants by her or anyone else, although it does include brief internal sections using the phrygian and lydian modes.[27] In the source on Hildegard that Kernis consulted during the compositional process, he found quotations relating to medieval theorists' ideas about music in the universe, thus giving rise to the movement's subtitle. This movement places a theme and variations structure within an arch form: an introduction precedes the statement of the theme, which is then followed by seven variations of different lengths. At the end the introduction returns, followed by a short coda. As in his passacaglia—and like many of Beethoven's variation movements—the theme becomes increasingly hidden as the variations progress. They become faster and decrease in length until, near the end, the theme reemerges in a homorhythmic setting in long notes.

In the year he wrote the quartet, Kernis arranged this slow movement for string orchestra, and it is now perhaps his most frequently performed work. Critics have repeatedly compared the orchestral *Musica Celestis* to Samuel Barber's Adagio for Strings. The association "makes me crazy," says Kernis. "I simply don't see it." The impetus for his concern is not any implication on the part of critics that he is trying to cash in on Barber's success, but rather that the similarities between the two works are superficial: "It's for strings, it's slow, and it ascends," he says, "but from a formal point of view, a harmonic point of view, the two pieces have nothing to do with one another." Indeed, the similarities are for the most part atmospheric. On the other hand, Barber—a lyrical composer whose music reflects elements of Sibelius, with whom Kernis does feel a close affinity—may have been a subconscious influence.

If the slow movement calls to mind the aesthetic of Sibelius or Barber, the scherzo pays tribute to Beethoven and Haydn. (The humor and structure of the fifth movement of Beethoven's C-sharp minor quartet op. 131 may come to mind, but Kernis was consciously recalling the scherzos of Haydn.) The movement opens with pizzicato: at first chords and then a catchy tune. The scherzo ends in G; then a mediant progression ushers in the contrasting trio in E. Here a simple melody line is set against drones. Adopting a typical Beethovenian strategy, Kernis inserts a short nine-measure transition back to the (altered) scherzo. The movement ends with a coda that references the opening theme of movement 1.

The quartet's finale is a rondo subtitled "Quasi una Danza." Four intermediary sections separate the varied returns of the A theme. Each time the opening melody recurs Kernis changes its harmonic setting, increasing its dissonance and hence its tension. The opening motive is, in its most basic form, simply the leading tone (D♯) to tonic (E), which eventually expands to become scalar, then octatonic, then chromatic. Intermediary sections are highly contrasting, one including repeated notes forming a type of drone, another (mm. 135–73) featuring a legato Romantic melody accompanied by undulating eighths that suggests the beginning of the first movement, another introducing elements of funk, boogie-woogie, and jazz. The final interlude section is marked "quasi fuga pomposo" and, indeed, forms a type of parody of a Beethoven fugato in long notes, beginning with the cello. Just before the end, the tempo suddenly changes to *tranquillo* (another strategy Beethoven often used) and, as in the scherzo, Kernis then inserts a recollection of the first movement's opening theme and eighth-note accompaniment, creating a cyclical form. A five-measure *molto allegro* romp ushers in the final E major cadence.

In summary, then, the first quartet marked a major turning point in Kernis's style. Even two years earlier, his program notes state, he had considered the Classical forms "outmoded and inapplicable to the music of our time." But building on his turn to tonality in the *Symphony in Waves* and searching for a new direction, he decided to explore these very forms and found them "rich in possibilities" and "conducive to the needs" of his own language. What attracted him most about pre-twentieth-century music—which he now found himself increasingly enjoying—was its "emotional inclusiveness,"[28] a characteristic he cultivated in his own works.

Critics evaluating the *Symphony in Waves*, the first quartet, and other compositions from this period often looked for influences: not only Bach, Barber, Beethoven, Berg, and Sibelius (already cited), but also Adams, Bernstein, Britten, Ravel, and Stravinsky, whose names pop up in written commentaries. This search for historical antecedence might in part have arisen from Kernis's own turn toward traditional forms, but on a broader scale it reflects the critics' need to categorize, pigeonhole, and historicize the work of contemporary artists. Such comparisons play into questions of originality, of course. Perhaps a composer's worst fear is to be labeled "derivative." At the same time, however, it is impossible to wipe the mind clean of any influence, either historical or contemporaneous. The difficulty facing the contemporary creator is, rather, to admit admiration for the accomplishments of the past but at the same time transform that admiration into something uniquely personal. Kernis's success in doing so may well have been a major factor prompting Holland to call his first symphony the most important orchestral work of 1991 and inspiring the Pulitzer, Grawemeyer, and Nemmers committees to honor his work.

Meeting Evelyne; New Works for Voice, Piano, and Chamber Ensembles

On November 13, 1990, the Lark Quartet presented the premiere of Kernis's new string quartet at Alice Tully Hall. Five days earlier, he had attended a concert of quite a different sort at the Greenwich House School of Music—twenty-nine songs by the Beatles arranged by Steven Blier. The concert was part of the third season of the New York Festival of Song, established in 1988 by Blier and Michael Barrett. Kernis found himself sitting next to a young pianist, Evelyne Luest, who had just moved to New York City and was a founding member of the newly established Eberli Ensemble, consisting of clarinet, violin, cello, and piano. (The name *Eberli* came from the cellist's instrument maker. The group changed its name to the Contrasts Quartet in 2001 after a new cellist joined.) In 1982 Luest had completed a bachelor's degree at the University of California, Santa Cruz, where she studied piano with Sylvia Jenkins and chamber music with Heiichiro Ohyama. She then moved to New York, where, under the tutelage of Gilbert Kalish, she earned a master's degree and a DMA at SUNY Stony Brook (the latter completed in 1992). In the meantime, on March 24, 1990, she presented her debut New York solo concert at Weill Recital Hall as one of the winners of the annual Artists International Competition. Her avid interest in contemporary music led to performances with various new music groups and festivals in the city.

Luest and Kernis conversed a bit at the concert but their relationship went no further until a surprise birthday party for Rohan Smith, husband of Lark Quartet first violinist Eva Gruesser, on April 13, 1992. As the guests hid in the kitchen of the party's host waiting to surprise Smith, Aaron and Evelyne became reacquainted. (Evelyne had just discovered *Invisible Mosaic I* for clarinet, violin, cello, and piano at the American Music Center and was anxious to discuss the piece with Aaron. His response, she recalls, was that the piece was much too dif-

Kernis with his wife, Evelyne Luest, at their apartment complex in Washington Heights, ca. 1998. (Photo by Caroline Brown. Used by permission.)

ficult to play. Eberli did eventually perform the middle movement, "Children's Games.")[29] They discovered that they were both living in Washington Heights, a few blocks apart. At the end of the party, Evelyne gave Aaron a ride home and the rest, as they say, is history. They began dating, soon moved in together, and were married on August 29, 1996. As a soloist or as a member of her quartet, Evelyne has continued to perform Aaron's music extensively and to record his chamber music works. In fact, she joked with Aaron that Contrasts should change its name to the "Kernis Quartet." The group has performed full recitals of Kernis's music (mixing solos, duos, trios, and quartets) and often brings him along on their tours and residencies.

In addition to his first symphony and his first string quartet, Kernis also composed in this period substantial works for voice, piano, and other chamber ensembles. Among the vocal works are *Songs of Innocents*, books 1 and 2, for soprano and piano (fifteen-minute cycles completed in 1989 and 1991 for Dawn Upshaw); *Brilliant Sky, Infinite Sky* for baritone, violin, percussion, and piano (1990, for Jorja Fleezanis and Sanford Sylvan); and *Simple Songs* for soprano and an ensemble of ten instruments (1991, for Susan Narucki).

Kernis sees *Brilliant Sky, Infinite Sky* as a companion piece to *Love Scenes*. Just as his own life turned from tension to success in this period, so *Love Scenes*' negative view of human relations is now transformed into a paean to life. For this work Kernis compiled texts by four different poets: George du Maurier, John Ash, Czesław Miłosz, and Jean Joubert. The first is a dream from which the poet awakens "in a mystic flutter of ecstasy." The two central movements celebrate nature. Ash's "The Sky My Husband," the longest poem of the four, in many ways resembles the Momaday text Kernis had used in *"dream of the morning sky"* years earlier: each of its seventy-nine lines begins with the words "the sky." Miłosz (movement 3) writes about the end of the world, in which there is no lightning, thunder, or archangels, but rather bees circling clover, women walking through fields, and "a white-haired old man" binding his tomatoes. Even the finale, in which Joubert talks of a friend "entering his death," has no despair: "when he looks up, suddenly the sky / is arrayed in . . . (vertiginous) clarity."

The stimulus for *Brilliant Sky* was the Schubert Club of St. Paul, which had been founded as a women's club (The Ladies' Musicale) in 1882. One project of the club was to sponsor New York recitals for Minnesota artists. Commissioned works often served to attract the critics to these performances.[30] Funding for two of these commissions came from a philanthropic couple in the city, Linda and John Hoeschler. In this case the recitalist was Jorja Fleezanis, who joined the Minnesota Orchestra as concertmaster in 1989. She told the Hoeschlers about Kernis's *Symphony in Waves* after its 1989 (partial) premiere and suggested him as a composer. Fleezanis performed the work for the first time at Weill Recital Hall on December 17, 1990, with baritone Sanford Sylvan, pianist Robert Helps, and percussionist Daniel Druckman (son of Jacob Druckman).

Simple Songs, which Kernis later arranged both for chamber orchestra and for piano, evinces a gentle, almost mystical spirituality that would resurface much later, most notably in his Third Symphony (2009). Like *Brilliant Sky*, it illustrates his love for making connections, not only among diverse musical styles but also among diverse texts. Hildegard von Bingen was again a major influence. Kernis used one of her poems along with texts from Sufi mystic Jalāl ad-Dīn Muhammad Rūmī (1207–73), Japanese Zen Buddhist monk Ryōkan Taigu (1758–1831), and two of the Hebrew psalms, all of them in English translation. Kernis's aim was not only to create a work with variety but also to make a political statement: "One religion is not better than another . . . ; these different ways of thinking are interconnected and equally valid." The resulting song cycle became, in contrast to the symphony and quartet, not a "monumental public work, but a personal reflection—not so much a cathedral as an intimate spiritual space."[31]

Four of the five texts were translated (or, more accurately, freely adapted) by Stephen Mitchell; the Rūmī poem was translated by Robert Bly. All five appear in *The Enlightened Heart*, a collection of 123 texts from various authors and religious traditions that Mitchell judged to be "poems of fulfillment."[32] In his single-page foreword, Mitchell juxtaposes quotations from Robert Frost ("We dance round in a ring and suppose, / But the Secret sits in the middle and knows") and Chuang-tzu (Zhuangzi), a Chinese poet of the fourth century BCE ("When we understand, we are at the center of the circle, and there we sit while Yes and No chase each other around the circumference"). The circle's center, Mitchell explains, is the unknowable God, Tao, Self, Buddha. All the poets whose works appear in his collection are found within the circle—some near the outside, others firmly in the center. "But really," he concludes, "there is no circumference. Everyone, everything, is joyfully included." Mitchell's brief introduction aptly embodies a universalist spiritualism that underlies much of Kernis's later work. His developing interest in mysticism, already suggested in the texts of *"dream"* and *Brilliant Sky*, "tended to enable relief and quiet reflection," he says, "while the larger-scale works [he would write during the 1990s] reflected tumult and empathy with grief on personal or moral terms."

After selecting the five texts from Mitchell's volume, Kernis arranged them to create a coherent musical form, embodying contrast but also a varied return. The piece opens with the Hildegard poem, which addresses the spirit as the root generator of life. Psalm 1:1–3 forms the basis for the peaceful second movement: the righteous, says the psalmist, will be nourished like trees. Ryōkan's humorous and earthy text about a monk playing with children forms a scherzo-like middle movement. The poet's joy in nature, in youth, in the simple things of life inspired Kernis to create an upbeat centerpiece for the cycle. Then follows the contemplative poem of Rūmī, who muses on the relation between free will and divine control: "You are the notes, and we are the flute," says the poet. "We are the mountain, you are the sounds coming down. / We are the pawns and kings and rooks / You set out on a board: we win or we lose. . . . / Your invisible wind carries us through the world."[33] The final movement sets Psalm 131, which compares the soul to a child in its mother's arms.

Mitchell's adaptation of Psalm 131 is extremely free, particularly in the first verse, which can be rendered literally as "Lord, my heart is not haughty, nor mine eyes lofty; / Neither do I exercise myself in things too great, or in things too wonderful for me."[34] Mitchell transformed this verse into the following: "My mind is not noisy with desires, Lord / and my heart has satisfied its longing. / I do not care about religion or anything that is not you." This paraphrase of the original text prompted an angry response from an audience member, who wrote to Kernis: "How dare you write this? It's not a translation!" But Mitchell's interpretation of the psalm resonated perfectly with Kernis's search for personal spiritual fulfillment in a context independent of any particular religious tradition. He dedicated this finale—in which he deliberately paid tribute to some Mahlerian harmonic changes and which he filled with quiet open spaces—to Leonard Bernstein. "My sense," says Kernis, is that Bernstein "was very tortured. Although it's good to not be satisfied and always pursue challenges and new things and have a kind of restlessness, I wanted to try to find a transcendent element in this piece that would give the sense of bestowing a moment of rest and peace on his spirit."

Simple Songs in some ways represents a cadential arrival point for Kernis himself. In it he aimed to use the simplest of harmonic elements but treat them in a manner that was at once free and yet bound by tonal function and return. The opening movement, for example, captures the ecstasy of Hildegard's melodies, as well as her frequent use of exuberant upward leaps, but places them in a contemporary harmonic context. The rising scale with a leap at the end, which had begun to form a melodic trope for Kernis, reappears at the beginning of the second movement, where it is graced with contrapuntal layering. A series of mediant progressions in the movement's center—C–A–f♯–D–B–G—adds poignancy to the text's images of nature: the righteous "are like trees planted near flowing rivers, which bear fruit when they are ready. Their leaves will not fall or wither." The slow rising scale, now extended to nearly an octave, reappears in the last movement. In the movement's center, the instruments drop out entirely, leaving the singer alone ("my mind is not noisy with desires"). And the entire work ends in E♭, which, as we have seen in the discussion of *Invisible Mosaic III*, Kernis considers one of the most beautiful and richest of keys. It also marked for him a very special affect. "I tend to gravitate to sharp keys," he notes, "and only used E♭ major or other flat keys in very special situations."

Other chamber music and piano works from this period include *Delicate Songs* for flute, violin, and cello (1988, eighteen minutes); *Before Sleep and Dreams*, a twenty-minute, five-movement work for piano solo (1990); and the playful three-minute miniature *Mozart En Route* for string trio (1991). *Before Sleep and Dreams* opens with a slow movement evoking bells in the manner of Debussy's piano prelude "La cathédrale engloutie," an inspiration that would become even clearer in the mid-1990s when Kernis orchestrated five of Debussy's piano etudes. Like the *Symphony in Waves* and the variation movement of the string quartet, the suite has an arch form. Two outer slow movements and lively second and fourth movements surround a central lullaby—the piece memorializing the victims of the Indian gas leak that Kernis had composed three years earlier. The second movement, a scherzo, starts with the effect of bouncing balls. The fourth, marked "very fast and mercurial," is highly virtuosic with quick repeated notes alternating in the left and right hands. The highlight of the set, though, is the lullaby, which, at eight minutes, dwarfs all of the other movements. Here Kernis pays musical tribute to both Debussy and Chopin (in his use of rubato cross-rhythms). The movement's origin as a memorial also marks it as the first of several important compositions prompted by contemporaneous world events that would dominate Kernis's creative output in the early 1990s, although here he has relinquished the work's concrete reference, allowing the world of children and musical innocence to replace the original grief-tinged stimulus.

Just as the accordion polka provided comic relief from *Love Scenes*, so *Mozart En Route* contrasts with the seriousness of the piano suite. The commission for this short piece came from Bravo! Colorado for its 1991 festival. To honor the two-hundredth anniversary of Mozart's death, the festival commissioned three composers to write pieces with a specific instrumentation and then coupled them in concert with works for the same instruments by Mozart. Kernis's assignment was a string trio, and his fanfare appeared on the program along with Mozart's trio, K. 563. Kernis took inspiration from a letter Mozart wrote about a painfully bumpy carriage ride from Salzburg to Munich. "For two whole stages I sat with my hands dug into the upholstery and my behind suspended in the air," Mozart wrote in 1780. "It will serve as a warning rather to go on foot than to drive in a mail coach."[35] Kernis imagined Mozart visiting the United States in 1991, speeding from place to place in high-tech transport ("the type of particle transmission and re-assemblage found in *Star Trek*") and in the process being "brought face to face with . . . diverse forms and sounds of music." Among these diverse encounters are "Richard Strauss, American folk fiddling, Hollywood curtain raising (or cartoon) music, blues, and funk," notes Kernis. The overall effect is a set of "micro-mini variations eclectic in their sources and fleeting in their length."

The trio opens with virtuosic downward scales in the violin that reference a similar figure in the opening movement of K. 563. But instead of the steady eighths that Mozart used to accompany the scale, Kernis gives the lower instruments repeated notes in syncopated jazzy rhythm. He quickly takes the scales through six keys in a circle of fifths (F–B♭–E♭–A♭–D♭–G♭) and then moves them down in range, assigning them to the viola and then the cello. A decisive arrival on D leads to a direct quote of the first eight bars of Mozart's fourth movement: a delightful little children's tune. Its rhythm is soon disrupted, however, as the eighth notes turn into triplets and then sixteenths. Then Mozart is completely overtaken by jazz, until everything is reduced to single pitches and the players one by one articulate an interrupted C major scale. A return to the original tempo brings another quote from the Mozart trio: a rhythm (two sixteenths and an eighth) that forms a prominent figure in K. 563's finale. Mozart's texture here is homorhythmic, but Kernis uses the motive in close three-voice imitation. After returning to the original scale in the violin (accompanied by a three-note figure in long notes also inspired by Mozart's finale), the trio ends with a decisive cadence on B♭, approached through contrary motion in sixteenth notes. At the risk of indulging myself in the critic's search for influences, I couldn't help but imagine at this point Mozart meeting Bartók: Kernis's ending brought to mind the dynamic ending of Bartók's fifth string quartet.

5 War, with Interludes (1991–1995)

BY THE END OF THE 1980S KERNIS had established a reputation as one of the most promising young composers on the contemporary scene. New York critics approached his concerts with their antennas up and pens poised. Allan Kozinn called him "an eloquent young composer [who] finds an excellent balance between abstraction and lyricism." John Rockwell characterized him as "exuberant" and "fecund," noting that he "happily mixes idioms."[1] Prizes and commissions continued to roll in as well: an NEA Composer Fellowship (1986), a Ludwig Vogelstein Foundation Grant (1987), awards from the Koussevitzky and Fromm Foundations (1988–89, for *Songs of Innocents*), and an ASCAP Young Composers Grant (1989), to name a few.

Considering such positive acclaim, the next period may seem more than a little surprising. The years 1991–95 are marked by a proliferation of dark, brooding works responding to world conflicts, most notably, the Second Symphony (1991), a reaction to the first Gulf War; *Still Movement with Hymn* (1993), provoked by the war in Bosnia; *Colored Field* (1994), inspired by his 1989 visit to Auschwitz and Birkenau; and *Lament and Prayer* (1995), a memorial to the Holocaust.

Was it, perhaps, the self-confidence brought on by increasing fame that in some sense empowered Kernis to take on these greater-than-life themes or to imagine that in some way he could, by his art, effect a change in the world around him? Such a viewpoint in no way indicates a misplaced self-importance. Rather, it is essential to the very art of composition, to the communicative goal that most composers pursue: the reaching out, through personal self-expression, to move and commune with listeners, and ultimately inspire a transformation in them; to raise consciousness about what links humans to one another; to overcome, at least momentarily, the divides of politics, culture, and language. Lou Harrison once noted that "big works, such as . . . symphonies, are efforts to embody a viewpoint of the world. One doesn't assemble a large orchestra and a large audience without feeling that in some sense the composer is, if not representing, at least expressing, some part of himself as the 'general citizen.' The composer becomes, in short, a kind of singer for others."[2] Harrison's response to the 1991 Gulf War was to shut down; as a spokesperson for the "general citizen," he simply lost his voice for several years. Kernis, on the other hand, cried out stridently in protest.

Other composers, in contrast, resolutely stuck to abstract works, maintaining a distance between their artistic creations and the all-too-present violence around them. "Charles Wuorinen, your former teacher . . ., claims that you're confusing art with politics," suggested Jenny Raymond in an interview with Kernis in 1998. Kernis responded that contemporary composers have been made uncomfortable "in feeling inspired by the world at large. . . . Whether it was the Second World War [or] socialist-realist art," it was deemed "too dangerous to take influences directly from the world, from events, from people's experiences." Historically, he reflected, "the rise of Darmstadt and post–World War II ultramodernism came as a specific response to Soviet-era repression. Writing music for the masses, writing music with a message, became connected in people's minds with fascism."[3] But Kernis already had a substantial history of writing music with a message, dating back to his early *Meditation (in Memory of John Lennon)* and *Death Fugue* in 1981. Indeed, human tragedies have served as catalysts for some of his most profound works.

Despite the predominance of war-inspired, sorrowful works in this period, Kernis also provided himself emotional relief by creating more buoyant ones. "I always need a break," he says, "to something lighter, something different." The virtuosic orchestral *New Era Dance* (1992) embodies that dichotomy within itself. Although it was fueled by images of the riots in Los Angeles following the announcement of the verdict in the Rodney King case, outbreaks of violence in Atlanta, and threats of the same in Kernis's own Washington Heights area, the piece is at many points exuberant and even, at its end, cautiously optimistic—although the exuberance is consistently tempered by the threat of chaos. This work and the comical *Superstar Etude no. 1* for piano followed immediately on the heels of the Second Symphony. A quintet for guitar and string quartet, *100 Greatest Dance Hits*, dates from 1993, the same year as *Still Movement with Hymn*. Indeed, the devastation at the end of the Second Symphony—which leaves the listener shattered—is not matched in Kernis's other war-inspired pieces. Both *Still Movement* and *Lament and Prayer* conclude instead with compassionate supplications, embodying in their dynamically restrained and unhurried musical expression the extreme effort needed to reach individual catharsis and collective peace amid the world's seemingly intractable conflicts. Any perceived resolution in these works, however, is hard-won. "In *Still Movement with Hymn*," Kernis notes, "it is reached at the last possible second and with great effort. *Lament* does reach full resolution, but neither in major nor minor—neither hopeful nor negating hope." The ultimate impression in both works is that of an unfulfilled quest.

Although these works were incited by concrete events, the resulting musical expression embodies, in the best historical tradition, more generalized human emotions. The works, in short, transcend their stimuli. None of them is defined by its catalyst. Rather, like the visual or verbal images that inspired many of Kernis's other works, the world events that prompted these compositions simply served as springboards for a more all-embracing human response.

Two Works with Narration: *The Four Seasons of Futurist Cooking* and *Goblin Market*

Among Kernis's compositions in this period are two large works with narration: *Le quattro stagioni dalla cucina futurismo* (*The Four Seasons of Futurist Cooking*, 1991) and *Goblin Market* (1995). The first originated at the period's outset, the second near its end, thus creating a frame for his output in these war-dominated years. *Le quattro stagioni* is a twenty-minute composition for piano trio and speaker, with texts (in English translation) from the *Futurist Cookbook* of Filippo Tommaso Marinetti. *Goblin Market* is a near-operatic setting of a lengthy poem by Christina Rossetti. Building on the diverse approaches to word-music interaction he had explored in earlier pieces, here Kernis took on the significant challenge of combining music with spoken narration, using two contrasting texts and finding two contrasting solutions.

In part, Kernis's choice of Marinetti's work stemmed from his own love of both cooking and parody. The *Futurist Cookbook* (1932), according to Lesley Chamberlain, was "one of the best artistic jokes of the century," aiming to "wrench food out of the nineteenth-century 'bourgeois' past and bring it into the dynamic, technological urban twentieth century."[4]

In 1930 Marinetti coauthored (with painter Luigi Columbo Fillìa) the revolutionary *Manifesto of Futurist Cooking*, which was published in Turin's *Gazzetta del Popolo*.[5] This manifesto was in part tongue-in-cheek, in part political satire, in part a serious condemnation of the Italian lifestyle. Marinetti particularly lambasted pasta, accusing it of inducing lassitude and a lack of courage. Not surprisingly, his challenge met with loud public outcries. He also advocated linking the senses by making cuisine appeal to tactile, auditory, and visual stimuli. He devised sculpted foods, for instance, advocated the use of perfumes, and favored the abolition of knives and forks.

Marinetti's highly controversial writing career had begun decades earlier with the *Futurist Manifesto*, which glorified speed, urbanization, and technology. "We stand on the last promontory of the centuries!" he proclaimed in 1909. Kernis, finding himself on the promontory of the next century, opened his own piece with these same words, introduced by a fanfare of *fortissimo* cluster chords in the piano interspersed with virtuosic figuration in the strings. But Marinetti's 1909 text had continued with a paean to violence and an outburst of misogyny and anti-intellectualism that Kernis excised. "We will glorify war," Marinetti wrote, "the world's only hygiene—militarism, patriotism, the destructive gesture of freedom-bringers, beautiful ideas worth dying for, and scorn for women." Bypassing these controversial sentiments, Kernis took up Marinetti's 1909 text again when he celebrated the era's technological revolution.

> We will sing of great crowds excited by work, by pleasure, and by riot; we will sing of the multi-colored, polyphonic tides of revolution in the modern capitals; we will sing of the vibrant nightly fervor of arsenals and shipyards blazing with violent electric moons; greedy railway stations that devour smoke-plumed serpents; . . . bridges that stride the rivers like giant gymnasts, flashing in the sun with a glitter of knives; . . . deep-chested locomotives that paw the tracks like the hooves of enormous steel horses bridled by tubing.[6]

From that point, Kernis cut to the 1930 cooking manifesto, quoting at length the essay's proposed revolution in language (injecting "agility into world literature with words-in-liberty"), in cinematography and photography, and, of course, in food. "While recognizing that badly or crudely nourished men have achieved great things in the past, we affirm this truth: men think dream and act according to what they eat and drink." Futurist cooking, Marinetti asserted grandly, "proposes a complete revolution in the nourishment of our race, with the aim of making it more joyful, spiritual and dynamic."[7]

The four movements that follow Kernis's introduction describe meals appropriate for the four seasons. In the first, "Heroic Winter Dinner," a group of soldiers about to go off to war consume, among other dishes, a "drum roll of colonial fish" and "raw meat torn by trumpet blasts." In the second, "Springtime Meal of the Word in Liberty," three young men sit outdoors at an arbor for a meal that begins with "a synoptic-syngustatory plate . . . of peppers, garlic, rose petals, bicarbonate of soda, peeled bananas and cod liver oil equidistant from each other." The third movement, "Nocturnal Love Feast" takes place on a terrace in Capri in August. In the concluding movement, "Autumn Musical Dinner," Marinetti describes a meal for two couples in a hunter's cabin in a forest. Accompanied by whistling wind and the wail of a violin, they are served chick peas, seven capers, twenty-five liqueur cherries, twelve fried potato chips, a sip of wine, and a roast quail that they look at and smell but do not eat. Four long handshakes with the peasant cook conclude the meal.

Thus Kernis created his own plot, extending the process we saw at work in *Love Scenes* and *Simple Songs*. After a glimpse into Marinetti's worldview he transitioned to food, cutting out, in the process, parts of the text that offended (or simply didn't appeal to) him, and rearranging other elements to form a new, coherent work.

Why, one might ask, did Kernis select the work of this controversial right-wing author, whose political affiliations and violent language have spawned extensive commentary and interpretation? (Marinetti loudly touted his military experiences, was a member of the Fascist party, and supported Mussolini. On the other hand, he was a devoted husband and father and strongly condemned anti-Semitism in 1938.) Kernis's choice of text had both pragmatic and symbolic stimuli. On a practical level, he set out to write something fun with immediate appeal to both performers and audiences and suited to the occasion of the premiere: a birthday event. More important, however, he was attracted by Marinetti's combination of music, politics, technology, and cuisine, as well as parallelisms between the twentieth century's beginning (symbolized by the 1909 manifesto) and its rapidly approaching end. In developing his own text from these sources, Kernis excised much that was distasteful in Marinetti's work. In short, he presented Marinetti de-fanged.

Musically, the opening movement, "Manifesto," shows connections to Kernis's previous harmonic language in its oscillation between consonance and dissonance. After the fanfare and the narrator's first exclamation, the piano begins a series of soft rising second-inversion triads, organized in groups of two and built on an ascending scale in the bass. As the chord-pairs continue, Kernis inserts melodic disjunctions between them. Then, in m. 15, the harmony becomes polytonal—the two hands play different triads—but at the same time the left-hand chords retain a connection to the beginning by appearing in pairs that rise by step. Simultaneously the strings play flurries of sixteenths until they are interrupted by a loud F♯ major chord in the piano (the pitch in the bass where the entire pattern of triads had begun). Thereafter a series of long-note chords in the piano, often creating mediant progressions, accompany quarter notes, then quarter-note triplets, then eighth-note triplets in the strings. The movement ends with a widely spaced A major chord (a fifth from the opening D). The introduction thus summarizes Kernisian traits: oscillation between consonance and dissonance, motives based on scales, changes in density, and gradual rhythmic acceleration. It also contains harmonic, textural, and rhythmic crescendos: increases in dissonance, speed, and density—typical strategies Kernis uses to build excitement.

The remaining four movements, the seasonal meals, can be seen as a traditional symphony or chamber music form: fast-moderate-slow-fast. The second one, "Springtime Meal of the Word in Liberty," parodies the nineteenth-century symphony and opera. It opens with a reference to the beginning of Beethoven's Ninth (inspired by the word *liberty*), although here the fifths rise instead of falling. Kernis subsequently makes stylistic reference to Bruckner in the guise of a Romantic melody accompanied by tremolos, and then quotes the Grail Leitmotif from Wagner's *Parsifal*—an allusion to the text's "cod liver oil." (Mendelssohn had previously used this same motive, known as the "Dresden Amen," in his Reformation Symphony.) Later in the movement Kernis inserts a reference to the opening of Mahler's Third Symphony as the narrator tells us that the diners "dutifully eat a bowl of traditional *tortellini in brodo*." Then, as their "palates take flight quickly to search . . . for an indispensable new harmony," chordal structures outside those previously explored gradually appear.

The "Nocturnal Love Feast" is in ternary form. In the opening section, and again near the end, the piano imitates a harp with arpeggiated figures that gradually evolve and change. At the movement's conclusion, the string players sing "O Sole Mio" and the piano concludes with an evocation of *Claire de lune*. The virtuosic finale features the pianist, who races around scalar patterns *presto* and in unison in the two hands.

The narrator in *Quattro stagioni* sometimes speaks unaccompanied, sometimes concurrently with the music. When music and speech occur simultaneously, Kernis aligns the beginnings of sentences with specific moments in the score, but generally leaves the precise rhythm up to the speaker. The narrator can thus exercise considerable freedom within the bounds of the musical structure.

In contrast to *Quattro stagioni*, *Goblin Market* is monumental in scale. This forty-five-minute work for narrator and chamber orchestra (the longest piece Kernis had written up to that time) is basically a short opera, using as its libretto a complete setting of Christina Rossetti's 1859 convention-busting narrative about two sisters tempted by goblins who offer to sell them luscious but poisonous fruit. "Dense with symbolism and sexual allusions, passionate and decadent—a . . . journey through the darkest areas of the psyche,"[8] the lengthy tale challenged established Victorian mores, to say nothing of poetic conventions. (The lines are irregular in terms of meter and length.)

The sisters are yin and yang, Apollonian and Dionysian. "Lizzie most placid in her look," writes Rossetti, "Laura most like a leaping flame." Indeed, cautious, sensible Lizzie resists the tempting cries of the goblins ("come buy, come buy"), whereas Laura, in modern psychological terms, is a reward-sensitive, dopamine-driven risk-taker. She succumbs to the goblins, paying for their fruit with a lock of her golden hair. She then eats gluttonously, sucking "until her lips [are] sore," and vows that night to return for more.

The following day, however, Laura can no longer hear the goblins, although Lizzie continues to be haunted by their cries. Longing to satisfy her craving, Laura returns day after day to no avail. "But when the noon waxed bright / Her hair grew thin and grey; / She dwindled, as the fair full moon doth turn / To swift decay and burn / Her fire away." In short, she "seemed knocking at Death's door."[9]

Lizzie, who had lovingly tended to her sister, decides in desperation to brave a meeting with the goblins and buy their fruit as a "fiery antidote." She approaches them with trepidation, offering money but steadfastly refusing to eat. The goblins, spying another conquest, at first swirl in images that suggest the furies in Gluck's *Orfeo*: "Flying, running, leaping, / Puffing and blowing, / Chuckling, clapping, crowing, / Clucking and gobbling, / Mopping and mowing. . . . / Fluttering like pigeons, / Gliding like fishes." But at Lizzie's refusal to eat, they become violent, and Rossetti's description has suggested to more than one commentator a rape: "They trod and hustled her, / Elbowed and jostled her, / Clawed with their nails, / Barking, mewing, hissing, mocking, / Tore her gown and soiled her stocking, / Twitched her hair out by the roots, / Stamped upon her tender feet, / Held her hands and squeezed their fruits / Against her mouth to make her eat." Still Lizzie resists. "Though the goblins cuffed and caught her, / Coaxed and fought her, / Bullied and besought her, / Scratched her, pinched her black as ink, / Kicked and knocked her, / Mauled and mocked her," Lizzie utters "not a word . . . / Lest they should cram a mouthful in."

Staggering home smeared with fruit, Lizzie begs Laura to lick the juice from her face. In a rite of exorcism, Laura does so and falls into a swoon. In the morning she is cured and returns to health. In the epilogue, years later, Laura tells her children and Lizzie's about her sister's bravery in the face of the "wicked, quaint fruit-merchant men, / Their fruits like honey to the throat / But poison in the blood."

The text has prompted commentators to cite diverse images: the temptation of Eve, the lure of the devil, Christ's sacrifice ("Whoso eateth my flesh, and drinketh my blood, hath eternal life"—John 6:54), *Song of Songs*, the AIDS epidemic, and lesbian love.[10] (In addition to the highly erotic scene in which Laura licks the juice from Lizzie, Rossetti earlier paints a blissful picture of the two sisters sleeping together, "Golden head by golden head, / Like two pigeons in one nest / Folded in each other's wings.") Kernis himself noted that the initial impulse for his music came from "the tangled roots of desire, seduction and the loss of innocence at the heart of the text, which connects to our own end-of-century lack of innocence."[11] In the end, however, Rossetti reverts to Victorian female roles: both women are "wives / With children of their own." Critics have variously responded to this ending as symbolizing the mastery of evil, maturation through learning self-control, progress from a fall from innocence into "an ascent into experience," female rites of passage, the redemptive role of human interdependence, and an overarching religious mandate.

In addition, most critics highlight autobiographical references. Rossetti's brother William encouraged readers to identify Lizzie with their older sister Maria (to whom Christina dedicated *Goblin Market*), strong-willed and over-protective with an imposing physical presence. At middle age, Maria entered an Anglican convent. Laura, on the other hand, evokes images of Dante Gabriel Rossetti's wife Lizzie Siddal, a sickly, beautiful woman addicted to narcotics who died of an overdose in 1862. Christina, for her part, never wed; she broke off one engagement and rejected a second marriage proposal on religious grounds. She also tamed her rebellious, wild-tempered spirit, transforming herself into the polite, humble, modest, self-denying (and, most probably, repressed) model of High Anglican womanhood expected of her.

In contrast to most of his previous vocal works, here Kernis set the 567 lines of Rossetti's text *in toto*, and the spoken narrative runs almost constantly through the lengthy piece. Furthermore, unlike *Quattro stagioni*, *Goblin Market* requires the narrator to execute precise rhythms, thus closely linking the text to its musical accompaniment. The narrator never recites unaccompanied, posing additional challenges in terms of the projection of the words. (In performance, the narrator must be amplified.)

Kernis's score calls for a chamber orchestra of fourteen players. In order to diversify timbral color, the two percussionists play twenty-three types of instruments. The harmonic and contrapuntal language is often dissonant and the texture dense. "I thought that such a dark story warranted a similarly gloomy musical language," Kernis told Carlo Boccadoro in 1999, "and as a matter of fact this is one of my most chromatic works, using harmony in a strongly expressionist way reminiscent of the spirit of early Schoenberg. . . . [Nevertheless] the climax of the piece is reached through the explosion of an ultra-consonant chorale, almost provocatively based on very simple tonal harmonies" ending in E major. Indeed, the chorale appears in the epilogue, where the texture thins noticeably; but, a bit like the mischievous prankster in Strauss's *Till Eulenspiegel*, the goblins, now playful, have the last word. A little woodwind flourish at the final moment recalls their earlier flying, running, leaping, puffing, blowing, chuckling, clasping, and crowing. Kernis reminds us (though Rossetti does not) that temptation and darkness always threaten.

Through his musical expression, Kernis thus added his own interpretation and rhythmic characterization to the poem. Conductor Rebecca Miller cites one of many examples: as the girls fall asleep together at the end of part I, she notes, the music settles into a sweet-sounding D major, but the oboe and glockenspiel add a tart dissonance to hint at darker things to come.[12] Leifmotifs unify the lengthy score, and instruments represent characters. The woodwinds often portray the goblins. The viola is the free-spirited protagonist (Laura), who sings in Romantic melodies. The high-strung violin, in contrast, represents the overprotective Lizzie, who assumes through Kernis's pen a sometimes frantic persona not evident in the written text. ("I saw Lizzie as constantly worried and shying away from confrontation until she finally finds her courage," says Kernis.) The contrast between the sisters is aptly shown in their first duet (part I, scene 2): long sweeping melodies in the viola are interrupted by frenetic disjunct outbursts in the violin. After Laura eats the goblin fruit, however, she is transformed; her romanticism becomes agitated frenzy.

As usual, Kernis's imagination finds voice in his colorful orchestration. One of the most striking sections is a passage of flutter tonguing in the winds (in part II, scene 1) that lasts for a full two minutes. Although Kernis had used a similar procedure in *Invisible Mosaic II*, in this case the individual pitches are sustained for a longer period and the flutter is more pervasive. Beginning with the flute and clarinet, he piles instrument upon instrument until the fluttering includes flute, English horn, clarinet, bass clarinet, bassoon, and horn; it is further enhanced by rolls on the bass drum. At the height of this section, the instruments begin to articulate shorter notes, entering at different times like daggers piercing Laura as she keeps watch "day after day, night after night" for the return of the goblins.[13]

Later, as the goblins retreat following their unsuccessful battle with Lizzie, the music thins and descends literally into nothingness. The higher instruments drop out, leaving only the bass clarinet and then the double bass, which descends in a slow glissando marked at its end by a *pianissimo* stroke on the bass drum. (A comparison might be drawn to the descent into a single gong stroke in *Invisible Mosaic II.*) A recording of the portions of *Goblin Market* discussed here is mounted on the book's Web site, http://www.press.uillinois.edu/books/miller/kernis/.

Quattro stagioni and *Goblin Market* reflect Kernis's growing international reputation but also his connections to the past and his ability to adapt to different dramatic situations. *Quattro stagioni* is in some ways an intimate work. Written for a chamber ensemble, it was commissioned for a private occasion: the piece was a fiftieth birthday present for John Gidwitz, president of the Baltimore Symphony, from family members. The work's premiere took place in a private concert at Martha's Vineyard on August 30, 1991. (Performers included Jorja Fleezanis, who had premiered *Brilliant Sky, Infinite Sky* the previous year, cellist André Emelianoff, who had commissioned and premiered *Love Scenes*, and pianist Christopher O'Riley. Michael Steinberg narrated.) Kernis wrote the work in the spring of 1991 in the privacy of a quiet artistic setting: the MacDowell Colony. Since its premiere, however, *Quattro stagioni* has had a highly public history; it is one of Kernis's most frequently performed works. In 2007 Copland House presented it as a fundraiser coordinated with a grandiose epicurean event: television chef Lidia Bastianich reconstructed a Futurist banquet based on the meals described in Kernis's piece. The banquet took place at her Del Posto restaurant in Manhattan for a capacity crowd of 150 guests. The musicians, with Fred Child (host of NPR's *Performance Today* series) as narrator, presented the individual movements between courses. "A dream evening for me!" Kernis recalls.

Goblin Market, in contrast, was highly public from the start. Commissioned by the Birmingham Contemporary Music Group, the piece began its performance life with a nine-city tour of England (January 12–22, 1995), including a performance at the Queen Elizabeth Hall in London and others in Shrewsbury, Barnstaple, Bath, Blackpool, Lancaster, York, Leicester, and Birmingham, all in halls appropriately suited for a chamber opera. (Audiences ranged from 180 to 471 for a total of 3,313 for the run.) The Birmingham ensemble presented a staged version of the piece, collaborating with the Trestle Theatre Group. They modernized the setting, portraying the sisters as drugged runaways taking shelter in a fruit and vegetable warehouse. Laura's encounter with the goblins became a hallucination. Reviewers praised Kernis's score, but some had trouble with the interaction of speech and music. The form itself "is problematic," wrote Alastair Macaulay in the *Times* of London. "Listeners have to choose between paying attention to text or music."[14] Indeed, making the text entirely comprehensible without subordinating the musical score to the background is an extremely difficult task.

Kernis's success is laudatory, but he himself may have realized the form's inherent dangers and ultimately irreconcilable demands. Since *Goblin Market* he has not written any other works with spoken narration.

The Second Symphony

Marinetti's cookbook had been a birthday gift to Kernis from his girlfriend Catherine Bush in January 1990. Kernis had met Bush at the MacDowell Colony in 1988, and a serious relationship developed that led him to live near her, first in Toronto and then in Provincetown, Massachusetts. In the summer of 1990 (a few months before he met Evelyne) the relationship foundered. At the same time, the threat of war in the Middle East loomed on the horizon: on August 2 Saddam Hussein's Iraqi army invaded Kuwait. Kernis was about to embark on writing his Second Symphony, which ultimately became a response to the war that erupted the following January. The emotional stress from his romantic breakup only added to the cataclysmic complexion of the new work.

The commission for the symphony came from Carillon Importers through their CEO, Michel Roux (with advice from Jeffrey Kaufman, head of Phoenix Records, and producers Ettore Stratta and Pat Philips). Carillon Importers brought Absolut vodka to the U.S. market. Roux persuaded the Swedish liquor manufacturer to fund commissions for the arts, both visual and aural. The musical part of the project began in 1989 with commissions to Joan Tower, Michael Torke, John Adams, and Lukas Foss. Each year a Wednesday evening concert at Avery Fisher Hall called "Absolut Concerto" featured the commissioned works. The proceeds benefited worthy non-profits, for example, Pro Musicis, the American Foundation for AIDS Research, and, for the concert with Kernis's symphony, the National Minority Business Council. The Second Symphony was the largest work in the third concert, which took place on Kernis's thirty-second birthday (January 15, 1992), two days shy of a year after the United States and its allied coalition partners began aerial bombing in Iraq.[15]

The political climate of the country during the half year or so Kernis spent composing his symphony was tense. The war itself did not erupt until January 1991, but it had been building steadily after Saddam Hussein sent troops into Kuwait, overrunning the country and declaring it a province of Iraq. Polls taken in the United States between November 1990 and January 1991 showed strongly divided opinion—both hesitation and substantial support for the war.[16] The villainy of Saddam was widely reported: his blatant violations of human rights, his use of biological and chemical weapons in the war against Iran and against the Kurds within his own nation, and his saber-rattling bravado. At the same time, many on the Left were enraged by the U.S. government's actions. Why was the nation becoming involved in a regional conflict in a volatile area of the globe? Were we going to witness another extended war like that in Vietnam? How much of the decision to go to war was motivated by protecting U.S. oil interests? These protests were countered by loud supportive rhetoric, bolstered by horrific tales of Iraqi atrocities in Kuwait (some of which turned out to be false). The sterile, antiseptic nature of modern warfare, with its up-to-the-minute, on-the-scene reporting by journalists, cast a surreal haze over the war and in effect muted, for many members of the public, the very real toll in human life. The world watched in detached wonder as live CNN reports showed smart bombs that found their targets using sophisticated technology. Some dubbed the conflict a "video game war," glorying in the coalition's ability to destroy critical structures and target "a modern Hitler" with virtually no danger to the attackers, and (they asserted) with minimal casualties on the ground.

The public, however, received a dose of brutal reality on February 13, 1991, when the United States bombed an air-raid shelter in the Amiriyah area of Baghdad. Two smart bombs were dropped on the facility in the 4:30 A.M. raid, killing more than four hundred sleeping civilians. The Pentagon insisted that the bunker was a command and communications center to which Saddam had deliberately sent civilians. Pictures of bloody, dismembered bodies caused outrage throughout the world, but the military's prestige survived the disaster, which has now become only a footnote in the war's history. Two weeks later, after a short ground assault, George Bush declared a ceasefire and proclaimed the war at an end.

Kernis wrote in the program notes for the Second Symphony: "The absurdity and cruelty of this war, in particular the 'surgical' nature of its reliance on gleaming new technological warfare used at a safe distance, made an enormous and lasting impression on me. It awoke me to the brutality and hollow moralizing of which nations are all too easily capable and led me to examine the culture of war and genocide in our time."

The twenty-six-minute, three-movement work opens "aggressively" with a movement titled "Alarm." A quick roll on the timpani accompanies a stark ascending line in the horns. It is a typical Kernis motive: a rising scalar figure followed by a leap of a fifth, beginning in f minor, historically a key of *Sturm und Drang* (example 2a). Kernis envisioned this line as a metaphor for the individual human voice struggling futilely against the war machine, represented by "unrelentingly brutal music" in the orchestra. As the symphony continues, the "mechanistic, crushing background" gradually overpowers the "breathing melody" until at the end the individual is annihilated.

Ex. 2: Second Symphony (1991): transformation of the opening motive.

The machine makes its appearance right from the start in the guise of an ominous series of agitated eighths and sixteenths in the strings and low winds underlying the rising line in the horns. That accompaniment also emphasizes the fifth, an interval that figures prominently throughout the symphony.

An explosion of percussion follows the opening statement.[17] As usual, Kernis calls for a huge array of instruments: four performers play a variety of drums (snares, tom toms, bass drums, log drum, brake drum, bongos, congas), bells (hand bells, cow bells), seven cymbals of various types, mallet instruments (vibraphone, xylophone, glockenspiel, marimba, chimes), wood blocks, thunder sheet, crotales, cabasa, reco reco (a Brazilian güiro), triangles, lead pipe, and four tam-tams. The piano, too, often functions as a percussion instrument, especially in the central part of the movement where, with the log drum, congas, and tom toms, it plays a continuous sixteenth-note pattern of clusters that underscores frantic call-and-response melodic motives in the winds and strings.

Although the first movement as a whole has a loose A–B–A'–Coda structure, the opening motive permeates it (and, in fact, the entire symphony). As shown in example 2b, the B theme is loosely related to A by its rising scalar trajectory. It appears first in a fugal texture, boldly stated in the horns followed by imitation in the trumpets and then the trombones. A winding-down before the movement's conclusion reintroduces the opening bass drum roll before being cut off by a violent ending.

At twelve minutes, the intermediary slow movement (the first one Kernis composed) is twice as long as the opening one—and it is this movement that reviewers most often cited. The title, "Air/Ground," simultaneously evokes the war and early music. The essential quality is that of a Baroque lament aria (the English term for *aria* at the time being *air*). Baroque laments traditionally featured ostinato bass lines (often, but not always, four notes descending), supporting an overlying freer melody. Among familiar examples are Monteverdi's *Lament of the Nymph*, which uses the simple four-note descent, and the "Crucifixus" portion of Bach's B Minor Mass, in which the descending fourth is filled in chromatically to portray more poignant weeping. Kernis's second movement begins with a motive in open fifths in contrary motion in the flutes and clarinets (example 2c) accompanied by handbells, suggesting both medieval music and Byzantine culture. The theme is a rising scalar motive in the clarinets, recalling the beginning of the first movement but now accompanied by its inversion. In addition, Kernis uses an additive process here reminiscent of his early works: the opening three-note figure is expanded to five, which then blossoms into an expanded line. After this introduction the viola presents the ground bass: a rising four-note motive that begins with a half step, referencing the phrygian mode (example 2d). The clarinet's solo lamenting air above it brings to mind the B theme of movement 1. Simultaneously, a subdued rhythmic accompaniment features throbbing chords in the contrabass supported by rolls on the bass drum. The ostinato in this movement evolves in the way Kernis had explored in earlier works, such as his *Passacaglia-Variations* (although in this case the motive is far more concise and controlled.) The rising scale becomes a descending one and expands in length. Eventually it takes on a form very similar to that of the opening melody of movement 1 (example 2e).

The February 13, 1991, bombing provided the catalyst for the symphony's finale, "Barricade." It opens by referencing, once again, movement 1, with rolls (this time on snare drum and cymbal) and a melody in the violin very similar to that at the beginning of the symphony (example 2f). This motive pervades the entire eight-minute finale. The complex layers of counterpoint that marked the earlier movements are now stripped away, leaving the line vulnerably exposed, only to be ultimately buried under the machine's final assault. In the middle it is punctuated by *fortissimo* gunshots. Somewhat later it is inverted, becoming a downward ostinato recalling the second movement. (Creating thematic connections among the various movements of a work became increasingly common for Kernis.) In the end, the music builds in intensity to an extended roll simultaneously on all four tam-tams, beginning *pianissimo* and increasing, over the course of eight measures, to *ffffff*. The players hold that volume for five seconds and then let the sound die out over the course of a half-minute. The effect is devastating, as well as ear-splitting. (In performance, virtually all the musicians need earplugs.)[18] Allan Ulrich, reviewing the San Francisco Symphony performance of 2002, wrote that the conclusion was greeted by thirty seconds of stunned silence before anyone dared to break the spell with applause.[19] The last minute, wrote Pierre Ruhe after a performance in Atlanta two years later, "is an end to everything, a percussion blast that obliterates all that came before it, and then silence. Nothingness. Finito. No catharsis, no resolution. Madmen, munitions, death."[20]

1992–1993: *New Era Dance, Superstar Etude no. 1,* and *100 Greatest Dance Hits*

Critics called Kernis's Second Symphony Mahlerian in scope (if not in length).[21] At the same time as it was unveiled in January 1992, the New York Philharmonic was entering a new era in its history. In celebration of its 150th anniversary (the oldest orchestra in the United States, it was founded in 1842) and in honor of its new music director Kurt Masur, the Philharmonic commissioned Kernis to write a symphonic work, *New Era Dance*. It shared the commission with the Baltimore Symphony, which presented the work's premiere on April 8, 1994, in a concert of twelve pieces by U.S. composers called "Dance Mix," conducted by David Zinman. Kernis took his (very appropriate) title from a World War I–era ragtime tune.

The violent features of *New Era Dance* highlighted by many reviewers appear immediately in the opening section. Taped electronic sounds (which Kernis derived from movie scenes and sound-effect recordings) accompany the orchestra, projecting explosions and strafing by fighter planes, while two police sirens and pistol shots accompany loud salsa music. (One of the percussionists shoots off blanks.) Following up on a comment by the composer, critics drew programmatic references to the six days of riots in Los Angeles in 1992—a response to the acquittal of four Los Angeles police officers in the beating of Rodney King—as well as to the urban noise in the Washington Heights area. (The neighborhood has since become rather gentrified.) At the same time, *New Era Dance* also projects a vibrant present and an urgent call for an inclusive future. The salsa reference has reminded more than one listener of Bernstein's *West Side Story* (thus evoking musical theater), and the work as a whole ends in an energetic chant by the full ensemble in anticipation of the new millennium, "in hope for a time of imperative political and social change in this country."[22] As David Wright succinctly put it in the program notes for the New York Philharmonic performance: "In *New Era Dance*, a piece seemingly ripped from the streets of today's New York . . ., Kernis powerfully evokes the rage of people left out of [the twentieth century's] vision of progress, and also the hope that springs from their energy and indomitable spirit."

In addition to his usual extensive battery of percussion (enhanced with sirens, a police whistle, and the pistol), Kernis included the collage of recorded sound effects mentioned above as well as a sampler attached to a MIDI keyboard. (His composer friend Eve Beglarian graciously helped with this electronic component.) Programmed into the sampler are additional sounds (for example, marimba, electric bass, and turntable scratching) and the noise of shouting crowds. The basic material of the eight-minute dance resembles that of the first movement of the symphony. In fact, its main theme is in essence a *presto* version of the rising scale with leap that opened the earlier work (example 2g). In tribute to the two renowned orchestras, *New Era Dance* is truly virtuosic. Among the highlights of the opening section is a canon at the quarter note for two trumpets, whose theme is characterized by notes interspersed with rests, inspired by fourteenth-century hocket, the virtuosic interlocking rhythmic patterns in gamelan music, and, most important for Kernis, the canons of Steve Reich. After twenty-four bars of hair-raising *presto* trumpet writing, Kernis ups the ante even further by introducing a third trumpet; the three play another canon for about fifteen bars, now an eighth-note apart. (One is reminded here of the close canonic imitation in the violins at the beginning of the fourth movement of the *Symphony in Waves*, cited in Chapter 4.)

The central section contains two parts, one slower and fugal, the other fast with flutter tonguing and salsa references. Then a recollection of A ushers in a section with the themes combined (much like the recapitulation in the opening movement of the symphony), leading to the reintroduction of the violence of the beginning. On the prerecorded tape are the "sounds of political protest, bombing, marching crowds, machine guns, and explosions." The sirens end in a dramatic moment of silence except for the blaring of a police whistle. Then the orchestra members begin to chant "New era, new new new new era," first in a whisper, then rising to a shout, accompanied only by the percussion section and the sampler. Growing in volume, the chant becomes rhythmically more complex, until it is transformed into an exuberant call for social change. The short coda recaps the beginning theme, followed by the sounds of fireworks instead of bombs.

In the same year as he composed *New Era Dance*, Kernis wrote *Superstar Etude no. 1* for piano solo, dedicated, "in admiration," to Alan Feinberg. The piece pays tribute to (but also parodies through exaggeration and the extraordinary use of the left foot on the keyboard) the pounding piano style of Jerry Lee Lewis, whom Kernis had already referenced in his *Symphony In Waves*. The three-minute etude features heavy repeated chords at the extreme ends of the keyboard, full-keyboard glissandos, clusters, and shouting ("Whoa, baby!"). At m. 77 begins a section marked "cluster city" requiring forearm tone clusters spanning two octaves alternating with smaller ones requiring only the flat palm. Four bars later Kernis instructs the performer to "swing foot up to bottom of keyboard." The left foot then plays repeated clusters at the bottom of the piano for the next nine bars, ending with a decisive "stomp on the floor." Thus the piece is as much a visual as an aural show. Indeed, numerous YouTube versions highlight its theatrical aspects.

Kernis continued to explore extended instrumental techniques, salsa, and vocal percussion in the four-movement *100 Greatest Dance Hits* for guitar and string quartet (1993). The opening movement is completely percussive, although the note D periodically emerges as a kind of tonic through the use of snap pizzicatos. To indicate his extended techniques, Kernis had to devise a new notation for both the guitar and the strings; he worked out the former with San Francisco guitarist David Tanenbaum. The second movement is a "Salsa Pasada" recalling elements of

New Era Dance. The third, titled "MOR [Middle of the Road] Easy Listening Slow Dance Ballad," recalls Mildred Kernis's favorite musical style. A moment of arpeggiated triads in contrary motion brings to mind the finale of Berg's *Lyric Suite*, but if the influence was there at all, it was subconscious; Kernis himself cites the harmonies in Ravel's string quartet and the instrumental interplay in Joaquín Rodrigo's guitar concerto as stimuli. The finale, "Dance Party on the Disco Motorboat," begins with a tonal four-measure ostinato that gradually becomes serialist. (Kernis calls it "a deconstruction of late-night TV music mixed with a parody of the New Complexity.") At the height of this complexity, with snap pizzicatos in the cello and guitar highlighting the important ur-line, the music suddenly stops and a section of "fake samba" (Kernis's term) intervenes before the contrapuntal texture resumes, this time culminating in various extended techniques and finishing off with vocal chanting. ("Do-it-yourself rap percussion," he says.) Unlike the chanting in *New Era Dance*, here the four string players articulate nonsense syllables that imitate a drum set: tsz tsz. . . . . . tih (violin 1), kih kuh, kih kuh (violin 2), chicka chika buh (viola), puh ss puh ss (cello). In a sudden interruption, they together yell "Dance party." Overall, then, this piece is simply fun, providing Kernis "refreshment after working in darker, more dramatic language."

Minneapolis–St. Paul Residency; New Works about War

In May 1993 Kernis received an appointment as composer-in-residence with three organizations in Minneapolis–St. Paul: the Minnesota Composers Forum, Minnesota Public Radio, and the St. Paul Chamber Orchestra (SPCO). The SPCO had just hired a new music director beginning in the 1992–93 season: Hugh Wolff had been part of the triumvirate of conductors working with the orchestra since 1988.[23] Wolff had met Kernis at the time of the SPCO's commission for the *Symphony in Waves* in 1989. Now, in his first year as sole director, he made a point of performing the entire work, which John Adams had presented only in part. In the same season Wolff conducted the New Jersey Symphony in the premiere of Kernis's Second Symphony, which he would subsequently record on an award-winning disc.[24] In future years, Wolff presented Kernis's orchestral works throughout the country and in Europe (for example, in San Francisco and Atlanta, at Tanglewood, and in Frankfurt, Stockholm, and Birmingham, England).

Kernis's three-year residency (September 1, 1993 to August 1, 1996)—the start of what would become a long-term relationship with the musical organizations of the Twin Cities—was one of five awarded in 1993 by Meet the Composer, which in this case provided a salary of $30,000.[25] The terms of the residency specified that he would "be responsible, in consultation with the Music Director, for the overall contemporary music programming." He would develop a process for reviewing scores for the SPCO and the Minnesota Composers Forum, participate in educational and outreach programs for all three organizations, and compose works specifically for them.[26]

Kernis's connection to these three prominent organizations significantly increased his national visibility. The thirty-four-member SPCO could boast of an impressive record of dedication to new music. A list of world premieres and commissions at the time of his appointment includes fifty-one works directly commissioned by the orchestra between 1961 and 1994, plus many others performed by the group for the first time.

The Minnesota Composers Forum, which dates back to 1973, was founded by a group of graduate students that included Libby Larsen and Stephen Paulus. By 1990 the organization was suffering from severe financial problems and the board asked Linda Hoeschler (a seasoned corporate executive who had been a vice president of Dayton Hudson, now Target) to take over the reins as executive director. Although she was hesitant, Hoeschler agreed to a six-month appointment beginning in May 1991. She soon found that she enjoyed the work immensely and ended up remaining at the helm for twelve years, during which time she not only restored the institution's financial health but also expanded it by establishing chapters all over the country. By the time Kernis began his residency in 1993, the forum was helping more than six hundred composers promote and disseminate their works. The organization eventually became the American Composers Forum, now one of the largest composer service organizations in the country.[27]

Minnesota Public Radio (MPR), for its part, was (and still is) a major producer of public radio programming. In 1983 MPR joined forces with several other program-producing public radio stations (for example, WGBH Boston, WNYC New York, WGUC Cincinnati, and KUSC Los Angeles) to form a cooperative arrangement called American Public Radio (APR). The aim, according to Senior Executive Producer Michael Barone, was to control more directly the distribution of their programs, without the restrictions of decision makers at National Public Radio. American Public Radio was based in the Twin Cities.[28]

This new network counted among its most prominent offerings *Saint Paul Sunday Morning*, a program designed to bring to listeners "an intimate and personal link to the classical music performance process."[29] (The word *Morning* was eventually dropped from the show's name to facilitate broadcasts in later hours of the day.) Host Bill McGlaughlin (a trombonist and composer) interviewed prominent musicians who were featured in a performance taped especially for the program. (Interviews and performances were recorded at the studio in advance and were subject to editing before broadcast.) In 1993 the series aired on 195 public radio stations throughout the country.

As Kernis began his residency, APR commissioned him to compose a new piano quartet in honor of the network's tenth anniversary, thereby reviving "a long-neglected role for radio [at least in the United States] as a medium that inspires and nourishes new classical music."[30]

Kernis's quartet, *Still Movement with Hymn*, received recital performances in several venues on the East Coast in the fall of 1993 and then a widely advertised radio premiere on *Saint Paul Sunday Morning* on March 20, 1994. Featured in the performance were four renowned musicians brought to Minnesota Public Radio especially for this project: Pamela Frank (violin), Paul Neubauer (viola), Carter Brey (cello), and Christopher O'Riley (piano). They had chosen Kernis to receive the APR commission through a mostly blind process. Along with the show's producer, the quartet members identified a group of young composers, each of whom submitted a recording of fifteen minutes of chamber music. These excerpts were assembled into an audition tape, with the composers identified only by number. Each member of the quartet reviewed the recording independently. Kernis was their unanimous choice. *Still Movement with Hymn* became a runner-up for the 1994 Pulitzer Prize.

In this piano quartet Kernis reverted to the dark aura of his previous war works, but without the anger of the Second Symphony. Instead, he created an extended thirty-minute lament expressing the "disbelief and loss of innocence that come from learning that the world that most of us believe we live in, one that's rational, compassionate and forgiving, seems so banal and fragile in light of the force of ethnic hatred and brutality."[31] His own grief arose not only from the genocide concurrently taking place in Bosnia but also from a personal loss: his friend, the composer Stephen Albert, was killed in a car accident in 1992.

Kernis's distress took the form of a slow lamentation broken only a few times by outbursts of protest. The piece opens with bell sounds in the piano, extremely slow and widely spaced. Time, here, is suspended. There is no sense of beat. The main thematic material then enters in the cello, and consists of a rising scalar motive with a leap of a third at its end, reminiscent in shape of the themes of the

Second Symphony and *New Era Dance*, but now showing none of the rage of the former or the exuberance of the latter. Instead, the scale is barren and forlorn, accompanied only by the bells in the piano that toll for the wanton loss of life—on both the grand scale of the Bosnian war and the small scale of a random accident.

The "ethnic cleansing" in Bosnia reminded Kernis of another genocide, that of his own people during World War II, a topic that had served as a catalyst for his works as early as the 1981 *Death Fugue*. That remembrance found voice in the second theme of the quartet (first introduced in m. 53), a descending scalar motive ornamented with grace notes that evoke the sobbing vocal style of a Chassidic cantor. This influence from his boyhood is directly referenced later in the piece when the cello plays a solo recitative. In one of the climactic moments, the three string instruments take up the cantorial second theme in unison, increasing in speed, intensity, and urgency (figure 9; this theme, with its poignant grace notes, begins in m. 233).

Still Movement with Hymn builds on expressive techniques Kernis had previously explored—cluster writing in the outburst sections, a passage featuring high string harmonics, a brief recollection of the traditional four-note descending passacaglia bass, the combining of the two main themes in a broad A B A' form—but now they are writ large in an expansive personal expression of heartache. The quartet's slow sections require impeccable ensemble coordination. In the few fast passages, Kernis notes, he drove his material to the breaking point. In these sections, he said, "I can't go any higher, get any louder, or get more intensity with the . . . number of notes per square inch."

The ending forms the work's most dramatic apotheosis: a seven-minute hymn that begins with two notes and expands to four and then to twelve (using the type of additive process he had found successful since *Stein Times Seven*). The hymn spins out slowly in the strings, accompanied, as in the opening, by bells in the piano. It uses as its source material a solo accordion piece Kernis had written the previous year for Guy Klusevsek. An extended work of nearly twenty minutes, the accordion hymn contains the same theme but includes, particularly in its central section, far more dissonant explosions than does the quartet. Like *Still Movement*, it ends with a melodic ascent and a dynamic descent into nothingness. Whereas the accordion hymn simply fades out at the end during a repetition of a two-note motive, *Still Movement* reaches a point of catharsis in a shimmering C major chord spread over six octaves, with the viola then climbing slowly to the hopeful major third of the chord. McGlaughlin, not usually at a loss for words, had nothing to say following the work's radio premiere. Silence was the only possible response.

Figure 9. *Still Movement with Hymn* (1993), mm. 231–35. (Copyright © 1993 by Associated Music Publishers, Inc. International Copyright Secured. All Rights Reserved. Used by Permission.)

The events in Bosnia brought to the fore a memory that had lain dormant for five years. During his visit to Birkenau in 1989, Kernis had met an American family from Brooklyn: a couple with two children. In the lush fields covering the former death camp, the children began to chew on blades of grass. Kernis suddenly realized with horror that the ground feeding that grass was soaked in the blood of innocents. "I . . . saw the fields rise up above me like a tidal wave, awash in a sea of blood and bones and bodies," he said.[32] That hallucination inspired the opening movement of the next work he wrote: a concerto for English horn and orchestra commissioned by attorney Hugh Taylor for Julie Giacobassi and the San Francisco Symphony.

Taylor was fond of the English horn and regretted not hearing it more often in concerts. Thus, when Giacobassi, who joined the San Francisco Symphony in 1981, suggested commissioning a concerto for the instrument, he greeted the idea with enthusiasm.[33] The symphony's management agreed, provided they approved of the composer. Over a period of eight months, Giacobassi listened to music by more than a hundred active composers, looking for one who could write something both interesting and challenging. She and the Symphony chose Kernis. After extensive negotiations, the completion date was fixed for September 1993, with a premiere scheduled for April 1994. The work was projected to last eighteen to twenty-one minutes.

Colored Field, however, turned out to be more than forty minutes long. Because Kernis sensed that the extended length was needed, the completion of the work was delayed; he did not finish the score until mid-March 1994. "My compositional process is always longer than expected," he reflects in retrospect. "My hopes for a more compact gestation and work period seem always to be foiled by the reality of truly getting to know my materials over time and working very meticulously." The premiere nevertheless took place as planned the following month, and the orchestra and Giacobassi recorded it for Argo a month later.

The concerto is in three movements, slow-fast-slow, the last of which, at twenty-two and a half minutes, overshadows in length and grandeur the other two combined. *Colored Field* is neither political nor programmatic despite movement titles that convey concrete images: "Colored Field," "Pandora Dance," and "Hymns and Tablets." The first recalls Kernis's vision of horror in the fields of Birkenau. The second evokes the world's evil forces, "little black things slithering out of a box." The finale has suggested tombstones to some reviewers, but the more important reference for Kernis is the stern voice of the God of the ancient Israelites, transmitted through Moses at Sinai as he delivered the tablets containing the laws of human behavior that have so often failed to curb the violent impulses of humankind.

Although the concerto thus contains "imagistic journeys," says Kernis, "there are no specific stories or dramatic scenarios" in it. Similarly, politics plays no role in its conception; rather, it is about "my identification with my ancestors, relatives, brothers and sisters . . ., a sense of personal grief, and the translation of wide-ranging emotion into musical form." A similar statement can be made about the Second Symphony. Although Kernis was in one sense protesting the actions of the U.S. government and the technological war effort, his symphony primarily conveys a sense of "sharing in the feeling of loss brought on by the destruction."

One preeminent visual impression that inspired *Colored Field* was the wind playing over the now-beautiful physical environment of Birkenau. "I had an image," Kernis says, of the way "the world keeps going, nature keeps growing. . . . Time keeps passing and the wind blows and things go on as they do, things are covered over." He captured this image quite directly in the set-up of the orchestra. The strings are divided into two sections, separated on the stage. The soloist stands between them as the music passes back and forth in evocation of the wind (perhaps most graphically illustrated in the middle movement). Just as the horrors of the death camp were eventually covered over, so here the soloist is gradually absorbed, not by volume as in the Second Symphony, but by the increasingly thick densities of the surrounding sounds. One way in which Kernis achieves this effect, most strikingly shown in the finale, is by layering triads a step apart. "The blanket of sound gets more and more clogged and clustery," he says.

In many ways *Colored Field* extends compositional processes and modes of expression that Kernis had explored during the previous decade. On a very direct level, the finale draws from the same accordion hymn that had appeared at the conclusion of *Still Movement*, but here he uses its loud, dissonant opening chords, rather than the ending prayer he tapped in the earlier work. Marked "stern and intense," this final movement opens with an image of the majestic stone tablets rising in a stark, grandiose *fortissimo* in the full orchestra. The chords appear in pairs, the second one rising by step while the first remains unchanged, thus creating a wrenching dissonance. The effect is in many ways similar to—but far more intense than—the opening of the slow movement of *Symphony in Waves*.

Colored Field, as one might expect, is a dark work. The Second Symphony's image of the individual, represented by a solo melodic line overpowered by the forces of evil, finds a similar expression here, but at the same time the despair is not quite as inexorable. At the end of the first movement, for example, the soloist emerges from the overwhelming density of the orchestral forces to speak alone, in an expression of grief that shows more affinity to the ending of *Still Movement with Hymn* than to the complete obliteration of the Second Symphony. The soloist descends slowly to a low A, reinforced by strokes on the timpani and in the lowest range of the piano. This ending prepares the listener for the conclusion of the entire concerto, where Kernis covers the tonicized theme with clusters.

Like other works preceding it, *Colored Field* contains ostinato figures, canonic sections, subtle pulsating accompaniment patterns, hocket-like interlocking figuration, and, most critical, references to vocal styles, both plainchant and cantorial. In the first and last movements Kernis experimented with unbarred sections in which players repeat short motives numerous times until cued by the conductor to move on—a device he had tried only rarely ("something I use when it's the only right solution," he says), for example, at the start of *Symphony in Waves*, briefly in *Goblin Market*, and in *America(n) (Day) Dreams*. The effect of this unmetered writing in the opening movement is a wash of background sound that accompanies the soloist's free cantorial line, which is filled with augmented seconds.

In this work Kernis once again proves imaginative in the combination of instruments and contrasts of sounds. Timbral modulation figures prominently at crucial moments: at the opening of the work, for example, where the oboe emerges almost imperceptibly from the viola's melody, and at the end of the first movement, where Kernis dramatically brings the soloist out from the texture by stripping away the surrounding sonic layers. Brass instruments are used coloristically and the piano often reinforces the percussion. To cite one of many notable moments: *fortissimo* interruptions of the soloist's cadenza in the middle of the finale combine chimes, crotales, glockenspiel, harp, and piano in quick flourishes, each instrument playing a different number of notes simultaneously. Nor does Kernis hesitate to call for extremes of range or dynamics. He makes full use of the English horn's technical and timbral capabilities.

Perhaps the most striking moment in the piece—and one that prompted frequent critical acclaim—occurs about seven minutes from the end of the finale. Huge rolls on tam-tams and gongs build to deafening volume as at the end of the Second Symphony; but here, some element of deliverance emerges from the devastation. As the huge resonance of the percussion subsides, a *tranquillo* section in the strings reveals a *pianississimo* F major chord that sounds like a quiet organ. Over this ethereal soundscape, the soloist enters with a supplication (later quoted in *Lament and Prayer*): a simple melody of three downward scales followed by a leap upwards. (The melody, in fact, is a simplified version of the one sung by the oboe at the beginning of the concerto, lending a cyclical nature to the piece.) As the slow prayer unfolds, the strings play a series of major and minor triads in long notes articulating mediant progressions and step-wise root movement (F–a–g–B♭–C–A♭). Six bars from the end, however, the "apocalyptic wind music" that opened the first movement returns, and the soloist is silenced by a brass cluster that rises from *pianissimo* to *fortissimo* followed by a final dissonant chord in the piano.

The End of the War Period

By March 1994 Kernis's life was becoming so busy that he had to type out a detailed schedule for himself, seeking time to compose while racing around the country to attend concerts, festivals, and recording sessions. In late March he was in St. Paul for the broadcast of *Still Movement with Hymn*. By early April he was in New York for a performance of *Delicate Songs* by the Chamber Music Society of Lincoln Center, and then immediately thereafter in Baltimore for the world premiere and recording of *New Era Dance*. A week later he was in San Francisco for the premiere of *Colored Field*, and he returned there in May for its recording following trips to St. Paul and New York. After a short respite, he served as composer-in-residence at the Yellow Barn Festival in Putney, Vermont, and then returned to Manhattan to switch apartments. (Aaron and Evelyne had bought an apartment in Hudson View Gardens and moved into it in December 1993, but the following day an electrical fire in the floor between their place and the apartment above forced them to move out again and sublet for several months while repairs were made.) In September the Pittsburgh Symphony performed *Invisible Mosaic III*, and the following month the Minnesota Orchestra played *Musica Celestis*. A week later, the New York Philharmonic gave its first performance of *New Era Dance*.

Goblin Market was scheduled for a January 1995 tour, and Kernis had not begun to write it when he compiled this schedule nine months earlier. He was, indeed, earning his living completely through composing, but as he had projected in his high school essay, the road—even with lucrative commissions and national recognition—was not easy. Where would he find the time and quiet to create new works?

At the bottom of his schedule page, Kernis laid out a projected composing calendar: March–May, a "work for the SPCO and Pamela Frank"; May–September, *Goblin Market*; September–January, a "work for Joshua Bell"; January–June, a double concerto for violin and guitar "if funded." (It was.)

The "work for Joshua Bell" became the twelve-minute Air for Violin and Piano, supported by a joint commission from the Society for the Performing Arts in Houston, UCLA's Center for the Performing Arts, and the University of Texas, Austin, Performing Arts Center. Bell first played it in Houston on March 11, 1995, and it has since been adapted for cello and for flute. The piano part has also been transcribed for orchestra.

The commission for Pamela Frank turned out to be *Lament and Prayer*, written not for the SPCO but for the Minnesota Orchestra. Both this work and the Air ultimately postdated *Goblin Market*, which Kernis now put on the front burner. Indeed, he managed to meet the premiere deadline for that work, but not by much. As he frantically completed various sections of *Goblin Market*, he fed them to Schirmer, which had them typeset and sent on to the Birmingham Contemporary Music Group, but the performers did not receive the final typeset score until January 6, 1995, six days before the first performance.[34]

Kernis turned his attention first to the Air for Bell and then to the piece for Frank. He composed *Lament and Prayer* during the first half of 1995, delivering the completed score to Schirmer in mid-June. The delay allowed him to cast the piece as a fifty-year commemoration of the end of the Holocaust. The orchestra first performed it the following year, on July 31, 1996.

The Double Concerto, on the other hand, took longer to materialize. Instead of the six months Kernis projected for it, the composition process consumed eight to nine. Funded by a joint commission from the Aspen Music Festival, the Los Angeles Chamber Orchestra, and the St. Paul Chamber Orchestra, the work was first performed in February 1997 instead of the original projected date of April 1996. It was the first piece for which he fell seriously behind schedule and the last work from his St. Paul residency.

All of these pieces are challenging, as even the most renowned performers admit. *Lament and Prayer* is "not easy to play," says Pamela Frank in a dramatic understatement. Guitarist Sharon Isbin relates that learning the Double Concerto was a challenge, and Diane Pascal, first violinist with the Lark Quartet after Eva Gruesser left in 1996, notes that Kernis is "not afraid to ask players to 'work hard.'"[35] All of these virtuosic players note, however, that the music was well worth the time expended in learning it. Kernis, for his part, finds it ironic that "the structural flow" of his music "makes it very comprehensible to the listener . . ., but the challenges to the performers are often very significant." Indeed, Hugh Wolff says that Kernis's music is often "more difficult than it sounds" but "to his credit the complexity is something that's part of the structure of the piece, not an end in itself." Marin Alsop, who has conducted numerous compositions by Kernis at the Cabrillo Music Festival, agrees. The music is highly complex due to its contrapuntal layering, she notes, and conductors need to be willing to commit extra time to studying the scores if they are to do justice to it. However, the difficulty of Kernis's music is no greater than that of many other contemporary composers, says Wolff. James Rushton agrees: The music is "virtuosic," he notes, "but not awkward." In part, the virtuosity of Kernis's scores results from his association with exceptional players. "I was seeing performers who were deeply versed in the performance of Babbitt, Wuorinen, Schoenberg," he says. "I took in an assumption that that's what performers in the late twentieth century did. . . . My music was infused by that sense of what was possible."[36]

A case in point is *Lament and Prayer*, which (in the admittedly biased opinion of this author) takes its place among the most beautiful half-hours of music in the contemporary literature. Like *Still Movement with Hymn*, it had a predecessor in a solo piece: *Aria-Lament* for unaccompanied violin, which Kernis had written in 1992. The demands of *Lament and Prayer* on both soloist and orchestra (in this case, strings, harp, percussion, and oboe) are substantial, not only in the fast passages but also in the extremes of tempo, dynamics, and range. (The soloist reaches repeatedly into the territory three octaves above middle C.) Kernis calls for dangerously slow tempi (quarter note equals 40–42 at the beginning, 36 at the end) and very soft playing, requiring incredible control (exemplified in the extraordinary performance by Frank on her recording with the Minnesota Orchestra.) But in fact, it is Kernis's demands for extremes of dynamics and tempi that make his works so compelling. Conductors cannot get away with playing it safe in the middle (not too loud, not too soft, not too fast, not too slow) without sacrificing the essential drama of the music.

The piece opens (after two bell-like unison As in the strings) with a solo line for the violin: a melody with cantorial inflections built of two- or three-note cells arranged in various patterns in the manner of the Jewish cantillations used for chanting the Torah. As in *Still Movement with Hymn*, these short cells are ornamented with grace notes imitating Chassidic chant. During its thirty-minute span, *Lament and Prayer* oscillates widely between consonance and dissonance (as we have seen in previous works) and among three diverse textures: solo or sparsely accompanied passages for the violin or unison strings, lush tonal sections, and highly dissonant dense counterpoint. Various members of the orchestra play as soloists, and the string section is frequently subdivided, in one place into twenty-five parts. In some sense, Kernis may have been obliquely drawing a parallel to Richard Strauss's *Metamorphosen*, but the image that was at the forefront of his consciousness was the responsorial nature of synagogue music: the dialogue between cantor (represented by the soloist) and congregation. The multiple string voices in *Lament and Prayer* thus reference the individuated roles of congregational heterophony. As in *Colored Field*, the central section contains several passages in which three- to five-beat patterns repeat numerous times until orchestra members are cued to proceed.

The harp only sounds two little flourishes during the first half of the piece and then enters in its own right at m. 115, at first reinforcing the violins, then playing fuller chords, and finally doubling the bass line. The oboe, which is offstage, does not play until twenty-two minutes into the work, entering after the soloist's two-minute-long cadenza. Its melody is a direct quote from the prayerful solo at the end of the finale of *Colored Field* cited above (but now transposed down a semitone), complete with the accompanying long chords in the orchestra that articulate mediant and stepwise progressions. From that point almost to the end of the piece the oboe engages the solo violin in a duet. Here each of the consonant chords in the strings is anticipated by arpeggios in the two harps, the whole underscored by a "soft blanket of percussion sounds." Kernis instructs the percussionists to select from a set of soft metal instruments such as triangles, jingles, metal shakers, sizzle cymbals, and small Asian bells and play them *tremolando* for one to four seconds each, very softly, varying the instruments and making occasional small swells. The work then ends with a motive by a solo cello marked by a rising major third (a hopeful sign in Kernis's music as early as the *Meditation [in memory of John Lennon]*) and a slowly ascending line that takes us to an open fifth (A/E).

Lament and Prayer, as the last of Kernis's war-period works, shows the journey the composer traveled during this time. "I could only move on after it was done," he now reflects. Gone now is the fury of the Second Symphony and even the sorrow of *Still Movement with Hymn*. Prayers for the future of humanity transcend the terrors of *Colored Field*, and we are left only with the solo voice arising from the horrors of a violent world.

6 Triumphs and Tribulations

Big Commissions, Big Risks, Big Rewards (1995–2001)

IN 1995 THE AMERICAN ACADEMY of arts and Letters honored Kernis with a $7,500 prize to facilitate a recording.[1] Accompanying the award was a tribute to the thirty-five-year-old composer noting his "Dickensian abundance" in pouring out "many remarkable large-scale pieces. . . . As each work grows in both precision and eloquence," said the tribute's author, "Kernis seems destined to prove that Blake's 'road of excess' leads indeed to the 'palace of wisdom.'" The extravagant prose proved more prescient than its author could have predicted. During the following five years Kernis would continue down the "road of excess," churning out new works at a prodigious rate, but he would also be led to "the palace of wisdom" by confronting (and meeting) some difficult challenges.

The period began auspiciously with a mushrooming in the number of performances of Kernis's works. In January the Birmingham Contemporary Music Group took *Goblin Market* on its English tour. In March the National Symphony played *New Era Dance*. In the same month Joshua Bell performed the new *Air* on his own U.S. tour and then took it to Germany that summer. In May Hugh Wolff conducted the European premiere of the Second Symphony with the City of Birmingham Symphony Orchestra, followed by the U.K. premieres of *Musica Celestis* and *Invisible Mosaic III*. Wolff then conducted the orchestra in all three works for a compact disc release.

The Birmingham performances and the recording were facilitated by Argo Records and its general manager and artistic director Andrew Cornall, who had signed Kernis to an exclusive recording contract. When he assumed the leadership position at Argo in 1989, Cornall began to refocus a label previously committed to traditional repertoire by developing a cutting-edge concentration on new music. "Labels were normally committed to an artist—to a pianist or a violinist," he says. "There was somebody missing in that list, the composer." Argo made long-term commitments to six young U.S. and U.K. composers: Graham Fitkin, Michael Nyman, Mark Anthony Turnage, Michael Torke, Michael Daugherty, and Aaron Jay Kernis. Prior to Wolff's recording, Argo had already issued three discs of Kernis's music. The *Symphony in Waves* and the first string quartet appeared in 1992, followed by recordings of *New Era Dance* and *Colored Field* in 1995 and 1996. The disc containing the Second Symphony, *Musica Celestis*, and *Invisible Mosaic III* was published in 1997. Argo would release one more Kernis recording in 1999 (featuring *Lament and Prayer* and the Double Concerto), but by that time the CD boom of the 1990s had collapsed and the label's groundbreaking support for young composers disintegrated.[2]

In the summer of 1995 Kernis appeared for the first time as one of the featured composers at the Cabrillo Music Festival in Santa Cruz, California, a two-week contemporary music extravaganza held annually since 1963. Director Marin Alsop had become of fan of Kernis's music after performing *New Era Dance* with her Concordia Orchestra in New York; for the 1995 Cabrillo Festival she programmed that piece along with *Quattro stagioni*. Alsop subsequently presented Kernis's works in six additional seasons: 1999 (*Lament and Prayer* with Yumi Hwang), 2004 (*Color Wheel*), 2005 (*Air*, in the cello version), 2006 (*Newly Drawn Sky*), 2007 (*Valentines* with Susan Narucki), and 2009 (*Invisible Mosaic III*).[3]

In the summer of 1995 Mark Swed wrote a feature article about Kernis, whom he characterized as "a young composer on the fast track." He titled it "Danger Ahead!" citing the music's combination of extravagance and eclecticism:

> An extravagant gesture is an extreme one that makes you feel that things can be only one way. Eclecticism, on the other hand, is the recognition that the world is never one way. For Kernis that means not just the altercations and/or syntheses of musical styles, but also a passionate look at the conflicts which affect our lives and probably can never be resolved. He is a composer who seems inescapably drawn to visions of childhood reverie, but unable to evade the darkest visions of our war-torn, AIDS-torn, Holocaust-haunted era.[4]

Commissions added to Kernis's increasing renown—he received one in August 1995 from the St. Paul Chamber Orchestra for an arrangement of piano music (with funding from Linda and John Hoeschler and Louis and Susan Hill), another in September from the Birmingham Bach Choir for a short choral work, and a third in October from the Chicago Symphony for a choral symphony. Meanwhile Kernis was frantically working on the Double Concerto for Violin and Guitar, which continued to give him trouble. "I blocked out five months to write the piece," he told Jim Tosone shortly after its premiere, but "for three of those months I was empty."[5] Hugh Wolff had scheduled the first performance with the St. Paul Chamber Orchestra for April 1996, but in March the piece was still not finished. So the SPCO moved the premiere to February 1997. Two months later Gerard Schwarz conducted the second performance at Lincoln Center with the New York Chamber Symphony. During the work's slow evolution, Kernis ended up discarding his original opening movement and writing an entirely new one.

While work on the Double Concerto proceeded in fits and starts, Kernis did manage to write the brief choral piece for the Birmingham choir. In "How God Answers the Soul" (1995), he set a translation of a text by Mechthild of Magdeburg (ca. 1207–ca. 1282/1294), a medieval nun whose poetry he found "unusually beautiful, sensual, and provocative."[6] His choice followed in a direct line from the inspiration of Mitchell's *Enlightened Heart* (whose translations he had used in *Simple Songs*) and from the texts and music of Hildegard von Bingen that had inspired the slow movement of his string quartet.

In 1996 Kernis also completed the orchestration of piano music for the SPCO. The orchestra's practice of commissioning arrangements had begun in the 1980s when Christopher Hogwood was associated with the organization. It was a way of expanding the limited repertoire for chamber orchestra, notes Hugh Wolff.[7] When the SPCO approached Kernis about making such an arrangement, he immediately recalled Druckman's orchestration class at Yale: the last assignment had been to create an instrumental version of Debussy's piano prelude "La cathédrale engloutie." Kernis thus decided to set five of Debussy's etudes and prepared for the task by closely studying the early twentieth-century French repertoire. This study later bore fruit as he considered various orchestration options in *Garden of Light* (1999), *Valentines* (2000), and *Color Wheel* (2001).

On the other hand, the last commission, the one for the choral symphony, did not materialize. "I was not ready to write the work at that time," he later recalled. He couldn't settle on a text; he couldn't find the motivation to proceed. Ultimately, the idea did not take concrete form until fourteen years later with his third symphony.

Meanwhile, however, much bigger commissions were in the works. The most grandiose of them came from the Walt Disney Company, stimulated by a spectacular performance of Mahler's Eighth Symphony on May 4 and 5, 1995. Mahler composed this work, the first symphony to use a chorus throughout, in 1906–7. It was so massive in terms of performing forces that the producer of the sold-out 1910 premiere dubbed it the "Symphony of a Thousand." The 1995 Carnegie Hall presentation did not involve a thousand people, but the forces were nevertheless huge: 688 musicians took part in it. On stage were a hundred choristers, a forty-eight-member children's chorus, the Cleveland Orchestra (expanded to more than a hundred players), a piano, an organ, and eight soloists. In the tiers were not only a brass ensemble but also 414 more singers from the Atlanta and Cleveland Symphony choruses, the Cincinnati May Festival Chorus, and Oberlin College. The audience, wrote Edward Rothstein in the *Times* the next day, heard the work "with all its bombast, vulgarity, kitsch, madness and brilliance intact. The floor shook, the space resonated with choral proclamations, the trombones and trumpets blared down from above, the heavens were invoked and redemption promised." He added that the symphony was "an ancestor to Cinemascope and the Sony Imax."[8]

One man in the audience apparently agreed: Michael Eisner, CEO of the Disney Company. What better way to celebrate the upcoming millennium, thought Eisner, than with a lavish gesture akin to Mahler's, a tribute in music, "the art closest to the idea of time"?[9] And what better organization to revive the old system of royal patronage to herald the coming of a new era than Disney? (Or, as Paul Lieberman put it in the *Los Angeles Times*: "Michael Eisner meets the Medicis.")[10] To help realize his vision, Eisner tapped Jean-Luc Choplin, vice president of Disneyland Paris. The choice was hardly capricious; Choplin had built an impressive record in the area of contemporary music and dance. As director of the Fêtes musicales de la Sainte Baume from 1976 to 1980, he developed an "interdisciplinary laboratory"[11] by bringing in artists such as John Cage, Yvonne Rainer, Henri Pousseur, and Takehisa Kosugi. In 1984 he joined the Paris Opera as general administrator of dance. Eisner now brought Choplin to Los Angeles as an artistic counselor to plan events for the turn of the century. Choplin proceeded to sift through the music of more than a hundred composers. Although several reviewers remarked that he had been searching for one who was returning to tonal roots, Choplin himself says that his primary goal was to find someone who could "tell a story," who could create a narrative work in the tradition of a vibrant oratorio.[12] The original idea was a single commission. But Choplin had trouble settling on one composer, and so he convinced Disney to contract with two: Kernis and Michael Torke. By the beginning of 1997, negotiations were under way. Contractual details consumed more than a year but ultimately led to a spectacular celebration in Avery Fisher Hall with the New York Philharmonic in October 1999.

The Double Concerto for Violin and Guitar and *Too Hot Toccata*

The Double Concerto, which had its first performance while the Disney contract was in negotiation, was stimulated by a request from guitarist Sharon Isbin and violinist Nadja Salerno-Sonnenberg. Their enthusiasm led to a joint commission from the St. Paul Chamber Orchestra, the Los Angeles Chamber Orchestra, and the Aspen Music Festival, with funding provided by the Meet The Composer/Reader's Digest Commissioning Program and the National Endowment for the Arts. Kernis had seen Salerno-Sonnenberg on the *Tonight Show* and was entranced by the project. But his work progressed slowly, mainly due to his struggle with the problem of balance—both between the two solo instruments and between the guitar and the orchestra. The guitar required amplification. The violin decidedly did not. Miking the former allowed both instruments to be audible but also created timbral problems. "It was difficult to equalize the registers on the guitar," says Kernis. Furthermore, notes conductor Gerard Schwarz, the "special speaker that sat under [Isbin's] chair . . . was necessarily directional," and therefore it projected differentially to various areas of the performance hall.[13]

In the work's three movements, Kernis experimented with altering the relationship between the soloists. In the first, they act independently, each with individual melodic sections. The guitar rarely plays chords. In the slow movement, they function as partners, most often playing in counterpoint. In the finale, they explore both relationships. The piece as a whole charts a new direction for Kernis, ushering in a series of upbeat works that seem to represent a catharsis after the previous period of darkness—as if the supplication of *Lament and Prayer* had capped his own journey from pessimism to hope and he could now indulge in a celebration of life. The change in spirit was fueled not only by his increasing professional recognition but also by the personal fulfillment of his marriage to Evelyne Luest on August 29, 1996.

The concerto's first movement begins with a jazzy motive in the orchestra, followed by a minute-long guitar solo with light accompaniment, including occasional riffs in the clarinets. Kernis had not listened seriously to jazz since his first year in college, and now he returned to that dormant interest. He notated the swing rhythms in detail, knowing that orchestral players would render precisely what was on the page, and he counted on the drum kit player and the double bassist to help bring those rhythms to life. After a brief passage in which the two soloists play in unison, the violin takes its turn for a solo passage equal in length to the guitarist's opening. The middle of the movement contains an extended cadenza for the soloists followed by "a big orchestral tutti"[14]—in effect a cadenza for the orchestra. The movement ends with an altered, shortened recapitulation.

The problems of combining guitar and violin involve not only the relative volume of the two instruments but also their characteristic sound qualities: the guitar with its quick decay and the violin with its long sustain. Kernis decided to take advantage of this contrast in the opening movement by alternating the two types of articulation. Lively staccato passages, which predominate, build on the inherent nature of the guitar; sections in which the orchestra plays long notes accompanying the soloists emphasize the strengths of the violin. And by having the two play passages in near unison he in effect created a "super-guitar" and a "super-violin": the violin acquired more attack, the guitar more sustain.

The fifteen-minute slow movement begins and ends in consonance (the final chord is an open fifth, like the end of *Lament and Prayer*) but becomes extremely dense and dissonant in its long central section. The most impressive movement is the six-and-a-half-minute finale, which starts with a jazz melody first in the solo violin and then in the guitar, accompanied by bongos and timbales (Cuban drums), while the violas play "alla guitarra (strummed)." The opening motive, a rising scale, first swung and then played in straight sixteenths with a leap at the end (a linear trajectory we have noted in several previous works), pervades the entire movement, except for a short slow section in the middle. A vibrant cadenza treats the motive in an additive fashion (see, for example, mm. 165ff. in figure 10). It becomes increasingly virtuosic as the percussion instruments re-enter (first quietly with only the high hat, and then adding drums, woodblocks, and cow bells). An exuberant altered recapitulation culminates in a noisy conclusion reminiscent of the end of *New Era Dance*.

As he finished the Double Concerto, Kernis received two more commissions. The first came from the St. Paul Chamber Orchestra in May 1996. Recognizing the potential of the Double Concerto's finale, Kernis transformed that movement into an overture for orchestra, renaming it *Too Hot Toccata*. He eliminated the cadenza but otherwise preserved the original composition, while making major alterations in instrumentation. One issue, of course, was the assignation of the guitar part to other instruments. Kernis sometimes gave its line to the strings, sometimes to a piano, and sometimes to the winds, creating virtuoso passages for trumpet, oboe, bassoon, and horn, inspired (typically) by particular performers in the SPCO. He also rethought the orchestration of many other parts of the movement. The result is a showpiece, a miniature concerto for orchestra.

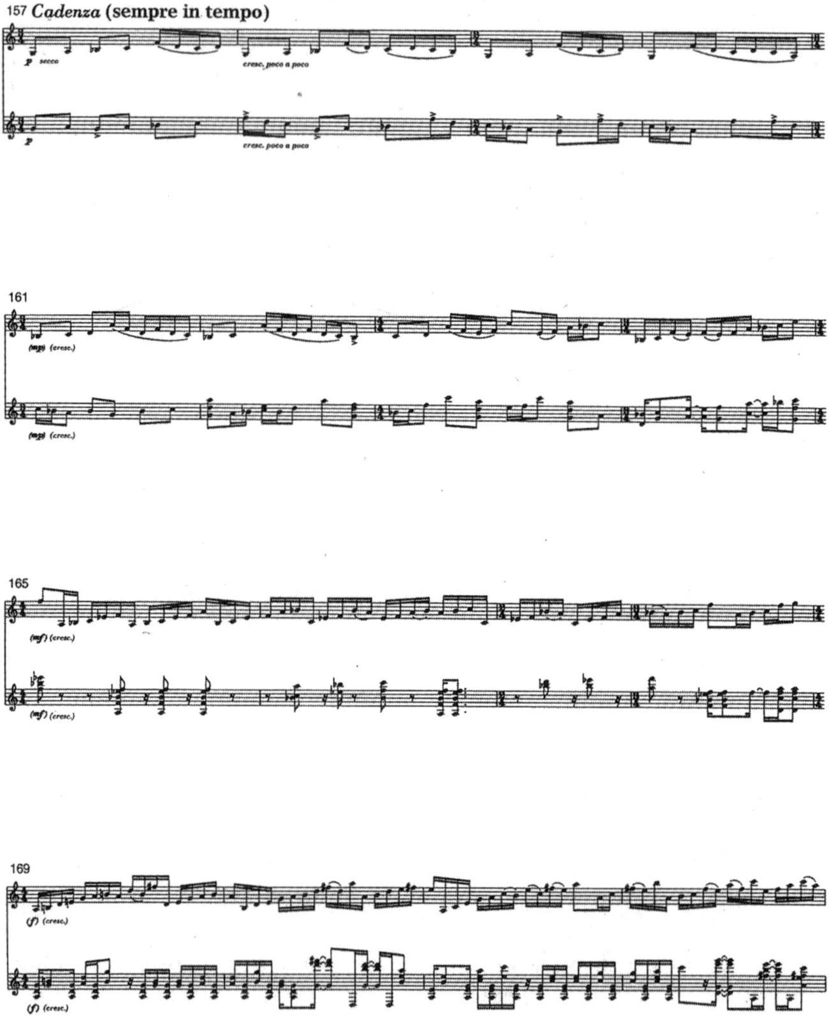

Figure 10. Double Concerto for Violin, Guitar, and Orchestra (1996), mvt. 3 cadenza.

Too Hot Toccata was the first of a number of successful arrangements in this period. True, Kernis had previously orchestrated the second movement of his String Quartet *musica celestis* for string orchestra and had allowed for alternative performances of the *Air* for violin by cello or flute (or with orchestral instead of piano accompaniment), but these arrangements required a minimum of alteration. *Too Hot Toccata*, in contrast, represented a major reworking of the original instrumentation and therefore a more fundamental rethinking of the piece. Kernis found the process so rewarding that other arrangements followed in the next few years, as the large number of substantial commissions began to overwhelm him. In addition to his orchestration of the Debussy etudes in 1998, he created a *Concierto de Dance Hits* from two movements of *100 Dance Hits* and an adapted version of a solo guitar piece named *Echo* (1999), he arranged *Colored Field* for cello (2000), and he developed an orchestral overture (*Overture in Feet and Meters*) from the first movement of his second string quartet (2000).

The Second String Quartet and the Pulitzer Prize

The second quartet turned out to be the most influential new piece Kernis would compose during the period 1995–2001. It arose from a commission in June 1995 by the Lark Quartet (now with altered personnel).[15] Funding for this commission again came from combined sources: the Elaine Kaufman Cultural Center, Ohio University, the Schubert Club of St. Paul, and Chamber Music America.

The Kaufman Center, on West 67th Street, had been founded in 1952 as the Hebrew Arts School, providing music training for pre-college youth. Since 1978 it has housed the Merkin Concert Hall and today offers, in partnership with the City of New York, a K–8 public school for musically gifted children. A year after the commission for the second quartet, the center appointed Kernis as its first "featured composer" for Merkin Hall. The two-year position was designed "to provide a forum for new music and new artists and to solidify Merkin's position as one of the city's foremost venues for the music of our times."[16] In this capacity Kernis attended concerts, advised in the programming of contemporary music, gave public lectures, and spoke with students in their classes. The center, in turn, presented performances of his works. The second string quartet had its premiere there on January 10, 1998.

Like the first quartet, the second has a subtitle referencing early music, in this case "musica instrumentalis," a term taken from *De institutione musica* of Anicius Manlius Severinus Boethius (ca. 480–ca. 524). The primary transmitter of

Greek music theory to the West during the Middle Ages, Boethius divided music into three classes: musica mundana (the music of the spheres), musica humana (music of the body and the soul), and musica instrumentalis (music produced by humans). As the tonal center for the work Kernis chose B♭, deliberately distant from the prominent A and E of his first quartet.

In this piece Kernis further explored his interest in dance, ever more present in the works he composed during the 1990s (for example, *New Era Dance* and *100 Greatest Dance Hits*). In fact, he characterizes the opening movement as "an overstuffed medley."[17] Like a typical eighteenth-century suite, it begins with a Prelude, but then continues with an unusual combination of sub-movements: an Air (a gentle song), a quick Corrente (here in 12/8 instead of the normal 3/4), a light Canzonetta filled with pizzicato playfulness, a short Musette (with the drone feature typical of such works present only occasionally), a Canzonetta Piccolo (recollecting the first canzonetta but then diverging into loud, agitated repeated notes), and Ritornelli Diversi e con Variazioni. The movement as a whole is strongly rooted in B♭. It opens and closes with repeated notes on the tonal center, somewhat like the beginning of Bartók's fifth quartet, except that here the notes function as pick-ups. A strong cadential arrival on B♭ comes at the end of the Corrente, almost exactly at the center of the movement.

The second movement, centered in F♯ minor (a mediant relationship to the outer fast movements), is titled "Sarabande Double, Sarabande Simple"—again a reference to the Baroque suite. The sarabande—a stately dance in triple meter with a stress on beat 2 in alternate bars—is an ever-present component of eighteenth-century suites and often constitutes its slowest and most expressive movement. A *double*, in the parlance of the French Baroque, indicates an ornamented variation on the previous dance. Such variations are traditionally followed by a return to the simpler dance, thus creating an A A' A form on the macrocosmic level. Kernis modeled his own sarabande on similar movements in two of Bach's suites: the sixth English suite in D minor (BWV 811) and the Suite in A minor (BWV 818). The rhythm of Kernis's first sarabande resembles that of the *double* in BWV 811. His second sarabande pays tribute to Bach's simple sarabande in BWV 818: a slow descending three-note scale (one note per bar) forms a backdrop for the theme. Kernis, however, reverses the typical form, beginning with the more complex *double*, followed by the simpler dance. The melodies of the two sarabandes are related through the pulsating rhythm of dotted quarter–eighth–quarter, but there is no variation or ornamentation scheme in the manner of the Baroque style. There are, simply, two sarabandes that alternate and then evolve each time they recur. Kernis separates their repetitions with four short, frenetic interruptions. The movement ends with a series of rhetorical statements: first the cello presents an unaccompanied cadenza, then the second violin plays a throbbing motive evoking cantorial chant, and finally the first violin articulates a muted upward-reaching cry. These melodies intertwine to arrive at a single bare F♯, bringing the movement to an introspective close.

The quartet's finale, a tour de force titled "Double Triple Gigue Fugue (after Beethoven)," not only references Baroque dance, but, more important, pays tribute to the finale of Beethoven's quartet op. 59, no. 3, which is a fugue embedded in a sonata form. Beethoven's finale begins with a standard fugal exposition, the subject strongly emphasizing tonic (C major) and dominant. After that opening, Beethoven introduces sonata-form elements: a transition section leads into a brief secondary area in the dominant with no distinct contrasting theme, followed by a lengthy development. The movement's recap brings back the fugal opening with the original subject graced with a new counterpoint in longer note values.

Kernis not only adopted several strategies Beethoven had explored in op. 59, no. 3 but also paid tribute to Bach, Haydn, and Bartók. Like Beethoven's finale, Kernis's is a fugue within a sonata form. Instead of 2/2 meter, his is in 12/8: hence the "gigue" in the title. Like Bach, Kernis explores complex invertible counterpoint. The first theme is immediately imitated by its inversion and then becomes linked to a consistently recurring countersubject (first appearing in m. 8–9 in the viola; see figure 11). As in Haydn's usage (for example, in op. 20, no. 5), the subject and its linked countersubject create the double fugue.

In contrast to Beethoven, whose quartet finale is for the most part monothematic, Kernis indulges his melodic imagination and his tendency to construct thematic groups within the exposition. After a strong B♭ major cadence, an exuberant third theme appears over a B♭ pedal point; it serves as a transition to the dominant F (also introduced with a pedal point). A recollection of the opening subject then rounds off the first thematic group. The secondary area is unrelated to the Beethoven quartet, but for the development Kernis returned to his model, using elements of all the material introduced previously. Closely following op. 59 no. 3, he brings back his opening subject in the recapitulation with a new counterpoint, thus giving rise to the "triple fugue" reference in the movement's title. This new counterpoint, like Beethoven's, is in longer note values than those of the main motive. The recapitulation features expressive alterations, such as snap pizzicati and glissandi (both Bartókian traits). Then, like Bach, Kernis combines several of his motives simultaneously in the coda. Reminiscent of some Beethoven works (but not op. 59 no. 3), the music slows dramatically before a sudden fast ending that first moves to E but then abruptly switches to B♭ to emphasize the

Figure 11. String Quartet no. 2, "musica instrumentalis" (1997), opening of the finale.

tritone relationship he had explored at the opening of the piece. To hammer home his debt to the classical quartet—and with tongue firmly in cheek—Kernis ends the entire quartet with a standard, unornamented V7–I cadence.

By this time Kernis was clearly comfortable not only with the formal structures of past centuries but also with what we might call an extended tonal language, which is functional, but not in the traditional sense of the word. He uses harmonic relationships as "an underlying device for pacing . . . , flow and narrative." Most important to him is to balance "extremes of harmonic weight," ranging from triads to diatonic clusters to all-interval chords.[18] Thus he built on, and expressed his debt to, his predecessors, but did so in his own distinctive language.

As Kernis's second quartet was taking shape, his international reputation expanded considerably via the dissemination of his orchestral works. In June 1997 Hubert Soudant conducted *Colored Field* in Nantes and Paris with the Orchestre National des Pays de la Loire (Christophe Grinel, English horn). Four months later *Diapason* honored Hugh Wolff's Argo recording of the Second Symphony, *Musica Celestis*, and *Invisible Mosaic III* with its Diapason d'Or de l'Année in the category of contemporary music. (Selections for these awards are made by French critics and broadcasters.)

In November 1997 Kernis received a commission from Philip Brunelle and the Plymouth Music Series chorus (now VocalEssence) in Minneapolis, allowing him to add three more movements to the setting of the Mechthild of Magdeburg text he had composed for the Birmingham choir in 1995. He completed *Ecstatic Meditations*, a four-movement piece for eight-part choir with soprano and tenor soloists, in 1998. In 2006 the National Endowment for the Arts named the work a "Masterpiece of American Choral Music." Kernis considers this set the best of his large *a cappella* works.

In December Kernis traveled to Israel as a judge in the Leonard Bernstein Composing Competition. In that same month the contract with Disney was at last finalized. At each step in the negotiation process, the commission fee had increased. The final figure was far higher than any he had previously received—well into six figures. According to Choplin, Disney hoped thereby to secure ownership of the pieces, but later abandoned this goal.[19]

In this same period the Glimmerglass summer opera festival, New York City Opera, and PBS's *Great Performances* invited Kernis to participate in an opera project centered on the theme of Central Park. The commissioners first chose three librettists: Wendy Wasserstein, Terrence McNally, and A. R. Gurney. None had previously written for opera. They then paired these authors with composers to create three independent one-act operas. Kernis was assigned to McNally. In three joint preliminary sessions in 1997, he found McNally an eager and cooperative collaborator. "I suggested an approach to the story that McNally generously took," Kernis recalls. When he attempted to express some concerns about details of the text, however, Kernis was summarily dismissed from the project. The notification arrived on February 4, 1998, without any warning or explanation. (The dismissal was particularly painful because he had declined several commissions and residencies to make time for the opera.) Despite a conciliatory letter to McNally and legal investigations by Schirmer, the decision remained firm. (No formal contract had been signed.) McNally issued a statement noting that he was a "passionate admirer" of Kernis's music.[20] The only elucidation Kernis ever received was that the libretto might receive "more compatible treatment" from another composer.[21] McNally ultimately wrote an entirely different libretto, set to music by Robert Beaser.

As if to thumb its nose at this turn of events, the following month the Pulitzer committee awarded its 1998 prize to Kernis's second string quartet. On April 14, 1998, Aaron and Evelyne were frantically packing for a trip to Majorca, where Evelyne's ensemble was scheduled to present a series of concerts. They knew that the Pulitzer was to be announced at 3 P.M., and Kernis assumed it would go to John Adams. At about 3:10 Susan Feder, vice president of Schirmer, phoned. "Are you sitting down?" she asked before conveying the news. "We both screamed," Kernis recalls.[22] And then the barrage of phone calls from the media began, delaying their departure for the airport by an hour. Fortunately, their plane was delayed as well. By the time they got on board, Kernis had received fifteen calls; he even gave one interview on board. During the flight he calmed his excitement by listening to Bach's B Minor Mass. "In the best way," he says, "it took the focus off of my own high." Once they were overseas, Kernis continued to enjoy from afar the hundreds of calls that filled his answering machine each day. The Pulitzer, however, also reawakened some self-doubts. "There was an outpouring of support," he told David Patrick Stearns in 2001, "but there also was a tension: Can I write a piece as good as the last one?"[23]

Garden of Light

The Pulitzer, of course, thrust Kernis further into the limelight; performances and publicity abounded. The Lark Quartet toured the United States and Europe playing the prize-winning work; the Aspen Festival presented the Double Concerto; the Boston Symphony played *Too Hot Toccata* at Tanglewood; a feature article on Kernis appeared in *Symphony* magazine. In July 1998 he was appointed new music adviser to the Minnesota Orchestra (to begin in September that year). According to Asadour Santourian, the orchestra's director of artistic planning, Kernis was selected to fill the new, anonymously endowed position because of his "selflessness," his "voracious appetite for listening to new music," and his "appreciation of an eclectic mix of styles and trends. We need his ears on the world," Santourian asserted.[24] Kernis's duties included composing four new pieces (including a song cycle for Renée Fleming and an arrangement of *Colored Field* for cello), reviewing new music scores for the orchestra and advising on commissions, overseeing new music programming, helping plan the orchestra's 2003 centennial and its annual Triple Play program (a collaboration with the Walker Art Center and the MacPhail Center for the Arts in which visiting composers wrote new pieces for student ensembles), and mentoring its Perfect Pitch program—a collaboration between the orchestra and the American Composers Forum. Under the auspices of this last program, the orchestra read through new scores that were then critiqued, much like Kernis's experience with the New York Philharmonic in 1983. Recalling the boost that early experience had given to his own career, he energetically promoted the Perfect Pitch program, which grew from a single day of readings to the retitled week-long annual Minnesota Orchestra Composer Institute. By 2006 the institute had seen readings of seventy-nine works by 75 composers. That year 143 composers applied for the nine openings.[25]

Meanwhile Kernis was busy writing the millennium symphony for Disney, which, at the time of the Pulitzer news in April 1998, was still "so secret it [hadn't] been announced yet."[26] Mahlerian in its genesis, the symphony became Mahlerian in its realization as well. Performing forces for the October 8, 1999, New York Philharmonic premiere were immense. Kernis calls for four flutes, four oboes, four clarinets, four bassoons, four saxophones, six horns, four trumpets, four trombones, and tuba. In addition to the normal string component are piano, celesta, synthesizer, electric guitar, electric bass, and harp. Six percussionists play so many instruments that the list of them takes up a full page: vibraphone, marimba, xylophone, glockenspiel, chimes, triangles, shakers, tambourines, various types of bells and cymbals, four tam tams, gongs, bell plates, crotales, an anvil, a lion's roar, clappers, woodblocks, bongos, timbales, tom-toms, snare drum, bass drums, maracas, whip, and ratchet. In addition there was, like the Mahler model, both an adult choir and a children's choir (a request from Disney), as well as adult vocal soloists and a boy soprano.

This huge ensemble had not been Kernis's first vision of the work, however. Originally he had pictured a small orchestra "with everyone mixed and amplified—putting forward a new manifestation for a twenty-first-century orchestra," he says.

Ultimately Disney opted for the traditional symphony, but Kernis supplemented it with the saxophones, sampler, electric bass, guitar, and that panoply of percussion.

On the plane, on his way home to Los Angeles after hearing the Mahler Eighth, Disney CEO Michael Eisner had sketched out "a rough treatment for a symphonic story line":[27] a history of an American family over a fifty-year period. Neither Kernis nor Torke was inspired by that "storybook," and Eisner, to his credit, did not push his idea. In fact, despite some speculation in the press to the contrary, the Disney staff largely gave the two composers free rein, along with lots of encouragement.

For the libretto Kernis tapped Welsh author Menna Elfyn, with whom he had collaborated during a workshop in England. A seasoned author, Elfyn had already published eight volumes of poetry, five stage plays, and a children's novel.[28] She had also developed a strong record of activism in support of children's rights, including work with the JUCONI Foundation (Junto con los Niños), a British-Mexican nongovernmental venture founded in 1989 with the aim of improving the lives of Mexican street children.[29] Thus her literary record and her experience with youth seemed well matched to the task of creating a meaningful libretto for Disney. As the collaboration proceeded, however, Elfyn's libretto took on an increasingly dark tone with an emphasis on broken homes that "didn't feel right for the piece or the occasion," says Kernis. Furthermore, she was not comfortable providing the type of rhythmicized text he needed to realize his musical concept. Kernis began to make some textual revisions himself.

In January 1999 Disney scheduled a workshop in Los Angeles with excerpts of the works-in-progress performed by the soloists, a chorus, and keyboard, conducted by the composers. Kernis prepared frantically, putting in fourteen-hour days, eating lots of chocolate, and turning off his phone.[30] Choplin was present at the event and, as he now recalls, felt uncomfortable with the text. Its quality, he says "was not of the level I was expecting."[31] Seeing his own role as a guide to the composers (a "utility, a kind of judge to help"), he encouraged Kernis's developing inclination to change librettists. Playwright David Simpatico (whose work had made a strong impression on Kernis) then entered the scene, first to collaborate with, and ultimately to replace, Elfyn. Thus nine months before the premiere, Kernis began almost anew. He discarded twelve minutes of music—about half of what he had already written—and he and Simpatico set out on a wholesale revision, retaining some portions of Elfyn's text, composing new words for large sections, and sometimes writing text to music that had already been composed.[32]

New York Philharmonic conductor Kurt Masur also wanted to have creative input, leading to additional discussions and modifications.[33] Disney paid for a week of rehearsals with the orchestra, chorus, and soloists during the summer so that the composers and conductor could continue to refine the scores. Choplin had worked very hard to convince Masur and the Philharmonic to participate. Their reluctance, he said, came not because the project was a collaboration with Disney but because the evening would consist of two new works by young composers. But once he was on board, Masur devoted himself to the project with energy. In fact, he developed the idea of commissioning other works: six new compositions written by composers from around the world were presented on two concerts in November, a month after the Kernis and Torke pieces were unveiled.[34]

The first movement of *Garden of Light* (thirteen minutes in length) begins with the world's creation, an orchestral big bang that leads into the men's chorus singing: "I am light / I bring on the day / bursting with sun, / seething with life." The parallels to the text of the finale of the 1983 *"dream of the morning sky"* ("I am the evening light / . . . I am the farthest star. . . . I am alive")—which also, of course, was first performed by the New York Philharmonic—are striking. Indeed, as we have seen, Kernis is often inspired by images of nature, and especially by the effects of light. Like Momaday's text in *"dream,"* and loosely following the creation story of Genesis, *Garden of Light* moves from the revelation of light to a section about animals (soaring eagles, singing dolphins, roaring lions), wind, lush fields, and tides. The soprano soloist emerges from this choral opening as a young child asking naïve questions: "I want to know why / Grass is green / Why rain is wet / Why the sky is blue / Why the sun must set." The movement ends with a return of the chorus, evoking again the power of nature: "Slumbering deserts . . . mountains unfurling . . . immeasurable oceans . . . Fiery starlight." At the end, the text resumes the creation myth: "I am Man and I am Woman / Brilliant with life" and concludes with the theme of the beginning: "I am Light, / I am the World."

The thirty-minute second movement begins with images of home as a "refuge / A harbor, a haven, a warm bed to sleep in / A door with a lock—your shelter." Then the vision of light that opened and closed the first movement returns in the form of nine stories, nine sparks of light—or, as the revised libretto reads, "A Journey in Nine Tableaux." That journey explores light's positive and negative manifestations: first, the child striking two rocks together to create fire, followed by the sparks of enlightenment (Buddha) and color (Michelangelo), then the Inquisition ("the blinding heat of the burning stake"), the sparks of love (Romeo and Juliet) and science (the discovery of electricity and the invention of the light bulb), the Holocaust ("The future is lost / in the raging glow / of six million ovens ablaze in the night") and the atom bomb, leading finally into the "blinding light of the greater good." These nine sparks are set for soloists with occasional choral interludes. When they are complete, the choir responds in the manner of a Greek chorus: "Where is the path that will lead us back / to the house we were born in, / to the Garden of Light?" Finally the children's chorus enters with the hope for a new century more peaceful than the one just past. In this utopian vision, the love of children leads home: "in our children's embrace, we are truly free."[35]

Highlights of the first movement include the opening section for men's chorus—a jazzy, rhythmic, spirited section that brings on the day, a scherzo for women's chorus at the first mention of animals, a dramatic climax with shimmering metal percussion preceding the child's first queries, and a *tranquillo* section with a beautiful flute cadenza (which then becomes a flute and soprano duet) over a drone and slow, held chords in the strings. The texture is extremely varied; imitation contrasts with chordal sections, staccato moments with legato.

The second movement opens with a hymn, the orchestra imitating an organ, the chorus in chorale style. After the premiere, Kernis created a version of this section for chorus and piano ("Home"), one of four pieces he extracted for more modest forces. Soft percussion and a dreamy flute cadenza introduce the first spark, sung by the boy soprano. Spark 2 features cadenzas for viola and cello, much like Kernis's writing in *Goblin Market*. Typical, too, is the virtuosity required of the players. One notable example is the orchestral interlude following spark 3, a tour de force for the horns. At the end of the frantic Inquisition section (spark 4), a downward rush ends in a long held note in the bass clarinet, contrabassoon, bass drum, and contrabasses—a dramatic effect Kernis had also used in *Goblin Market* and *Invisible Mosaic II.* The terrifying Holocaust section recalls similar outbursts during Kernis's "war" period of the 1990s. Racing upward scales suggest the flames of the Nazi ovens. Perhaps the most striking moment of the sparks section, however, is the beginning of the atom bomb reference. Here Kernis gives us near silence, an empty, dead landscape. The four soloists and the boy soprano sing in homorhythm with almost no accompaniment and a static melody, beginning with an open fourth that becomes a third and then evolves into dissonance; as we have seen, such movement from consonance to dissonance had characterized Kernis's music as far back as "*dream of the morning sky.*" Just before the final section, "Is There a Place?" (from which Kernis also extracted a piece for chorus and piano) there is a massive rolled crescendo in the timpani, cymbals, and tam tams reminiscent of the end of the Second Symphony. But here, instead of climaxing in devastation, the baritone enters with a recitative and then a final aria sung over a wordless choral background.

The premiere of the two millennium symphonies on October 8, 1999, was a sumptuous affair, with red carpet laid out for Disney dignitaries, media, and socialites. The audience, by all reports, was jubilant. Many of the critics, however, seized the opportunity to shoot barbs at both pieces. Perhaps it was the "Mahler meets Mickey Mouse" factor,[36] but for one of the rare times in his career, Kernis received strong critiques from the press. The main area of criticism—for both his work and Torke's—was the text. Even David Patrick Stearns, who wrote that the two pieces had "more taste than bombast" and complimented Kernis's "sumptuous" music, targeted the words, which sounded to him like "a greeting card" (the Kernis piece) and "bad Bertolt Brecht" (the Torke work).[37] Choplin, in retrospect, notes that *Garden of Light* "was not conventional . . . ; people were not ready for that kind of text."[38] Evaluation of the music, on the other hand, was more balanced. Reviewers noted the score's "effusive lyricism" and "exultant rhythms," although one commented that climaxes came too often and another found the work too big to hold together well.[39]

Some of the reviewers also reinforced the traditional divide between classical music and popular culture: Philip Kennicott accused the New York Philharmonic of selling "its soul for the weekend" and the composers of trying to please "la-la-land Medicis." Greg Sandow in the *Wall Street Journal* took a more thoughtful view, noting that Disney had not corrupted the composers by asking for "huge, optimistic scores" but, rather, had sought to reach larger audiences through "big, plain and highly public" statements. "I think classical music needs to widen its appeal," Sandow concluded. "So I hope that Disney gives us more commissions."[40]

Early plans on Disney's part to adapt parts of the symphonies for use in its theme parks came to naught. And the huge forces required made repeat performances extremely expensive. Choplin's original vision was to use the works in conjunction with animation, as in *Fantasia*, and he still holds out hope that the idea is not dead—citing, as support, the numerous occasions in music history when now-iconic works were greeted with negative initial reviews. Kernis, for his part, used the experience to revise the piece. In addition to extracting four short works for chorus and piano from it, he trimmed the orchestra a bit, "strengthened the orchestration," tightened several sections, and, with Simpatico's collaboration, instituted numerous text revisions in an attempt to "make the text more poetic, less naïve—in part to answer the critics and my own concerns." The text of the opening movement is heavily revised; that of the second less so except near the end. But the concluding words, articulating the hope for the future, remain essentially unchanged:

> In our children's embrace, we are truly free
> In our children's hearts, we are forever alive
> With our children's love, the world sings.
> . . .
> In their loving embrace, we are home.

The revised version had a highly successful performance in Minnesota three years later.[41]

Successes and Disappointments: *Valentines* and a New Plan for an Opera

Kernis was soon off writing another major work: a song cycle for soprano, commissioned for Renée Fleming by Great Performers at Lincoln Center (in the piano version) and the Minnesota Orchestra (in the orchestral form). He dedicated the piece to Jacob Druckman, who had died of lung cancer in 1996. This time Kernis mined the poetry of British author Carol Ann Duffy, selecting texts from several of her collections that were loosely related by the theme of frustrated love. In some ways the texts are similar in character to those of *Morningsongs* and *Love Scenes* in expressing both the desire for romantic fulfillment and its failure to materialize.

Valentines is a major work in four movements of varying lengths. Because Kernis rarely repeats words in his vocal settings, the length of each movement is directly related to the length of the text. Movements 1, 2, and 4 use relatively

Kernis, Renée Fleming, and the Minnesota Orchestra at the premiere of *Valentines*, April 2000. (Photo by Greg Helgeson. Courtesy of the Minnesota Orchestra.)

short poems and range from three to six minutes. The third movement, "Mrs. Midas," on the other hand, resembles a scene from an opera. Its lengthy narrative, told in the first person, sets the familiar Midas tale in a modern context. When a man who wishes for wealth is condemned to turning everything he touches to gold, his beleaguered wife separates from him in fear for her safety, banishing him first to another bedroom and ultimately to a remote glade in the forest. At twelve minutes, this movement dwarfs the others in length and has been performed separately from the rest of the set.

Valentines opens with a *presto* explosion reminiscent in some ways of *New Era Dance*, but it quickly turns "languorous" when the singer enters. The movement ends with a return of the *presto* instrumental section, at first identical to the opening (an unusual event with Kernis) but then diverging to create a conclusive ending. "Miles Away" (movement 2) is slow throughout. It begins with a melody in the English horn, played very high in its range. The timbre is so nearly vocal that at first the listener wonders if he or she is hearing the singer on an open vowel. Indeed, timbre is the governing parameter of this movement, with glistening scales and arpeggios simultaneously in celesta, harp, flutes, and clarinets at one point, accompanying the words "I hold you closer, miles away," and a piccolo solo at the end embedded in a triadic cloud as the stars glimmer at the close.

"Mrs. Midas" begins with a repeating figure that in some ways suggests an Indonesian gamelan. This type of writing actually harks back to Kernis's interest in minimalism, as well as to the additive procedures and ostinato patterns he had explored in his early works. In the first two measures the pianist plays a three-note figure, A–F♯–E, six times while the harp simultaneously plays its retrograde (E–F♯–A). In m. 2, the vibraphone and piano begin the same figure at a different pitch level (C♯–B–G♯ and G♯–B–C♯), overlapping with the first ostinato. This "answer" is sounded five times. Then, on the last beat of m. 2, the marimba and harp begin the pattern a third time, now on B–D–E and E–D–B, playing it four times. This opening recalls to a degree the process-oriented middle movement of "*dream of the morning sky*," but here, Kernis says, he used repetition and "tranquil intervals" to represent "domestic calm." A hint of them returns at the movement's end. As the voice enters, Kernis gradually introduces the woodwinds; the melodic shapes evolve and the level of dissonance increases. The quasi-minimalism soon gives way to other textures, but the three-note motive reappears occasionally as a type of leitmotif. As befits the narrative text, the music of this movement alternates among lyric passages, recitative, and action scenes, the orchestra often illustrating the text in the best historical tradition of opera and lieder. (For example, pings in flutes and percussion along with perfect fifths accompany transformations into gold.) Because the story line is so important, Kernis carefully controls the orchestral texture so that the audibility of the words is assured. The full ensemble plays only in interludes between the vocal stanzas.

Valentines concludes with a slow movement ("Who Loves You?") that begins with a tonal melody in B♭ sung by the clarinet over a gentle accompaniment in the harp. Moments of strong dissonance appear within the movement, the dynamic rising at one point to *fortississimo* followed by complete silence and a sudden *pianissimo*. The piece ends with the orchestra sounding a B♭ major triad, as the soprano sings an octave leap up to a *pianissimo* high B♭ (again evoking "*dream*"), but with a gentle dissonant counterpoint in the violin, harp, and timpani. The choice of B♭ to end *Valentines* not only reflects Kernis's perception of that key as warm (thus casting the finale in a mood of relaxation) but also takes advantage of Fleming's remarkable control of soft high notes. He handed her, he says, the high B♭ "as destination and anchor."

The coloristic relationship between music and text in *Valentines* reflects Kernis's study of Debussy and Ravel as he prepared for his arrangement of the Debussy piano etudes. This disciplined study, along with the influence of Druckman's teachings, further enhanced his sensitivity to timbre—already a strong point cited by critics, performers, and conductors. The premiere of the work took place on April 26, 2000, during an "orgy" of Kernis's works in the Twin Cities.[42] A week earlier the Minnesota Orchestra had presented the new cello version of the English horn concerto *Colored Field*, featuring the Norwegian cellist Truls Mørk. In the same concert the orchestra played *Musica Celestis*, as well as a transcription for cello and orchestra of the *Air* for violin Kernis had written for Joshua Bell in 1995. The ensemble recorded all three pieces during the concert for a compact disc that was released on Virgin Classics the following year. To top off the celebration, the St. Paul Chamber Orchestra performed the premiere of *Overture in Feet and Meters* on May 5. Kernis dedicated the piece to Hugh Wolff, who was leaving the SPCO at the end of the month and moving to Europe as chief conductor of the Frankfurt Radio Orchestra.

In the same year, Kernis also received a commission from the Santa Fe Opera to create a work for 2006, its fiftieth-anniversary season. He chose a topic (Ann Patchett's book *Bel Canto*) and a librettist (Philip Littell, who had written the text for Torke's millennium symphony). He also proposed British director Deborah Warner. Ultimately, however, the project dissolved before Kernis had written a single note. Although he invested six months in initial collaboration with Littell, the librettist, says Kernis, was disinclined to complete the significant tightening and structural focus that the multi-layered novel required in order to work for the operatic stage. In addition, the unanticipated deaths of both of Kernis's parents in 2004 ultimately made the time frame unrealistic.

For many years Kernis had been heading toward opera, a path forged not only in his vocal works from *Love Scenes* to *Valentines* and his compositions with spoken text (especially *Goblin Market*), but also in many of the instrumental works that were stimulated by narrative elements outside the music (for example, the Second Symphony and *Colored Field*). But for a composer as heavily involved with literature as Kernis, and one who cares deeply about finding in a libretto more than just "a serviceable treatment of a story line," the choice of text is necessarily difficult. The writer must not only hold an artistic vision compatible with that of the composer but must also have considerable artistic modesty: what works well in a play or a novel might prove disastrous in an opera. Furthermore, the librettist must be willing to accept the fact that audiences will often view the text as subordinate to the sound. Few writers are skilled at functioning under such strictures, one reason why the history of music is filled with difficult writer-composer collaborations. Indeed, some composers simply decided to write their own texts. (Wagner is the most illustrious example, but others, such as Berlioz and Berg, occasionally did so as well.) At this writing, the creation of an opera remains an unrealized dream for Kernis, one that demands the right team, the right story, and the right commissioner.

Trio in Red, *Color Wheel*, and the Grawemeyer Award

At the turn of the century Kernis received two more large commissions. The first was for a trio for clarinet, cello, and piano, funded by ninety-three-year-old philanthropist Milton Muelder for the Wharton Center for the Performing Arts at Michigan State University. The piece was written in collaboration with the Chamber Music Society of Lincoln Center, whose musicians were scheduled to perform at Michigan State. Bill Wright, the Wharton Center's executive director, proposed the commission. The musicians nominated Kernis.

The result was *Trio in Red*, written for clarinetist David Shifrin, pianist Anne-Marie McDermott, and cellist Fred Sherry. In a very real sense this piece moves away from the optimistic works of this period to revisit the strong emotions of Kernis's war years. The seventeen-minute work is in two movements, designated by colors that reflect his synesthesia: "Orange Circle, Yellow Line" and "Red Whirl." (Red is the dominant color, yellow and orange more muted and lyrical.) The first movement is mostly slow, at times bringing to mind the prayerful spirit of *Lament and Prayer* and *Still Movement with Hymn* but now influenced by the harmonic language of Messiaen. The movement's tone becomes very dark prior to a *presto* central section that ends by tapering off to a few held chords in the piano before the opening section's affect is regained. Near the end is a striking passage in which the clarinet sings a plaintive line over a series of whole notes in the piano (see figure 12). These chords move mainly by mediant progressions, reinforced by the cellist, who sounds the bass pitch in repeated notes interspersed with harmonics.

"Red Whirl," in contrast, is a virtuosic romp for all three instruments, "always on the edge, unyielding."[43] Indeed, like *New Era Dance*, "Red Whirl" is at once electrifying and frightening. A klezmer section comes off as a grotesque parody of this eastern European dance music. An intermediary passage features fragmentary motives in dialogue among the three instruments, interrupted by rests (the irony of the devil's dance from Stravinsky's *L'Histoire du soldat* comes to mind, as do the polkas of Shostakovich). The movement is full of slides (in double stops in the cello at times), and at the end the pianist plays *presto molto* in large "extended hand" clusters. Behind this work lies another literary inspiration and another link to Kernis's Jewish heritage: he had just read *Constantine's Sword* by James Carroll, a former priest who documents the violent history of Catholic anti-Semitism.

The second commission in this period stemmed from big plans afoot in Kernis's home town: the opening of a new music auditorium to replace the venerable Academy of Music as the Philadelphia Orchestra's home. The new building, which opened in December 2001, was largely funded by Sidney Kimmel, a film producer and the CEO of the Jones Apparel Group (parent company of such upscale brands as Jones New York, Nine West, and Evan Picone). Kimmel himself was a classic self-made man. The son of a cab driver, he had become one of the richest men in the country, and he expressed his gratitude for his good fortune through philanthropy. In the ten years preceding the hall's inauguration, Kimmel had given away or pledged more than $340 million, endowing not only the auditorium but also cancer research centers in Philadelphia, San Diego, and Baltimore.[44]

In honor of the event, the Philadelphia Orchestra commissioned three works that year. Michael Daugherty wrote *Philadelphia Stories*, celebrating the city; Jennifer Higdon composed Concerto for Orchestra, celebrating the musicians; and Kernis wrote *Color Wheel*, celebrating the new hall. A preview article in the symphony's fall program assessed Kernis's strengths as "a keen ear for orchestral color, an ability to write idiomatically for large forces, and a broad emotional spectrum."

Before the Kimmel Center's opening in December, the orchestra had some other major news to add to this publicity. In November the Grawemeyer Foundation announced its composition award for 2002: the cello version of Kernis's

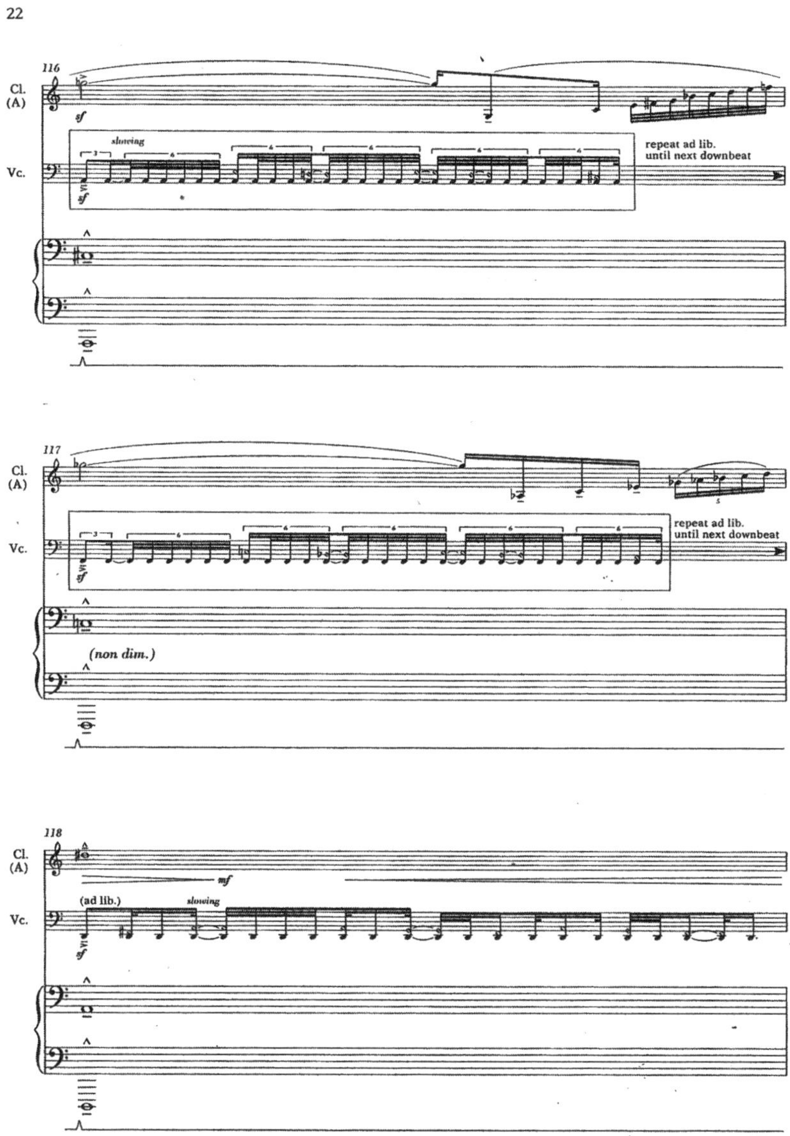

Figure 12. *Trio in Red* (2001), mvt. 1, mm. 116–18. (Copyright © 2001 by Associated Music Publishers, Inc. International Copyright Secured. All Rights Reserved. Used by Permission.)

Colored Field. The foundation's awards, founded by H. Charles Grawemeyer "to help make the world a better place,"[45] consist of five prizes administered by the University of Louisville in music, political science, psychology, education, and religion. The music award honors a composition in a large genre premiered during the previous five years. It is one of the most substantial prizes in the field: in the year Kernis won it there were about two hundred nominations, and the prize was $200,000. The award's three-stage intensive screening process was designed to ensure the independence of the judges. First, members of the composition faculty at the University of Louisville make an initial selection, narrowing the field to about 8–12 percent of the applicants. Next, three judges (a critic, a conductor, and a composer—who is often the previous year's winner) independently choose a group of finalists, normally five to seven, but sometimes as many as nine. Finally, a group of highly knowledgeable laypeople "who are very serious about music in general, and contemporary music in particular" select the winner. As in the semifinals, each member of the lay panel makes an independent judgment, ranking the works numerically. In this final stage, composers are not identified. The inclusion of lay people in the process, highly unusual in the world of composition, ensures that the chosen work will "appeal to an informed classical music audience as well as to seasoned professionals," in the words of current director Marc Satterwhite.[46]

Kernis composed *Color Wheel* in a manner that would take advantage of the celebrated Philadelphia Orchestra, an influence on him since his youth and renowned for its lush, luxuriant string sound and the virtuosity of its wind players. In addition, he met with architect Rafael Viñoly and the acousticians to understand the attributes of the Kimmel Center's new Verizon Hall.

The opulence of the opening weekend rivaled that of the Disney millennium concert. The events began Friday night with a "glitzy black tie gala show and buffet dinner";[47] the top ticket price was $5,000. The evening included an hour-long performance by Elton John, who, according to a report in the *New York Times*, received a fee of $2 million paid by Sidney Kimmel. Saturday night was directed to general audiences. The orchestra opened the program with *Color Wheel*, after which Yo-Yo Ma, Emanuel Ax, and Itzhak Perlman performed Beethoven's triple concerto. (In the middle of the third movement Ma's chair fell backwards off its riser. He tumbled on his back but immediately arose and played the next passage standing while one of the violinists replaced his chair.) The concert ended with Ravel's Suite no. 2 from *Daphnis et Chloé.*

Color Wheel is a true concerto for orchestra, highlighting, at various times, individual players or sections of the orchestra. It opens with a *fortissimo* series of four chords in the winds and brass, played in chorale style. In contrast, the strings enter with a legato theme, an upward, (mostly) scalar ascent of the type that had fascinated Kernis for years. These two motives form the basis for the twenty-two-minute work. A *presto* scherzo, beginning about two minutes into the piece, introduces a series of variations featuring different players. After a grand pause (at about nine and a half minutes), the slow, chorale-like music returns in spirit, though (typically) transformed in details. A new scherzo-like set of variations appears about four minutes later and eventually devolves into a recollection once again of the opening chorale, here heralded by chimes, horns, and trumpets. Kernis ends the work with a consonant version of the central motive, now turned into a long melody treated in canon. Vibrant scales and arpeggios begin in the lower strings and woodwinds and eventually embrace the whole string section, rising to an brilliant A major chord. The work's title refers both to varied orchestral colors and to Kernis's tendency to associate keys with hues, which he had mentioned to commentators as early as the 1980s in his reaction to the Ravenna mosaics. The tonal center of A major, he wrote in his program notes, appeared to him as bright yellow.

"Big comes naturally to [Kernis]," Mark Swed wrote in response to Disney's millennium symphony project. Indeed, the word aptly describes Kernis's output in the 1995–2001 period: four original orchestral works—the Double Concerto (30 minutes), *Garden of Light* (52 minutes), *Valentines* (25 minutes), and *Color Wheel* (22 minutes); five orchestral arrangements—*Too Hot Toccata*, the Debussy etudes, *Concierto de Dance Hits*, *Colored Field*, and *Overture in Feet and Meters*; and two major chamber works—the second String Quartet (39 minutes) and *Trio in Red* (17 minutes). Big also describes these works' impact, evidenced by the Pulitzer Prize and Grawemeyer Award, commissions from Disney, the Philadelphia Orchestra, and the Chamber Music Society of Lincoln Center, and strong reactions of audiences. Despite some disappointing bumps in the road, Kernis now found himself in the forefront of the new wave of composers, reaching out to audiences with a personal message, as he had envisioned in high school when he determined that he would devote his life to musical composition.

7 Family Matters (2002–2009)

KERNIS'S MILLENNIUM PRAYER THAT the twenty-first century, through its children, would usher in a "new era" of humanitarianism and peace shattered almost immediately after the century dawned in the devastating terrorism of 9/11. Aaron and Evelyne had just returned from California on the evening of September 10, 2001. Like many others around the country, they heard about the disaster after the first crash and watched on television as the other plane slammed into the second tower. From the George Washington Bridge, they could see the clouds of smoke downtown; the smell engulfed them as the wind blew north. That night they huddled with neighbors and a cousin visiting from Belgium.[1]

Although Kernis had previously written some of his most powerful compositions in reaction to war and devastation, this time he was "very certain" that he "could not and would not write music in direct response to the attack." But after many months, he said, when the initial numbness had become "somewhat internalized, parts of the slow movement of my second string quartet suddenly re-sounded in my ears and expanded in sound and mass for a large . . . group."[2]

It was two years before that expansion materialized, spurred by the efforts of Linda Hoeschler—to whom Kernis had dedicated the entire Second String Quartet. In 1990 Hoeschler had organized six couples into the "Minnesota Commissioning Club." Each couple contributed $2,000 per year (later raised to $3,000) with the express purpose of commissioning new works. The club now gave its resources to Kernis to create an orchestral version of his "Sarabande Double, Sarabande Simple," originally dedicated to the memory of arts supporter and friend Bette Snapp. Thus the quartet movement grew from a "private mourning for four instruments" and one individual into a public "sonic mass" for "far too many victims."[3] The Orchestra of St. Luke's, conducted by Donald Runnicles, first performed *Sarabanda in Memoriam* on February 26, 2004, in a 9/11 memorial concert at Carnegie Hall. Runnicles programmed it along with Strauss's *Metamorphosen* (composed in 1945 as a memorial to the destruction of Dresden), Karl Amadeus Hartmann's *Concerto funebre* ("a lamentation against the 1938 Munich agreement that allowed Hitler to annex the Czech Sudentenland"), and Shostakovich's Ninth Symphony. Poetry readings separated the musical works.

Perhaps in part to dispel those 2001 images of death—and with fatherhood on the horizon—Kernis composed two buoyant works the next year, the Concerto for Toy Piano and Orchestra, commissioned for Margaret Leng Tan, and the second Superstar Etude. The Toy Piano Concerto had its premiere in Singapore in January 2003 and its U.S. premiere in New York the following December (in a version for chamber ensemble). Kernis's interest in this project stemmed not only from owning a toy piano as a child but also from his love of John Cage's Suite for Toy Piano, which he calls "the essential ur-composition of the instrument."[4] During the composition process, he also recalled Henry Cowell's 1934 percussion octet *Ostinato Pianissimo*, in which eight ostinato figures of different lengths interact simultaneously.[5] Kernis, who had used ostinato patterns as an organizing principle since his student days, based the opening movement on the model of the Indonesian gamelan. Throughout the five-minute movement a series of repeating motives freely overlap. He referenced gamelan music in other ways as well: a pseudo-pentatonic melody at the beginning, a texture evoking the polyphonic stratification of Indonesian music, the use of metallic percussion, and the ending stroke on the low gong. (In gamelan music, gong strokes mark the ends of major sections.) As usual, though, Kernis combined cultural influences. The slow movement is a gentle lullaby, and the finale introduces jazz and a whirling surface similar to those in some of his earlier works. He has since recast the concerto for standard grand piano with the title *Three Flavors*.

Superstar Etude no. 2 celebrates Thelonious Monk's 1944 jazz standard "Round Midnight." The Italian pianist Emanuele Arciuli commissioned it as one of twenty short pieces based on the same tune. He played all twenty in a concert at Columbia University on November 14, 2002. Kernis, in his version, made use of the principal five-note motive of "Round Midnight," introducing it in various guises and clothing it in increasingly virtuosic attire. Arciuli characterizes the piece as "funny, crazily—even paradoxically—fast, humorous, and full of irony."[6] Indeed, the four-minute etude is a tour de force; it was, after all, influenced by, and written for, a "superstar."[7]

If in the 1990s Kernis's works had been stimulated, to a large degree, by public happenings (whether the opening of a new concert hall, urban riots, or wars past and present), those of the first decade of the twenty-first century drew primarily on private experiences, the most important being the birth of his twins and the death of his parents. Jonah David and Delphine Emalyah Kernis were born on February 23, 2003. (Both children now attend an advanced music school. Jonah plays the cello and Delphine plays the violin.) At the time of their birth, Aaron was in the midst of writing a choral work for the Dale Warland Singers, a three-movement composition, *The Wheel of Time, the Dance*, setting secular texts by Wendell Berry. The poems, says Kernis, celebrate the "dream of America's heartland, an America concerned with good air, unpolluted food and water . . . a love and respect for nature."[8] They also deal with cycles of life, a topic that had attracted Kernis since his college years and now, in addition, reflected his new role as a father. On the private, personal plane, those new young lives helped combat the recurring images of the deaths of so many others.

Unfortunately, Mildred and Frank only enjoyed their grandchildren for one year before they too died. Mildred had developed recurring lymphoma, which subsided but then re-emerged in the form of uterine cancer. Frank, for his part, had not had an easy life after the family returned to Pennsylvania in 1970. When Aaron was in high school, Frank suffered a heart attack after slipping on the floor in a supermarket. The postal service assigned him to office work and then laid him off after determining that he couldn't walk a full route. He found work in other areas (for example, in delicatessens and factories), but he had lost the job he loved. Then he suffered a second heart attack and required double bypass surgery, which "left him mentally and physically compromised," says Kernis. By the time Mildred's cancer returned, Frank was nearly eighty and was "getting a little far away." During the final stages of Mildred's illness, Aaron arranged for twenty-four-hour hospice care for her in the family home. Frank, at one point, stepped outside for the newspaper, neglecting to tie his shoes. He tripped on the concrete, hit his head, and never emerged from a vegetative state. Mildred died on March 26, 2004, at age seventy-seven; Frank passed away four months later, on July 7, at the age of eighty.

In addition to the personal events that stimulated Kernis's change in direction during this period, he also instituted alterations to his working methods and his artistic representation. While he was composing *Garden of Light*, Kernis began to use the computer to help him sort through preliminary ideas. For previous works he had simply made "zillions of hand-written sketches." Now he tried "writing hundreds of sketches on paper, and when I was happy with some, I would put them into the computer and start printing them out." Using the Sibelius music engraving program with a MIDI interface, he could then listen to these ideas, "testing counterpoint or voice leading" in situations where he "couldn't hold all the notes" in his head (or in his fingers). The ability to reproduce complex counterpoint immediately in sound was, of course, attractive, but Kernis found that the computer-generated output could also prove frustrating. "It's utterly wrong when it comes to balance," he notes. Thus, although the new technology was seductive, in some ways it made the compositional process more difficult by creating "an artificial orchestra that, once heard, had to be forgotten." Nor did it reduce the volume of paper he generated. He would end up with piles of print-outs by the time a piece was finished.

The change in artistic representation also turned out to be less than successful. In January 2002 he signed an exclusive contract with Boosey and Hawkes. His motivation for leaving Schirmer at this point was to keep ownership of his copyrights. In this regard, Kernis cites the advice of Philip Glass, who served as a model and guide for many younger composers. Ultimately, however, Kernis was attracted by the Schirmer staff's enthusiasm, knowledge, and support, and he soon returned to the firm. At the same time, however, he heeded Glass's advice. In 2007 he established "AJK Music" and designated Schirmer as his exclusive representative and administrative agent.

Newly Drawn Sky

When the twins were six months old Kernis began another orchestral work, *Newly Drawn Sky*, a seventeen-minute tone poem stimulated by a commission from the Ravinia Festival in honor of James Conlon's first year as music director. Welz Kauffman, president of the festival, had been artistic administrator of the New York Philharmonic during the millennium symphonies project. He chose Kernis for the Ravinia commission, he says, because of "Aaron's rigorous technical mastery, orchestration skills, and Romantic sensibility."[9] Kernis described the new work as "a lyrical, reflective piece for orchestra, a reminiscence of the first summer night by the ocean spent with my young twins . . . and of the changing colors of the summer sky at dusk."

Newly Drawn Sky (2005) has a very different cast to it than Kernis's previous works. There are no Jewish influences, nor any references to popular musics. Jazz—such a strong force in other recent works—is nearly absent. Even dance has a limited influence, and Kernis's beloved mediant progressions are rare (although there is a lovely one near the end, at mm. 248–49). Kauffman's faith in Kernis's imaginative orchestration is well rewarded, but the individual virtuosity seen in many previous works is less in evidence here.

Despite the lack of some previous stylistic markers, Kernis's individual voice—in the language he had come to find compelling—shines through clearly. The opening melody in the celli, for example, is formed from a rising scale with an upward leap at its end. In shape it resembles many others that had inspired him over the years, while paying tribute, in particular, to the beginning of the *Symphony in Waves*. And as in previous works, Kernis introduces this melody in an additive fashion: Two notes, G–A♭, then G–A♮, grow into a longer scalar line combining half and whole steps. The melody rises to the tritone C♯ and then exuberantly leaps up a fifth. This theme forms the basis for the opening and closing sections of the work, always evolving and transforming, taking on the different hues of the waning light of evening. Its reemergence near the end in two significant moments of arrival (mm. 163 and 198) gives an overall A B A' form to the piece.

With regard to harmony the work is also typically Kernisean. The guiding principle, presented at the outset, is a series of three-note, nontriadic chords in close harmony whose progression is governed by voice leading. As in previous works, Kernis uses cadential points to signal sectional divisions, although they come less frequently here than in other recent works (for instance, *Garden of Light*). At the same time, Kernis does not shy away from the grand gestures so apparent in other compositions. The orchestral sound is lush, and he gives vibrant solo passages to some of his favorite instruments: the trumpet, the English horn, the cellos, the violas, and the horns. And in typical fashion he frequently subdivides the violins to provide a dense texture. Contrapuntal elements predominate for most of the piece, but imitation (in contrast to his earlier works) is rare. The pervasive polyphonic texture makes the few moments of homorhythm stand out dramatically. One, in which almost the entire orchestra plays in unison, emerges starkly as a bold gesture. Another, near the end, features the opening theme in the winds and strings in hymn-like fashion. During this two-minute section the theme is underscored by rolls on tam-tams and cymbals that repeatedly swell and subside. The effect here, however, is nothing like that in the Second Symphony. Rather, it resembles the wash of metallic sounds at the end of *Lament and Prayer*. And like *Lament* as well, the end introduces a shimmering A major triad, over which the horns quietly articulate repeated chords based on A lydian. The final sonority mixes elements of A and E. This mixing of tonal and modal elements brings back images of the opening of the piece.

Overall, *Newly Drawn Sky* is a big, serious work, yet it is in no way sorrowful. Rather, the piece is grandiose and majestic, reflecting an awe of life on both the macro and the micro scale: the changing colors in the evening sky and the wonder of the new lives developing in Kernis's private domain.

In Memory of Mildred and Frank

In five works from this period Kernis paid tribute to his parents: a ballad for cello solo and seven cellos (or recorded cellos, or piano, 2004), the third Superstar Etude for piano (2004, revised in 2007), *Two Meditations* for chorus and organ (2005–6), *Two Movements (with Bells)* for violin and piano (2007), and the *Symphony of Meditations* (Symphony no. 3, 2009). Mildred Kernis loved ballads, and Aaron had acknowledged her preference as early as 1993 in the third movement of *100 Greatest Dance Hits* ("MOR Easy Listening Slow Dance Ballad"). Now, reflecting on her life, he explored the style at greater length, both in the cello piece and in *Superstar Etude no. 3*, which is titled *Ballad(e) Out of the Blues* (a live recording by Mihaela Ursuleasa is included on the book's Web site).[10] At ten minutes, it is the longest of the three superstar piano etudes, and it is also the most technically difficult. (To a great extent it is a study for the left hand.) Compared to *Newly Drawn Sky*, *Superstar Etude no. 3* shows much greater affinity with previous works. There are overt references to popular musics (in this case blues) and to Debussy, Messiaen, Ives, and Gershwin. Strong tonal elements devolve into dissonance. Here, as elsewhere, Kernis looks at color, exploiting the many hues possible on the piano.

After a short introduction, Kernis brings in his blues melody, complete with ninth chords and other characteristic jazz harmonies. Over it he lays virtuosic improvisatory-sounding passagework that creates a filigree winding over the tune. Although the harmonies reference the musics of black Americans (at one point he gives the instruction "with a gospel feel"), Kernis casts these iconic models in his own idiosyncratic language. He directly evokes Gershwin in the central section with hints of the piano preludes, *Porgy and Bess*, and *Rhapsody in Blue*. After a build-up to extreme dissonance, the piano imitates a harp (Kernis imagined an "Ivesian haze" here), and then the influence of Gershwin reappears for one more fleeting moment. The most unusual effect, however, comes during the last minute of the piece. Here Kernis uses the piano's lowest range to create a growling sound akin to the percussion parts in many of his orchestral works. The similarity to rolls on metal percussion instruments is enhanced by his instruction that this section be "heavily pedaled, somewhat blurry." Beginning *pianissimo*, the rumbling low scales build dynamically to *ffff*, much like the effect he called for on the tam-tams and cymbals in the *Symphony in Waves*, the Second Symphony, and other works. The piece ends, however, not with this crescendo, but with two shimmering tremolos and a long held note (a typical feature of jazz improvisations on standard tunes), followed by a quick afterthought: the pianist, with the *una corda* pedal depressed, rushes "subito presto" down to the bottom of the keyboard.

The year after he completed the third *Superstar Etude*, Kernis composed *Two Meditations* for choir and organ. The occasion was historic—the rededication of an organ at the Plum Street Temple in Cincinnati—and the commission came from the College-Conservatory of Music, University of Cincinnati, through its Tangeman Sacred Music Center. The Vocal Arts Ensemble, a long-running professional chamber choir in the city, performed the premiere on April 1, 2006. The Plum Street Temple has a long and illustrious history in the evolution of Reform Judaism in the United States. Its grandiose building was dedicated in 1866 as the place of worship for the Lodge Street Synagogue, which dates its founding back to 1840. In 1853 the congregation arranged to hire as its rabbi Isaac Mayer Wise (1819–1900), who is now widely recognized as one of the most influential leaders in the U.S. Reform movement. Wise was instrumental in the founding of the Union of American Hebrew Congregations—an umbrella organization for U.S. Reform synagogues that was established in 1873—and Hebrew Union College, which opened its doors two years later. (The college is still the Reform movement's seminary, but now also has branches in New York and Los Angeles). From the start of his tenure in Cincinnati, Wise was concerned about synagogue music. He introduced a choir in 1854 (directing it with his violin) and the following year began advocating for installation of an organ.[11] Choirs and organs are not part of traditional Jewish worship; in fact, musical instruments are proscribed in Orthodox practice. Early nineteenth-century German-Jewish reforms, however, reinstated the use of instruments,[12] and a choral music tradition began to take hold first in Germany and Austria, and then elsewhere. In a very real sense, these reforms—including buildings such as the Plum Street Temple—imitated Protestant practices and were designed to bring Judaic rituals into conformity with modern religious worship in the Christian world. The Plum Street building was placed on the National Register of Historic Places by the Department of the Interior in 1975. The rededication of its organ capped a wholesale reconstruction of the building and was thus a major event in the life of the congregation.

For texts, Kernis turned once again to Stephen Mitchell, whose *Enlightened Heart* had inspired *Simple Songs* in 1991. This time he selected two of Mitchell's psalm adaptations, contained in a volume of fifty psalms from the Hebrew Bible.[13] As in the *Enlightened Heart*, Mitchell's poems are not translations but, rather, interpretations. He noted in his preface that he "paraphrased, expanded, contracted, deleted, shuffled the order of verses, and freely improvised on the themes of the originals." Responding to the deaths of his parents, Kernis chose two psalms that "speak to the acceptance of death and the loving presence of God." In Psalm 39, the poet notes the transience of life. Mitchell freely renders verses 5–6 as "All of us flash into being, / as insubstantial as breath. / Our lives are a fleeting shadow; / then we vanish into the night." The second (Psalm 84) concerns the journey to "the place of perfect repose."

Kernis set both psalms for choir either *a cappella* or with organ accompaniment. In the first one he applied his practice of moving between tonal or consonant and atonal or dissonant language to individual phrases rather than to the piece as a whole. Numerous phrases begin and end on unisons, triads, or thirds but become dissonant at their midpoints. The movement overall is slow and meditative, with the organ version containing a striking *a cappella* section near the end.

In the second piece the consonant-dissonant dichotomy plays out on the level of the overall structure. (Again the influences of Messiaen and Pärt are apparent.) It begins and ends with strong tonal statements in D♭ major but becomes highly dissonant at the movement's center. Also making this movement difficult for the singers are the extended *a cappella* sections. The texture consists of an alternation between unaccompanied and accompanied sections, requiring excellent choral intonation. In both works Kernis periodically subdivides the choir into as many as eight parts. The writing here, both in style and musical language, anticipates that of the third symphony, which he would begin the following year.

The year 2006 proved extremely productive for Kernis. Not only did he complete the *Two Meditations* for Cincinnati, but he also wrote a twenty-minute chamber ensemble piece for the San Francisco Conservatory and received a commission for a violin and piano duo from the BBC Proms. The former honored the inauguration of a new dynamic facility in the heart of San Francisco, around the corner from the city's major performing arts venues. The San Francisco Conservatory had been incorporated in 1923 as an outgrowth of a piano school founded by Ada Clement in 1917, and, since the 1950s, it had been located in the western part of town near Golden Gate Park. Long an artistic bulwark of the city, the conservatory now moved front and center geographically as well. To honor the opening of the facility's new concert hall, the school turned to its former student Aaron Jay Kernis to compose a new work. The commission was funded by the Fleishhacker Foundation, established by a family with a long history of support for the arts in San Francisco. Banker brothers Herbert and Mortimer Fleishhacker had been among the initial two hundred founders of the San Francisco Symphony in 1911, and Herbert had worked tirelessly to bring about the construction of War Memorial Opera House. (He was part of a two-decade-long political fight to replace an auditorium destroyed in the devastating fires of 1906; the opera house finally opened in 1932.)[14]

Two Awakenings and a Double Lullaby, for soprano, violin, guitar, and piano (2006),[15] honors Kernis's twins. The first movement's text, by the English poet Thomas Traherne (1636–74), celebrates in metaphysical language the wonder of the birth of a baby boy. The setting begins and ends quietly (and tonally, in A) with bell sounds but rises in the center to impassioned excitement. For the second movement Kernis again turned to Carol Ann Duffy, author of the texts of *Valentines*. "The Light Gatherer" centers on the poet's wonder concerning her young daughter. This movement, in contrast to the first, is lively, energetic, sparkling, and agile. It exudes an exuberance evoking running, playing, swinging, and dancing. For the third movement Kernis chose two texts about angels, recalling, perhaps, the slow movement of his first quartet (*musica celestis*). Englebert Humperdinck's famous "When at night I go to sleep" talks of fourteen angels in seven pairs: two at the head, two at the feet, two on the right, two on the left, two warmly covering, two hovering above, and two guiding "my steps to heaven." The emphasis on the number two clearly references the twins, and the setting at first intertwines violin and soprano in an extended duet. (The piano accompanies this section but plays a role subsidiary to the two treble lines; the guitar does not enter until the last two minutes of the movement.) The second text used in this movement, from an American spiritual, contains the phrase "angels watching over me." This movement, arguably the highlight of the set, is thus a double lullaby. It begins with a gentle hymn, features in the middle one of Kernis's favorite mediant progressions taking us to E (the key with which he will also end his third symphony), and eventually winds its way back to the A where the entire work began, as the soprano sings "two, two, two."

The commission Kernis received in 2006 came from the BBC Promenade Concerts (familiarly known as the Proms), London's renowned eight-week series of daily concerts, most of which are held in the 5,500-seat Royal Albert Hall. The previous year the Proms had begun to offer a series of chamber music performances as well, held in the more modest Cadogan Hall; for this series the BBC commissioned Kernis to write a piece for violin and piano. The renowned Canadian violinist James Ehnes performed *Two Movements (with Bells)* with pianist Eduard Laurel on July 23, 2007. Kernis dedicated the seventeen-minute piece to his father, whose "favorite music was jazz and American popular song of the 40's and 50's."[16] His program notes state that he was surprised to see how strongly the influence of improvisation in jazz, blues, and ballad singing had emerged in recent years, and he traced the thread back to *New Era Dance* with its evocations of big band jazz. But *Two Movements (with Bells)* is very different in character from *New Era Dance*. It is largely introspective but is interrupted by sections of "restless, often uneasy lines and silences" and wild "outbursts of activity." In the first movement Kernis evokes bell sounds in the piano part, first underlying *leggiero* skittering motives in the violin and then broadly dominating the texture in the movement's extended coda. Bells had figured in earlier works such as the opening of *Before Sleep and Dreams*, the second movement of the Second Symphony, and, most prominent, the end of *Still Movement with Hymn*. Furthermore, the overall lamenting character of the piece brings to mind Kernis's history of works about death. Here, however, there is sadness but none of the anger or bitterness of these earlier works. Frank's death, though painful, was not unexpected, not the result of violence, not untimely in the broad scheme of life. Indeed, Kernis refuses to link the bell sounds specifically to death. "Are they funeral bells," he asks in his notes, "bells of distant memory, bells made of dense clusters of overtones which fracture and fragment from the intensity of their physical attack?"

Kernis notes that the first movement of this work is "a free interpretation of sonata form in five sections: slow opening with intensification, an active and improvisatory middle, a return of pensive slow music, a shortened section of faster music, and a calming coda." In the second movement he provides variations on an original jazzy ballad-like tune.

There is no room for improvisation in the performance of this piece, yet many sections give the impression of written-out extemporizations; they were stimulated, Kernis notes, by the "improvisatory impetuousness" of free jazz. If the bell sounds and lamenting characterization recall earlier pieces, the harmonic language here is more akin to that of recent works such as *Newly Drawn Sky*. Although this language is, overall, more chromatic and consistently dissonant than that of his earlier pieces, Kernis retains from the past his practice of moving from consonance to dissonance and back to consonance within each movement.

The use of variations on a small motive again forms a theme through the work. In this case that motive consists of three notes. The first two form a sigh motive such as that found in many Baroque works; the third is a long note that usually enters after an intervening rest (see figure 13a, mm. 1–4 and 13–17 in the piano and 12–14 in the violin). The sigh recurs intermittently throughout the piece, making its final appearance at the very end of the second movement. (In figure 13b, note that the sigh appears four times in the piano in mm. 89–91.) Then a gentle cluster in the piano introduces rising lines filled with fourths in both instruments and ending with prominent G♯s and C♯s and a soft piano bell.

Figure 13. *Two Movements (with Bells)*, 2007. (Copyright © 2007 by Associated Music Publishers, Inc. International Copyright Secured. All Rights Reserved. Used by Permission.)

a. beginning

A New Choral Symphony on a Medieval Text

In August 2007 Kernis began work on his third and longest symphony: the *Symphony of Meditations* for chorus and orchestra. For this piece he assembled a lengthy text from the work of the eleventh-century Sephardic philosopher and poet Solomon Ibn Gabirol (ca. 1021–ca. 1058), using translations by Peter

Figure 13. (*Continued*)
b. ending

Cole. (The text of the symphony is in English except for a few lines in Hebrew near the end.) The composition process ended up consuming nearly two years; the Seattle Symphony and chorus, conducted by Gerard Schwarz, presented the premiere on June 25, 2009. Kernis dedicated the symphony to Jeff and Lara Sanderson (the commissioners) "in profound appreciation of their support and belief in the transformative power of music," to Schwarz and his wife Jody, and to his own parents.

Kernis's third symphony forms a logical extension of (and in some ways an ending to) the direction in which he had been moving for years. Meditative themes had increasingly attracted his attention, from the prayers that concluded *Still Movement with Hymn* and *Lament and Prayer* through the universalist spirituality in *Garden of Light* and *Two Movements (with Bells)*. As we have seen, medieval texts, from Hildegard von Bingen to Mechthild of Magdeburg, had often been the vehicles for these meditations, speaking to Kernis in mystical images that stimulated his musical expression, both vocal and instrumental. But in the words of Ibn Gabirol, Kernis found this medieval mysticism not in the Christian tradition but, rather, in his own. Judaic themes, of course, had motivated him as early as 1981, inspired by Jewish history (especially the Holocaust) and ritual practice (cantorial vocal styles and congregational heterophony). Now this heritage took on a new dimension, for Ibn Gabirol imbued his poetry with neo-Platonist philosophy: the existence, if not the essence, of God can be known, he argues, and the universe, from the divine soul to the material world, is a unity. Kernis emphasized this theme through a cyclical return throughout the symphony to the words "God is One."

The Third Symphony also builds on Kernis's attraction to narrative and his unfulfilled desire to write an opera. He constructed his own story line by choosing and intermingling excerpts from thirteen of Ibn Gabirol's texts: four independent poems and nine sections of the poet's major work, *Keter Malkhut (Kingdom's Crown)*.

When the Chicago Symphony had proposed a commission for a choral symphony back in 1995, Kernis was not ready to write one (see Chapter 6). Now, however, after the birth of his children and the death of his parents—and especially after discovering Cole's work—the task became for him a fundamental necessity. The Seattle Symphony's request for a large composition provided the opportunity to fill that need.

In many respects Ibn Gabirol's themes were foreign to Kernis: praise of and supplication to God; preparation for death and a belief in the afterlife; sin and the seeking of divine mercy. But at the same time he found it "compelling and nurturing to embrace these words . . . while attempting to grapple honestly with their content. . . . In crucial ways," he wrote, "this piece represents to me a statement of my faith and has made me ruminate . . . upon how it is that we human beings and our souls are created and shaped."[17]

Kernis and Cole had met in the early 1990s through a mutual friend. At the time, Cole was guest-editing a volume of *Conjunctions* and invited Kernis to conduct the interview with John Adams quoted in Chapter 2. When Aaron and Evelyne traveled to Jerusalem in 1997 in order for Aaron to judge the (now defunct) Bernstein competition, Cole acted as their guide. He also showed Kernis the text of *Kingdom's Crown*, which he was translating. Kernis was stunned. The poem was "magnificent . . . symphonic in scope and proportion," he thought.[18]

Cole's collection of translations appeared in print four years later. It contains not only *Kingdom's Crown* but also some of Ibn Gabirol's independent shorter poems.[19] Following the death of his parents, Kernis reread Cole's collection and was strongly moved by it. The symphony "started out to be about twenty minutes," recalls Gerard Schwarz, "and Aaron said he wanted to use a text. I said, 'Fine.' Then he said he'd like to use a sixteen-voice professional choir from Canada . . . and of course I said, 'Fine.' Then he said he'd like to amplify the choir so that he could write freely for the orchestra. I was less enthusiastic about that."[20] The *Symphony of Meditations* turned out to be sixty-eight minutes long and requires a large (and skilled) chorus along with three soloists. (The small Canadian chorus "was fabulous," Kernis recalls, but it would not have worked with the massive orchestral forces he ultimately used.) Because the Seattle Symphony Chorus was not on board in 2007–8, Schwarz postponed the premiere until 2009.

As shown in table 6, Kernis pieced together the text by cutting and pasting elements from various parts of Cole's book. (Cole was supportive of this process and made himself available for extensive consultation about the background of, and symbolism in, the poetry.) Despite the symphony's narrative structure, Kernis did not assemble the lyrics in the order of the original, nor did he select all parts of the text before he began composing the music. He was first drawn to the words that form the central part of the second movement, which consist of a series of four-line stanzas preceded and followed by this three-line refrain:[21]

> All the creatures of earth and heaven
> together as one bear witness in saying:
> the Lord is One and One is his name.

The final line of this refrain not only reflects Ibn Gabirol's postulate concerning the unity of God but also refers quite directly to the Shema, a central prayer in the Jewish service, often referred to as the "watchword" of the faith: "Shema Yisrael, Adonai elohenu, Adonai echad" (Hear, O Israel, the Lord our God, the

TABLE 6. *Symphony of Meditations* (Symphony no. 3): movements, text sources, and scoring

Movement, measures	Text title, line numbers	Cole pp.*	Vocal scoring
Mvt 1: Invocation (7.5 minutes)			
Section 1	"I look for you early," complete (lines 1–16)	113	Baritone
mm. 1–35			
Section 2			Chorus
mm. 35–56	"I look for you early," 1	113	
	"Haven't I hidden your name," 1–2, 5–8	130	
mm. 56–75	*Kingdom's Crown*, VIII, 1–3, 29–33	147–48	
mm. 75–79	*Kingdom's Crown*, I, 1 ("You are One")	141	
Section 3	Simultaneous texts:		Baritone and chorus
mm. 80–112	"I look for you early," end (lines 14–16)	113	(Baritone)
	"Haven't I hidden your name," end (lines 9–10)	130	(Chorus)
Mvt 2: Meditation on Oneness (14.25 minutes)			
Section 1	"Three things," complete (lines 1–8)	112	Soprano
mm. 1–59			
Section 2	"All the creatures of earth and heaven," 1–10, 18–31. (Lines 1–3, 8–10, 22–24, 29–31 are identical, forming a refrain that ends in a paraphrase of the Shema, "The Lord is One and One is his name.")	124–25	Chorus
mm. 60–249			
Section 3			
mm. 250–79	"Three things," lines 3–8	112	Soprano and chorus
mm. 279–86	"All the creatures of earth," 3, beginning (Shema paraphrase)	124	
Mvt 3: Supplication (46.25 minutes)			
Section 1a			
mm. 1–114	*Kingdom's Crown*, XXXIII, 1–33 with minor excisions	177–78	Baritone; baritone and chorus; baritone

Section 1b			
mm. 115–47	*Kingdom's Crown*, XXXVII, 1, 4–13	184	Baritone aria
mm. 148–227	*Kingdom's Crown*, XXXV, 5–15, 17–24, 30–41	180–81	Chorus; short baritone interlude; chorus
mm. 228–65	*Kingdom's Crown*, XXXVII, 16–20 with excision	184	
	Kingdom's Crown, XXXVIII, 41–44 with excision	189	
	Kingdom's Crown, XXXV, 40–41	181	
mm. 265–332	*Kingdom's Crown*, XXXIV, complete (lines 1–22)	179	Baritone aria
	Kingdom's Crown, XXXIII, 23–26	178	
Interlude (instrumental)			
mm. 333–66	No text		None (orchestra only)
Section 2a			
mm. 366–419	*Kingdom's Crown*, XXXIX, 1–17	191	Chorus
Section 2b			
mm. 420–48	*Kingdom's Crown*, XXXIX, 19–30	191–2	Soprano solo
Section 2c			
mm. 449–526	*Kingdom's Crown*, XL, 4–21, 23–28	193–94	Baritone; baritone and tenor
mm. 527–91	*Kingdom's Crown*, XL, 29–39, 43–47	194	Baritone with choral interjections
Section 2d			
mm. 592–683	*Kingdom's Crown*, XL, 48–58, English, then Hebrew, then English continuation	194–95	Chorus; soprano and chorus
mm. 684–716	Simultaneous texts:	195	Baritone and chorus
	Kingdom's Crown, XL, 59–62 (Yih'yu paraphrase)		(Baritone)
	Shema paraphrase ("The Lord is one")		(Chorus)

* This column provides page numbers in the source text: *Selected Poems of Solomon Ibn Gabirol*, translated from the Hebrew by Peter Cole (Princeton: Princeton University Press, 2001).

Lord is One). This text proclaiming God's oneness creates a unity in Kernis's symphony as well. He incorporates versions of it in movement 1 at the end of the central choral section, in the middle part of movement 2 as the refrain for each stanza, and in the final moments of the forty-six-minute finale (in this case, in the Hebrew original: "Adonai echad," God is One).

Kernis composed the second movement first and then the finale (whose texts are drawn exclusively from *Kingdom's Crown*) before he selected the poetry for the opening movement whose text puts the emphasis on the speaker: "I look for you early"; "I come confused / and afraid"; "I seek you every evening and dawn"; "I'll praise the name of the Lord." Reflecting Ibn Gabirol's philosophy, Kernis structured his symphony to progress from the individual's relation to the divine in movement 1 to three manifestations of God (sky, earth, and heart) and the oneness of nature in movement 2 to divine mercy in movement 3.

In addition to the Shema paraphrase, other poems that Kernis selected—in particular, those from *Kingdom's Crown* (*KC*)—contain references to the Jewish liturgy. Several of the texts in the finale will immediately remind modern Jews of prayers found in the service for Yom Kippur, the Day of Atonement. On this fast day congregants reflect on the previous year, acknowledging their individual failings, and vow to improve themselves in the year to come. The traditional prayers evoke divine judgment through the metaphor of a book in which names are inscribed for the coming year as destined for good or for ill. Although one's fate can be altered through repentance and meritorious deeds, at the end of the atonement day the gates of mercy symbolically close, sealing the future. (The balance between predestination and free will in this context has absorbed biblical scholars' attention for centuries.) Cole's translation of *KC* XXXVII reads, in part, "For what is man that you'd judge him, / but haunted vanity and breath pursued." This text brings to mind the fifth verse of Psalm 5, traditionally read on Yom Kippur: "What is man, that Thou art mindful of him? / And the son of man, that Thou thinkest of him?" A hint of the twenty-third psalm appears in *KC* XXXIX, and a direct reference to the liturgy comes in *KC* XXXIV, whose text closely resembles the "Ashamnu" confessional prayer, traditionally recited ten times during the Yom Kippur services. During the public recitations of this prayer, the congregation rises as a body and confesses to a list of twenty-four sins: "We have trespassed; we have dealt treacherously; we have robbed; we have spoken slander; we have acted perversely; we have done wrong; we have acted presumptuously; we have done violence; we have practiced deceit; we have counseled evil; we have spoken falsehood; we have scoffed; we have revolted; we have blasphemed; we have rebelled; we have committed iniquity; we have transgressed; we have oppressed; we have been stiff-necked; we have acted wickedly; we have dealt corruptly; we have committed abomination; we have gone astray; we have led others astray." The communal confession recognizes society's common culpability for all transgressive acts and allows individual confession without public embarrassment. Compare the text of *KC* XXXIV, which reads in part: "and too often I've uttered blasphemy— / and been perverse and lawless; / fractious and full of violence; / I've lied and counseled evil—deceived, scoffed and rebelled; // been scornful, perverse and intransigent, / stubborn, harsh and senseless; / I've cut off your reproach and been cruel. / I've committed abominable acts / and wandered far from my path." The wording of the Ashamnu prayer as we know it today was already in use several centuries before Ibn Gabirol wrote *Keter Malkhut*; indeed, here and elsewhere he was in effect glossing on material that would have been familiar to his readers.[22]

The right-hand column in table 6 shows that movements 1 and 2 have a similar musical and textual structure. Each has a tripartite form, beginning with a section for soloist and orchestra, followed by a choral section, and finally by an altered return that combines soloist with chorus and uses texts already sung in sections 1 and 2. The first movement, though the shortest of the three, is imposing in style, dynamics, and emotional affect. If it could be compared to anything that Kernis previously created, it might be the music evoking huge stone tablets that begins the finale of *Colored Field*. That movement opens with a stark rising melodic second. Here, too, the rising step figures prominently, marking the end of each of the three sections. The opening section for baritone ends with a dramatic arrival on E (m. 35), which Kernis transforms, in a transcendent moment, into a B major triad via the soloist's step up to the dominant F♯. The choral section that follows concludes with another climactic arrival, on the words "You are One." Kernis leads into this outburst with a chromatic unison ascent from E to B♭ and then, on the repetition of the text, the B♭ rises to a C major chord, historically a key symbolizing triumph. A grand pause greets this exclamation. The concluding section ends with two rising seconds in long notes in the solo part: C♯–D♯–E♯. The last two notes are sung over an iridescent C♯ major chord in the orchestra.

As in his previous works, Kernis moves back and forth between diatonic and chromatic language. The opening motive in the baritone part centers on A, but by measure 6 it has already shifted to A♭. This opening melody is for the most part angular and disjunct, with prominent descending and ascending leaps of fourths and fifths that convey strength and solidity. At the chorus's entry in m. 36, the unison melody is identical to the opening but now transposed a step higher. The third section opens with the contrabasses playing a version of the same theme on F♯, now, however, with a soft and subdued character.

In shape this movement thus forms an arch with a double climax in the middle, at the start and the end of the choral section. The second climax emphasizes the symphony's idée fixe through the twofold repetition of "You are One." The trajectory of most of the melodic lines is upward, the overall affect suggesting the majesty of God and human arms lifted in praise.

The second movement can stand on its own as a separate piece; Kernis has authorized its independent performance. (The live performance by the Yale Philharmonia and choral ensembles, conducted by Kernis, appears on this book's Web site.) In contrast to the first movement, it begins introspectively with the high strings divided into seven parts followed by a plaintive melody in the oboe. After the succeeding soprano solo section, the instrumental elements return in reverse order: first the oboe, then the strings. The highlight of the movement, however, is the central choral section, "All the creatures of earth," which is dance-like and exuberant, centered strongly in B♭ (a mediant relationship to the movement's opening in F♯). Each time the refrain text appears, its musical setting becomes more ecstatic. In the final rendition, Kernis repeats the last line, "the Lord is One," forty-four times using jazzy changing meters and a homorhythmic texture in the voices that renders the words clear and the style declamatory. The surrounding orchestral texture becomes increasingly thick and excited, reaching a climactic moment with the piano, strings, and woodwinds in a kind of varied ostinato in repeated notes while the brass and percussion underscore the choral parts. The whole section comes to a crashing arrival on B♭ for the final words of the text: "and One is his name." The bass instruments and chorus then repeat this pitch in long notes for another twenty-one measures, grounding fragmentary melodic motives in the rest of the orchestra. Then the B♭ continues in the chorus, winding down over the course of another nineteen bars to introduce the tranquil final section for soprano and chorus.

The finale is essentially a forty-six-minute cantata for baritone, soprano, and chorus (with a brief passage for solo tenor) divided into two large sections of nearly equal length, separated by an instrumental interlude. (Kernis envisioned this movement as a gigantic symphonic form.) The narrative structure recounts the journey of the individual from shame and guilt in the first section to redemption through repentance and faith in the second.

The first half of the movement is itself subdivided into two discrete sections, each of which has a tripartite structure. In the first of them (1a), the three parts are defined by their vocal scoring: a section for baritone solo, a choral interlude, and a return of the soloist. The movement opens with a sixteen-measure melody in the unaccompanied solo timpani. The timpanist executes fourteen different pitches by retuning the drums during the course of playing them. Although this highly challenging technique has been used by other twentieth-century composers, the foregrounding of the timpani in such a central and exposed role is highly unusual. Its melody features minor thirds and a series of tritones—an interval that historically has stood as the symbol of sin. The baritone solo section that follows rises to a climax on the words "you are One" (repeated Cs in the voice) and "you are the Lord my God" (a rising third and then a tritone). Kernis juxtaposes the light of the third with the darkness of the tritone to suggest uncertainty and doubt, as the speaker laments his weakness and his shame at his own failings. The choral section reinforces this negative self-image (here Kernis extracts individual words and phrases from Cole's text: "dust . . . vessel . . . shame. . . . a spider's poison; a lying heart"), ushering in a slow and introspective solo section with the singer accompanied by harp, piccolo, and soft, sustained strings.

In the next part (section 1b), the three-part structure is defined not only by scoring but also by melodic character. Two arias for baritone surround a central section that is primarily for chorus. Preceding both arias are instrumental passages featuring the cello. In the first case, the cello's line is cantorial, with recitative-like melodic motion and repeated notes in the style of a chant. The first aria is gentle, as the singer appeals to God to allow repentance and spiritual transformation before death: "for if I depart from the world as I entered, / and naked and empty return as I came, / why was I made— / or called to bear witness to struggle and pain?" The soloist's line begins with a minor third, recollecting the opening motive of the movement in the timpani, but now the tritones have disappeared, replaced by the solidity of rising and falling fifths. The second aria evokes Bach, in part owing to its A B A' form, typical for Baroque arias. It opens with a rising fifth, recalling the first aria's melody. The B section introduces the Ashamnu confessional—the frightful admission of human frailty and failure—underscored by angry outbursts in the orchestra. Then the melody of the A section returns, its pleading fifths accompanied again by the cello, but now in such a high register that it almost sounds like a violin. That Kernis chose to use the high cello rather than a violin has both aural and symbolic implications. The musical effect creates a rise from a "natural" human plane to an elevated transfiguration, as the cellist literally reaches up the fingerboard to the instrument's highest notes. "My God," sings the soloist, "What am I or my life? / What is my might and my righteousness? / Throughout the days of my being I'm nothing / and what then after I die?" The choral section that separates the two arias focuses on the compassion of God and the ability of humans to alter their behavior. A lovely *a cappella* setting accompanies the text "How much trouble my eyes / have overlooked as you helped me," and the music builds to a *fortissimo* outburst in an evocation of the day of judgment. Here Kernis condenses Cole's translation considerably, eliminating in the process Ibn Gabirol's original balance between mercy and anger. Kernis retains only the latter. Cole's original—"Judge me, Lord, by the standard of mercy, / and not in your anger, / unless you'd bring me to nothing"—becomes in the symphony the far harsher "Judge me not, Lord, / not in your anger, / unless you'd bring me to nothing." Befitting this fearful vision, the section ends with a persistent hammering on E♭ for six *fortissimo* measures before its energy dissipates to usher in the second aria.

If the first half the movement is filled with self-recrimination, the second half focuses on praise of the divine and the unity of the world. It begins with an *a cappella* choral prayer (section 2a): open my heart to repentance; protect and shelter me with mercy. The soprano soloist then appeals, at first with the women of the choir and then alone, for the power to see good in the world and to take pleasure in creation (a reflection of Kernis's personal worldview, articulated in many previous compositions). Section 2b ends with a duet between the solo soprano and the flute leading into a decorative, effusive flute cadenza. (The flute-soprano duet in *Garden of Light* comes to mind.) The baritone then reenters in humility (2c), but eventually rises to a tonal, melodious exclamation: "Bring me to peace," which the chorus takes up as the soloist yearns to be placed "among the righteous" after death.

The final part of the movement (section 2d) extols and glorifies God. The chorus breaks into Hebrew at the end of this paean of praise, and then the baritone reenters singing a paraphrase of Psalm 19:15: "May the words of my mouth and my heart's meditation / before you be pleasing— / my rock— / and my redemption." These words are nearly identical to those of the "Yih'yu l'ratzon" ("May the words of my mouth"), traditionally recited at the end of the Amida, the central part of the Jewish Sabbath and High Holy Day services. The Yih'yu expresses the hope that the supplications just offered will prove acceptable to God. In Kernis's symphony, the baritone sings the Yih'yu paraphrase to a stately melody filled with upward leaps of fourths and fifths while the choir chants "Adonai elohenu, Adonai echad" ("The Lord our God, the Lord is One"—the Shema paraphrase) in unison on repeated Es. These repeated notes persist continuously for the final two minutes of the symphony, gradually joined by the instrumental forces and the soloist, who ascends from B to E, sliding between pitches to lend a Semitic inflection to the melodic line. The music builds in density and volume to a triumphant ending on the open fifth E–B (see figure 14).

Given Kernis's upbringing as a cultural Jew—with a spiritual link to his heritage but without its ritualistic trimmings—the Third Symphony begs the question of his own religious beliefs. It is not a matter for which he has a clear

Figure 14. *Symphony of Meditations (Symphony no. 3)*, 2009, end. (Copyright © 2009 by Associated Music Publishers, Inc. International Copyright Secured. All Rights Reserved. Used by Permission.)

answer. "By no means have I been able to integrate my love for spiritual texts and feelings of inner spiritual experience with rationalism and believing only in what one observes empirically," he says. "They simply exist side by side; so when my children ask me if I believe in God, I either answer that I believe in people's desire to have belief in what they feel but cannot explain, or say that sometimes I do believe in God, and feel that the Divine is a source of energy of all things, a life-force that all beings and nature draw upon."[23]

At the Decade's End

In the same year in which the Third Symphony was performed (first in Seattle and then at Yale), Kernis completed two concerti: *Concerto with Echoes* for chamber orchestra and *a voice, a messenger* for trumpet solo and wind ensemble (dedicated to the memory of his cousin Michael Kernis, 1955–2009). The first work was commissioned by the Orpheus Chamber Orchestra as part of its New Brandenburg Project, the second by the New York Philharmonic and the Big 10 Band Association for Philip Smith, principal trumpeter of the Philharmonic. The Orpheus Chamber Orchestra performed *Concerto with Echoes* on October 8, 2009, only a month before the second performance of the Third Symphony at Yale, but the trumpet concerto was not performed until April 2, 2013. The Philharmonic had programmed it for December 28–30, 2010, but unfortunately Mother Nature intervened to cause a cancellation—a very rare occurrence in the annals of Philharmonic concerts. The orchestra members had had the previous week off, and so a double rehearsal was scheduled on December 27. But on the 26th a massive blizzard hit the area and players were stranded. Kernis's concerto was canceled, as was a performance of Christopher Rouse's oboe concerto and Hindemith's horn concerto. In their place, the audience heard familiar selections by Sibelius, Debussy, and Tchaikovsky.[24]

If the Third Symphony is lavish in terms of length and performance forces, paying tribute to Kernis's Jewish roots, the *Concerto with Echoes* is quite the opposite: a rather succinct (seventeen-minute) instrumental work for chamber orchestra with no Jewish references, projecting instead his admiration for the German Baroque. The work was inspired directly by Bach's sixth Brandenburg concerto, which calls for violas, violas da gamba, cellos, bass, and harpsichord, and indirectly by the keyboard toccatas, the C minor passacaglia, and the first ricercar from the *Musical Offering* (in reality a three-voiced fugue). As in the sixth Brandenburg, Kernis uses violas, cellos, and basses, but no violins. In the second and third movements, he introduces pairs of oboes, horns, and bassoons, as well as a single trumpet and a few percussion instruments such as vibraphone and tuned gongs.

The first movement begins quietly with "two spiraling solo violas [and then two cellos], like identical twins following each other breathlessly through a hall of mirrors."[25] This introduction leads into an extroverted toccata—designated as such in the score. It bears a distinct resemblance to the ritornello form characteristic of the Baroque concerto grosso. A virtuosic tutti theme characterized by fast sixteenth notes, repeated pitches, and contrapuntal interplay alternates with somewhat quieter sections scored for soloists. The three-minute movement is a breathless showpiece for the orchestra, which is divided into anywhere from four to nine separate lines.

The slow second movement is a passacaglia in eleven sections. Its principal four-note theme is introduced by the first violas in the opening nine-measure section. Ten variations follow, which vary in length from four to fourteen measures and, typically, move further from the original theme as the movement progresses. The final section—as in previous works by Kernis but also as in variation sets from Haydn to Brahms—returns to a simple but altered version of the opening. Within the variations Kernis uses procedures typical of Baroque music, for example, thematic augmentation in the fourth and eighth sections and partial diminution in the ninth. Mood and texture vary greatly, from the gentle fourth section, which features long notes and a theme in the oboe, to the fast, nearly homorhythmic sixth section, to a *grave* mood in the seventh, which highlights chimes and trumpet. The savage tenth section contrasts strongly with the quiet meditative return to the theme in the last variation. The movement ends with a tender mediant progression, the final shimmering C major chord embellished with rising fifths in the horns.

The concerto concludes with an aria marked "dolente, grazioso" in 6/8. It is, in fact, like a Baroque siciliano, which is often compared to a lilting cradle song. The second oboist changes to English horn, lending a more subdued tone to the work, but overall the spirit is graceful and even, at times, pastoral. The texture, as usual with Kernis, is contrapuntal and intricate but at the same time features a clarity that makes the movement comprehensible even to novice listeners. The work comes to a conclusion in the very depths of the string range, with the melodic movement in the double basses reaching down to a low D.

In contrast to *Concerto with Echoes*, the trumpet concerto draws deeply on Kernis's Jewish heritage, particularly in the finale, whose inspiration was the shofar, a ram's horn blown on Rosh Hashanah (the Jewish New Year). The blowing of the shofar recalls a ritual practice from the biblical era. The instrument sounds with trumpet-like blasts to herald the coming year and to call urgently on congregants to turn their thoughts to righteous deeds in the future. (Smith, when he asked Kernis to write the concerto, had suggested using the trumpet-like instruments mentioned in scripture as an inspiration.) During the service for Rosh Hashanah and at the end of the Yom Kippur fast, the shofar is sounded publicly, articulating three motives, each of which is preceded by a verbal call by the rabbi or cantor: "tekiah," answered by a rising fifth (or fourth, depending on the instrument), "shevarim," followed the same interval sounded three times in a row, and "teruah," answered by eight repeated notes.[26] Kernis titled the finale of his four-movement concerto "Monument—Tekiah Teruah," and he uses a rising fourth and repeated-note figures as motivic elements.

The first and third movements have a less direct relation to Kernis's faith, although Jewish elements were always in the back of his mind. "The mood of these movements contains much typically Jewish soul-searching," he notes. The first is "Morning Prayer," the third "Night Prayer." Both are slow. Between them is the lively "Timbrel Psalm." The timbrel is the biblical precursor to the tambourine. Here Kernis directly references the 150th psalm, a text used by numerous composers because it urges praise of God through music. "Praise God with the blast of the shofar," writes the Psalmist. "Praise him with psaltery and harp / Praise Him with timbrel and dance / Praise Him with stringed instruments and pipes / Praise Him with resounding cymbals / Praise Him with clanging cymbals / Let everything that has breath praise God" (Psalm 150:3–6).

The timbrel is also associated with women: Miriam, sister of Moses, led the female Israelites in joyous singing and dancing accompanied by timbrels after the people had crossed the Red Sea, freeing them from Egyptian slavery:

> For the horses of Pharaoh went in with his chariots and with his horsemen into the sea, and the Lord brought back the waters of the sea on them; but the children of Israel went on dry land in the midst of the sea. And Miriam the prophetess, the sister of Aaron, took a timbrel in her hand; and all the women went out after her with timbrels and with dances. And Miriam sang to them, "Sing to the Lord, for He is highly exalted; the horse and his rider has he thrown into the sea." (Exodus 15:19–21).

The title "Timbrel Psalm" evokes both the tambourine and Kernis's exploration of orchestral color (that is, timbre; the pun on timbrel/timbral was deliberate). Rhythmic and lively, the movement also recalls his fascination with jazz.

The concerto thus has a basic slow-fast-slow-fast structure. The first movement, "Morning Prayer," features melodic lines embellished with grace notes in the cantorial style we have seen in, for example, *Lament and Prayer* and *Still Movement with Hymn*. Kernis introduces true heterophony at one point, perhaps recalling congregational singing. In "Timbrel Psalm" the harp and one register of the piano are prepared by threading paper through the strings to create a jangling sound evoking the tambourine. A virtuosic solo trumpet cadenza features repeated notes requiring triple tonguing and fast passages calling for exceptional technical control. The third movement ("Night Prayer"), in which the soloist plays flugelhorn, is in A B C A' form. It starts with a hymn in the brass followed by an expressive melody in the solo part; the intermediary sections gradually increase in tempo. Before the return to A' the timpani and bass drum lead into a roll and a crescendo on the tam-tam, and then huge block chords recall the opening of the finale of *Colored Field*. The finale is mostly quick, though it has a *lento tranquillo* section before the conclusion, which reintroduces elements of the opening before drawing to a punchy, hymn-like conclusion. Two additional solo trumpets here flank the soloist, "floridly mirroring the use of trumpets that purportedly was typical during festival celebrations in the Second Temple in Jerusalem before its destruction," says Kernis.

The sheer breadth of material Kernis produced in this decade—ranging from the four-minute, jazz-inspired *Superstar Etude no. 2* for piano to the monumental sixty-eight-minute *Symphony of Meditations* for orchestra and chorus—make it difficult to draw conclusions about his compositional direction. The works of this period (and others not discussed, such as the miniature orchestral showpiece *On Wings of Light*, which Gerard Schwarz calls "three minutes of the most colorful, energetic, jet-propelled music" for orchestra)[27] show the assured hand of a seasoned creator, who has refined a distinctive personal style, come to grips with the problems of text and music, built on previous harmonic explorations, and reinforced his own aesthetic principles. Whether his medium was solo instrument, voice, orchestra, chorus, band, or chamber ensemble, Kernis's sensitivity to color, his balance of consonance and dissonance, and his integration of the varied influences that had shaped his compositional language over the past quarter-century contributed to his maturation as a composer with a unique, articulate, and passionate voice. At the same time, however, the diversity of his output points at new directions, which we will see him beginning to explore in his latest works.

8 Looking to the Future

PERHAPS THE MOST FREQUENTLY QUOTED comment by Kernis is his expressed desire to "include everything" in his music. "I want . . . soaring melody, consonance, tension, dissonance, drive, relaxation, color, strong harmony, and form—and for every possible emotion to be elicited actively by the passionate use of those elements."[1] Critics have made much of his embrace of diversity, noting the influence of tonality and atonality, jazz, pop, and Baroque music, modernism and minimalism, intricate counterpoint and static ostinati—or as Mark Swed put it succinctly in 1995, "extravagance and eclecticism."

Kernis, however, resists the word *eclecticism* because implicit in it is the image of collage. Inclusivity, yes; a welcoming of diversity, certainly: but never with the aim of creating a static mixture, however bold it might be. Rather, Kernis's music—even in its slowest and most introverted manifestation—always emphasizes directionality. Each work, he says, is like a landscape. "There's a horizon and there's a point that I'm heading to. . . . I'm going to travel through a number of different kinds of roads, different kinds of hills, and [I might encounter] a terrifying moment on the side of the road, but I'm still always looking to that destination, however many miles or however many minutes away."[2]

Occasionally, as Kernis creates a new work, that end point is clear from the start. At other times he can see only halfway, or he can envision the end without a clear concept of the beginning. And sometimes he simply starts out without a set goal, allowing the horizon to emerge gradually. But before the work is completed, he has embedded in it that requisite momentum: "I try to make everything from beginning to end connect . . . emotionally, to be part of a larger experience."[3]

In short, the element of narrative is always present, whether a text guides the journey or whether the experience unfolds in sound alone. Hence the importance for Kernis of the motivating stimuli, be they political events, mosaics, life-cycle experiences, poetry, paintings, or simply an emotional state. Unlike many other contemporary composers, he does not use a predetermined system to delimit his choices. In fact, only in his early years did he make any attempt to devise such a system; his process pieces of the 1980s turned out to be but stepping stones to a less circumscribed compositional method. As he moved away from these self-imposed controls, Kernis began to place more trust in his intuition, while keeping it firmly embedded in a carefully crafted overall plan. Although he did not devise a system for choosing pitches, he created large, harmonically based formal shapes. Now, in his most recent work, that intuitive approach is coming even more strongly to the fore. He does not always need to see the endpoint as he works. "More and more I allow the music I'm creating to lead me to find the ongoing direction and shape of the whole," he reflects. "I no longer tend to expect that I can see the outcome or destination from the start."[4]

In the second decade of the new century, this increasing self-trust may well signal the start of still another new creative period. In addition, Kernis seems to be turning toward shorter works for smaller ensembles. Since 2011 he has rescored and expanded his *Air* to create a version for solo cello, oboe, piano, and string quartet (*On Distant Shores*, a collaboration with choreographer Pascal Rioult); composed two quintets with mixed instrumentation, one including a solo voice, the other instrumental; written a sextet for flute, clarinet, violin, cello, percussion, and piano; and completed a twenty-minute concerto for cello and chamber orchestra.[5] In part, of course, this trend reflects the commissions he has received. But there also may be both practical and aesthetic motivations. On the pragmatic level, these works have a greater chance for repeated performance than do lengthy orchestral compositions. On the personal level, they seem to be the expression of a composer who is increasingly looking within to reexamine and reevaluate his personal language and to find more compact shapes for his work.

A brief look at four of these works sheds light on the direction in which Kernis appears to be heading. In *L'arte della danssar*, for soprano, flute, viola, percussion, and harp (2011), he chose a text from a collection called *Fifteenth-Century Dance and Music*.[6] This hefty volume contains transcriptions of Italian dance treatises from the early Renaissance. As in many of his previous vocal works (for example, the Third Symphony, *Valentines*, and *Goblin Market*) the text is lengthy and Kernis does not repeat the words. Although he used English in his prior vocal works, in this case he set the words in the original Italian. (In fact, except for a four-minute choral setting of a tune drawing on a traditional Portuguese folk melody, this piece is his only vocal work that is not in English).[7] The opening movement presents an extended anonymous text from 1459 describing a dance festival. For the second and third movements Kernis selected writings by Giovanni Ambrosio, an influential dancer and dance-master whose original name was Guglielmo Ebreo da Pesaro (Guglielmo, Jew of Pesaro). The text of the second movement describes the passion and emotion of dance; that of the third enumerates the specific steps of the basse danse. For the final movement Kernis chose a poem by Lorenzo de' Medici, leader of the ruling family in Florence from 1469 until his death in 1492. Titled "The Triumph of Bacchus and Ariadne," the text celebrates youth, pleasure, song, and dance.

L'arte della danssar continues Kernis's long-term interest in dance, previously manifest in works such as the Second String Quartet, *New Era Dance*, *100 Dance Hits*, and many movements within his large orchestral and chamber works. Texts with concrete descriptions (the festival described in the first movement and the dance directions of the third) rub shoulders with those exploring the emotional character of dance—and it is these latter movements that seem to capture the essence of Kernis's fascination with the art. In the text of the second movement, for instance, Ambrosio tells us that dance is born of passion and expressed through rich harmony and sweet melody. Six principles will give glory to dance, he says:

> Misura e prima & seco vuol Mimoria
> Partir puo di teren con ayre bella
> Dolce meynera e movimento.
>
> Rhythm is first and it demands memory with it
> Elevation [lit: "leaving the ground"] with beautiful poise
> Sweet style and motion.[8]

Kernis's setting is strongly grounded in diatonicism. The texture is transparent, but he calls for virtuosity in the instrumental accompaniment. Musical references to Monteverdi (though more than a century removed from the poet) are strongly in evidence—in both the "speaking in music" style of much of the vocal line and the decorative ornamental flourishes in the flute and viola. But these recollections of sixteenth- and early seventeenth-century music are embedded in Kernis's individualistic language, extending elements of his earlier work: the ramping up of dissonance in the center of the movement, the occasional mediant progression, the moments of cadential arrival signaling a new section, the declamatory setting of the words, and the sweeping improvisational-sounding, cadenza-like passages in the flute. The piece also extends Kernis's attraction to modal music, manifest in works such as *Ecstatic Meditations* and *Musica Celestis*.

The text by Lorenzo de' Medici used in the finale is in the style of a sixteenth-century frottola, cast in the form of a refrain and seven stanzas. Frottola texts traditionally have a lilting, dance-like quality rendered in lines of eight syllables with strong accents on 3 and 7. The refrain is given here with the accented syllables in boldface:

> Quant'è **bel**la giovi**ne**zza
> Che si **fug**ge tutta**vi**a!
> Chi vuol **es**ser lieto, **si**a:
> Di do**man** non d'è cer**te**zza.
>
> How beautiful is youth
> That nevertheless so flees from us!
> Those who wish to be happy say:
> "Nothing is certain about tomorrow."[9]

The percussionist plays a hand drum and tambourine at the start, with the flute and soprano articulating a tune in 6/8 that captures the accents of the text. The melody closely resembles those of the early sixteenth-century composer Marchetto Cara. The last lines of the refrain recur at the end of each stanza, but, as customary with Kernis, the music is related but never identical. One of the most delightful moments is the fourth stanza, with its description of the drunken Silenus, tutor and companion to the Greek god Dionysos, patron of wine. Here Kernis drops the regular meter as Silenus staggers through the stanza and the instruments slide around to illustrate his instability. Midas (stanza 5) is accompanied by a virtuoso piccolo line (and a reminiscence of the "Mrs. Midas" movement from *Valentines*). The movement ends in a fury of harp glissandos and scales in the flute and viola, along with hand drum and tambourine accompanying florid, joyful melismas in the voice (see figure 15).

Similarly, *Perpetual Chaconne* for clarinet and string quartet (2012) has links to Kernis's previous compositional history, dating back to his first confrontation with variation form in the 1980s. True to its name, the piece is a set of variations whose theme starts with a descending but chromatically wayward scale that brings to mind Pachelbel's famous Canon (see figure 16). Thirteen variations follow, and then a "coda-chorale," which in effect functions as a fourteenth. Kernis treats the

Figure 15. *L'arte della danssar* (2011), last five measures. (Copyright © 2011 by Associated Music Publishers, Inc. International Copyright Secured. All Rights Reserved. Used by Permission.)

Figure 16. *Perpetual Chaconne* (2012), beginning. (Copyright © 2012 by Associated Music Publishers, Inc. International Copyright Secured. All Rights Reserved. Used by Permission.)

theme freely. It makes its appearance in fragmentary form in the variations as the surrounding contrapuntal textures are characterized by diverse rhythmic figures (triplets, sixteenths, and so on). As usual, in the central portion of the work the theme is less obvious and the dissonance level increases, but the original simple line reappears more distinctly at the end, in this case in augmentation. Overall the spirit of the *Chaconne* is sorrowful, drawing perhaps from the same emotional font as *Two Movements (with Bells)*. At the same time, the piece contains outbursts of anguish akin to Kernis's war-period works, for instance in the thirteenth variation, marked "strident," in which each note of the melody is accented.

L'arte della danssar and *Perpetual Chaconne* connect to Kernis's previous works in significant ways: for instance, the mixture of consonance and dissonance, the emphasis on counterpoint, the interest in dance, the influence of early musics, the invocation of tonality, the scalar melodic lines, the focus on melody, and the contrasts in texture. Notably absent, however, are references to American popular musics and to Jewish music, areas that had characterized—one might almost say, helped define—Kernis's earlier musical language. "I used to believe that rock and pop could be forces for social change," Kernis says, "but now I more cynically see much of it as purely commerce." James Rushton, the British publisher who first boosted Kernis's music in the 1980s, recently articulated the factors that made his music feel particularly "American," including "the influence of the blues [and] other standard American genres, . . . the clear tonal references, . . . the exuberance, . . . the variety, [and] the use of other idioms, like jazz . . . [and] Latin music."[10]

Are the specifically "American" elements of Kernis's style now taking a back seat to a less geographically specific, more universalist trend? As with his compositional process itself, it is too soon for us (and perhaps even for him) to see the horizon. The works that have appeared between 2011 and the time of the present writing, however, tend to reinforce this hypothesis. One example is *Pieces of Winter Sky* for flute, clarinet, violin, cello, percussion, and piano (2012), which continues in the more abstract language of *L'arte della danssar* and *Perpetual Chaconne*, while moving in a new direction that Kernis sees as critical. This piece involves extended techniques he had not previously explored, including bowing the strings of the piano, slap tonguing in the flute, and drumming with one hand on the fingerboard of the violin and cello. At the same time, there is no doubt that the piece is by Kernis. Distinctive traits highlighted throughout this book continue to find voice here, even if (in this case) they don't constitute its primary features. For example, a luxurious tonal melody emerges several times out of extreme dissonance; he calls for harmonics and very high notes on the violin and cello; he makes coloristic use of flutter tonguing; and mediant progressions appear occasionally. More important, however, in Kernis's view, are the new generative elements: his engaging with the personalities of the musicians for whom he was composing and the opening up of new realms in the areas of timbre and form.

Kernis's concerto for cello and chamber orchestra, *Dreamsongs* (2013), unites his past and present aesthetic directions. In character and expression, its opening slow movement builds on the lyricism of pieces such as *Air*, *Musica Celestis*, *Lament and Prayer*, and *Still Movement with Hymn*, but its second movement draws on world music traditions, in this case the kora, a twenty-one-string bridge-harp indigenous to West Africa. The kora consists of a body made from half of a calabash covered in skin, on which is placed a bridge. The twenty-one strings pass over this bridge in two ranks. From the top of the calabash extends a neck, as well as two handles which the player grasps with the third, fourth, and fifth fingers, holding the instrument firmly with the strings facing toward him- or herself. The player then plucks the strings with the thumbs and index fingers, performing elaborate counterpoint and polyrhythms. The thumbs pluck the strings closest to the player and the index fingers pluck the row immediately behind them. Advanced players can simultaneously perform an accompaniment figure and simple melody with the thumbs, along with virtuosic ornamentation with the index fingers.

"Floating Dreamsongs," the concerto's first movement, opens with expansive melodic writing for the soloist set over soft counterpoint in the orchestra. A recitative-like section in the middle leads into an orchestral tutti and then a solo cadenza. As in many earlier works, Kernis then recalls the spirit of the opening in an altered recapitulation that takes the soloist to the upper reaches of the instrument's range. The harmonic content mixes cluster-filled dissonances with strong periods of consonance.

In the second movement, titled "Kora Song," Kernis uses pizzicato and polyrhythms to imitate the African instrument. For large sections of the movement, he even has the cellist use a pick. Djembe drums and cabasa (a shaker consisting of loops of steel-ball chain wrapped around a cylinder) add to the African flavor, and the strings at one point are strummed "a la guitarra." These sections contrast with melodic arco passages. The cadenza section is not only virtuosic but also extended, almost like two cadenzas with a light orchestral accompaniment in between. The first is all pizzicato, the second bowed. The concerto ends in a grand flourish with orchestral tuttis alternating with passages for the solo cello and drums.

Although it is too soon to predict Kernis's future path, might it nevertheless be possible to draw conclusions about his place within late twentieth- and early twenty-first-century musical developments? Some preliminary observations at this stage are certainly warranted. In 1983 Druckman included Kernis in the New York Philharmonic's Horizons festival not only because of his strong technique and imagination but also because the spirit of *"dream of the morning sky"* fit the aesthetic of Romanticism that Druckman aimed to illustrate. In doing so, he placed Kernis alongside composers whom he saw turning away from the Apollonian intellectualism that had dominated postwar academic composition to embrace a more intuitive, emotional content—the same element that struck Rolf Liebermann, as we saw in his comments about Kernis's Mahlerian model at the conclusion of the ISCM film.

Like eclecticism, Kernis rejects Romanticism as a label for his style, but at the same time, when asked by an interviewer at the Disney concert how he would characterize his music, the terms that sprang to his mind were "expansive melody," "long lines," "emotional, expressive"—words that have become descriptors for the aesthetic of nineteenth-century music. In the notes to the first quartet (1990), when Kernis began to turn to Classical styles, he wrote: "I've been gradually realizing that the music I keep on going back to—the music I really love—was written before 1945 and especially before 1911. I love the emotional inclusiveness of music of the past." That statement still holds true and, in fact, marks one of the distinctive elements of his sound world. Certainly he is aware of, and has made use of, the -isms of his time, but his individual voice emerges through their adaptation, transformation, and combination.

Stylistic synthesis—the ability to cull, combine, and reconfigure elements from diverse sources—forms the essence of Kernis's language. In an era of stylistic openness, when there are seemingly no bounds, no regulatory restrictions, no limitations on creativity, Kernis has searched for coherence while welcoming diversity. In 1995 Philip Collins noted this "dynamic tension" in Kernis's music. Furthermore, wrote Collins, his scores evince "a profound complicity between order and freedom."[11]

The openness to diversity characterizes what many scholars now call postmodernism, another term that gives Kernis pause, because, he says, "it often presupposes an ironic stance toward the past. My approach," he emphasizes, "is anything but." In addition, he insists that the combination of varied influences functions in service of directionality. In short, Kernis seeks lucidity within difference. This path is not an easy one, and he often questions his own creation. Wherein lies his individuality, his distinctive voice? he asks himself. What would make a listener recognize that a particular piece could not be by anyone else? "On my better days," he remarked in 1993, "I'll say, 'No combination of these styles could exist at any other time in musical history or this century.' And on my bad days I'll say, 'This is too disjunct; where's my voice? Who am I? What's going on here? And how do I hear myself?'"[12]

Little has changed in that self-reflective attitude in the years since Kernis made this statement. He continues to question himself intensively. And composition is still something of a struggle. "He is extraordinarily self-critical," notes his wife Evelyne (although Aaron claims that recently the process has become far more enjoyable). She says,

> He writes and rewrites (sometimes spending hours, days and weeks on small sections), often throwing out all of his ideas until he has no choice but to use one of them because of a deadline coming up. Even then, there have been times when he wanted to throw out a finished movement or work. For example, when he finished the second movement of the second string quartet, he told me that it was garbage and that he wanted to start again.

I asked him to play the movement for me. I . . . told him it was one of the most beautiful things he had ever written. The quartet, of course, won the Pulitzer prize.[13]

Other awards keep rolling in. In 2011 Kernis was elected to the American Academy of Arts and Letters. In 2012 he was awarded the $100,000 Nemmers Prize from Northwestern University, a biennial prize that honors a composer who has made "a significant impact" in the world of contemporary composition.[14] But he considers these awards "secondary to the goals of the work." They are, he notes, "signposts on the journey rather than the destination."

In addition, Kernis continues to mentor young composers. Since 2003 he has taught at the Yale School of Music, and he remained passionate about the Minnesota Orchestra Composers Institute, which until 2012 attracted the best in aspiring young creative minds. (Although scheduled, the institute did not take place in 2013 due to a bitter and long-lasting labor dispute between the Minnesota Orchestra's administration and its musicians. The orchestra did not perform at all during the 2012–13 season. After the resignation of its conductor in the fall of 2013, Kernis followed suit and resigned as director of the institute.) Kernis's advice to these young people, as he stated in a 1995 interview, still stands: Don't go into the field unless you are absolutely committed; learn all kinds of techniques; "always strive to reach the unknown"; and "search to know yourself as deeply as possible. There can be no better inspiration for composing than life."[15]

Ultimately, in his own musical expression, Kernis's goal remains communication, reaching out to audiences with an individual, passionate, but at the same time understandable voice. "He's never been trying to find the next new chord," remarks Gerard Schwarz. "He tries to be expressive and write great music."[16] Indeed, Kernis's objective is emotional expressivity coupled with solid and convincing technique. "I want to write music that is visceral," he told Peter Occhiogrosso in 1995, music "that is moving and [at the same time] impeccably put together."[17] Kernis still adheres to that dual goal today. "The experience of new classical music should not be purely passive and respectful," he says. "Rather, I aim to create a richly emotional and sensual impact." Judging from the responses of his audiences and critics, that's exactly what he has achieved.

APPENDIX

Chronological list of works discussed in this book. (For a complete works list, see the G. Schirmer Kernis Web site: http://www.schirmer.com/default.aspx?TabId=2419&State_2872=2&ComposerId_2872=824.)

Year completed	Title	Scoring	Approximate length in minutes	Text author	Commissioner (or performer for whom the work was written)	Comments; arrangements; awards
1980	*Stein Times Seven*	5 solo singers (or SSATB chorus with soloists), piano	13	Gertrude Stein		Special distinction, National Federation of Music Clubs
1981	*Meditation (In Memory of John Lennon)*	cello, piano	10			
1981	*Death Fugue*	bass/baritone, double bass, percussion	11	Paul Celan, trans. Joachim Neugroschel		
1982	Music for Trio (Cycle IV)	flute (doubling alto flute, piccolo), cello, piano	22			BMI Student Composer Award
1983	*"dream of the morning sky"* (Cycle V)	soprano, orchestra	23	N. Scott Momaday		Public read-through, NY Philharmonic, 1983; BMI Student Composer Award
1983	*Morningsongs*	baritone, chamber ememsble or chamber orchestra	15	Jon Anderson	(Robert Osborne)	
1984	*America(n) (Day) Dreams*	mezzo-soprano, chamber ensemble	18	May Swenson	Musical Elements	
1985	*Passacaglia-Variations*	viola, piano	19		(Leslie Tomkins and Michael Barrett)	
1987	*Invisible Mosaic I*	clarinet, violin, cello, piano	30		Dartington Festival	
1987	*Love Scenes*	soprano, cello	27	Anna Swir, trans. Czesław Miłosz and Leonard Nathan	André Emelianoff (and Dawn Upshaw)	
1988	*Invisible Mosaic II*	large chamber ensemble	20		(Ensemble InterContemporain and Kent Nagano)	
1988	*Invisible Mosaic III*	orchestra	17		American Composers Orchestra	

1989	*Symphony in Waves*	orchestra	38		St Paul Chamber Orchestra (SPCO)	
1990	String Quartet no. 1 "musica celestis"	string quartet	35		Naumburg Foundation (Lark Quartet)	Mvt 2 arranged for string orchestra (1990)
1990	*Brilliant Sky, Infinite Sky*	baritone, violin, percussion, piano	25	Jean Joubert, George du Maurier, John Ash, Czesław Miłosz	Jorja Fleezanis	
1990	*Before Sleep and Dreams*	piano	24		(Anthony de Mare)	Slow mvt ("Lullaby") composed in 1987 for Anthony de Mare
1991	*Simple Songs*	soprano, chamber ensemble; second version: soprano, chamber orchestra; also: piano reduction	21	Book of Psalms, Rumi, Hildegard von Bingen, Ryokan, trans./adap. Stephen Mitchell	New Music Consort (Susan Narucki); chamber orchestra version: SPCO	Chamber orch. version, 1995; version for voice and piano, 1998
1991	*Mozart En Route*	string trio	3		Bravo! Colorado	
1991	*Le quattro stagioni dalla cucina futurismo (The Four Seasons of Futurist Cuisine)*	violin, cello, piano, narrator	20	Filippo Tomasso Marinetti, trans. Lesley Chamberlain	Adele and Susan Gidwitz for John Gidwitz's 50th birthday	
1991	Second Symphony	orchestra	27		Carillon Importers	
1992	*New Era Dance*	orchestra	8		New York Philharmonic; Baltimore Symphony	
1992	*Superstar Etude no. 1*	piano	3		(Alan Feinberg)	
1993	*Hymn*	accordion	18		Meet the Composer/Readers' Digest (Guy Klusevcek)	
1993	*100 Greatest Dance Hits*	string quartet, guitar	15		Music from Angel Fire	
1993	*Still Movement with Hymn*	piano quartet	30		American Public Radio (Pamela Frank, Paul Neubauer, Carter Brey, and Christopher O'Riley)	Runner-up for Pulitzer Prize

Year completed	Title	Scoring	Approximate length in minutes	Text author	Commissioner (or performer for whom the work was written)	Comments; arrangements; awards
1994, revised 2000	*Colored Field*	English horn, orchestra second version: cello, orchestra	40		Original: Hugh and Eugenie Taylor (Julie Giacobassi and the San Francisco Symphony) Second version: Minnesota Orchestra (Truls Mørk)	Arranged for cello, 2000; winner, Grawemeyer Award, 2002
1995 (Jan.)	*Goblin Market*	chamber orchestra, narrator	45	Christina Rossetti	Birmingham Contemporary Music Group; SPCO	
1995 (Feb.)	*Air*	violin, piano	11		Houston Society for the Performing Arts; UCLA Center for the Performing Arts; University of Texas Performing Arts Center (Joshua Bell)	Later arrangements for cello and piano, flute and piano (and string quartet), and orchestra accompaniment
1995 (June)	*Lament and Prayer*	solo violin, orchestra (strings, percussion, harp, oboe)	26		Minnesota Orchestra (Pamela Frank)	
1996	Claude Debussy, Five Etudes (arr. for orchestra by Kernis)	chamber orchestra	20		SPCO	
1996	Double Concerto for Violin and Guitar	violin, guitar, chamber orchestra	30		SPCO; Aspen Music Festival; Los Angeles Chamber Orchestra (Nadja Salerno-Sonnenberg and Sharon Isbin)	Last mvt arranged for orchestra as *Too Hot Toccata*
1996	*Too Hot Toccata*	orchestra	6		SPCO and Susan M. Halby	An arrangement of the finale of the Double Concerto

1997	String Quartet no. 2, "musica instrumentalis"	string quartet	38		Merkin Concert Hall, Schubert Club of St. Paul, Ohio University, Chamber Music America (Lark Quartet)	Pulitzer Prize; mvt. 1 orch: *Overture in Feet and Meters*; mvt. 2 orch: *Sarabanda in Memoriam*
1998 (1st mvt 1995)	*Ecstatic Meditations*	chorus, solo soprano, solo tenor	17	Mechthild of Magdeburg, trans. Jane Hirshfield and Oliver Davies	Birmingham Bach Choir; Plymouth Music Series Ensemble Singers and Choir	Named "Masterpiece of American Choral Music" by the NEA
1999	*Garden of Light*	large orchestra, choir, children's choir, vocal soloists	52	David Simpatico, Menna Elfyn	Disney Enterprises	
2000	*Valentines*	soprano, piano; or soprano, orchestra	25	Carol Ann Duffy	Great Performers at Lincoln Center (Renée Fleming); Minnesota Orchestra	
2001 (Mar.)	*Trio in Red*	clarinet, cello, piano	17		Chamber Music Society of Lincoln Center; Wharton Center for the Performing Arts, Michigan State University; and Milton Muelder (David Shifrin, Fred Sherry, and Ann-Marie McDermott)	
2001 (Nov.)	*Color Wheel*	orchestra	22		Philadelphia Orchestra	For the opening of Verizon Hall at the Kimmel Center, Philadelphia
2002	Concerto for Toy Piano	toy piano, grand piano, orchestra; alternate version: toy piano, grand piano, chamber ensemble	28		Singapore Symphony and Minnesota Orchestra (Margaret Leng Tan); alternate version: WNYC Radio	Revision (2013) for solo piano and orchestra with new title "Three Flavors—Concerto for Piano and Orchestra" (commissioned by Andrew Russo)
2002	*Superstar Etude no. 2*	piano	4		Emanuele Arciuli	

Year completed	Title	Scoring	Approximate length in minutes	Text author	Commissioner (or performer for whom the work was written)	Comments; arrangements; awards
2003	*Sarabanda in Memoriam*	string orchestra	16		Minnesota Commissioning Club (Orchestra of St. Luke's)	Arrangement of the slow movement of String Quartet no. 2
2004, revised 2007	*Ballad(e) out of the Blue(s)—Superstar Etude no. 3*	piano	10		Frederic Chopin Society of Minneapolis/St. Paul, Minnesota (Mihaela Ursuleasa)	
2005	*Newly Drawn Sky*	orchestra	17		Ravinia Festival (in honor of James Conlon)	
2006	*Two Meditations*	chorus, organ	15	Psalms, interpreted by Stephen Mitchell	Tangeman Sacred Music Center, College-Conservatory of Music, Univ. of Cincinnati (the Cincinnati Vocal Arts Ensemble)	
2006	*Two Awakenings and a Double Lullaby*	soprano, violin, guitar, piano (or without guitar)	22		San Francisco Conservatory and the Fleishhacker Foundation	
2007	*Two Movements (with Bells)*	violin, piano	17		BBC Proms (James Ehnes and Eduard Laurel)	
2009	*Symphony of Meditations* (Symphony no. 3)	orchestra and chorus, with baritone, tenor, and soprano soloists	68	Solomon Ibn Gabirol, trans. Peter Cole	Seattle Symphony; Jeff and Lara Sanderson	

2009, revised 2012	*a voice, a messenger*	trumpet and wind ensemble	25		NY Philharmonic and the Big 10 Band Association (Philip Smith)	
2009	*Concerto with Echoes*	chamber orchestra	17		Orpheus Chamber Orchestra	
2011	*L'arte della danssar*	soprano, flute, viola, harp, percussion	27	Anonymous (15th century), Giovanni Ambrosio, Lorenzo de' Medici	Astral Artists	
2012	*Pieces of Winter Sky*	flute, clarinet, violin, cello, percussion, piano	23		Music Accord for eighth blackbird	Finalist for the Pulitzer Prize
2012	*Perpetual Chaconne*	clarinet and string quartet	18		Chamber Music Northwest, La Jolla Music Society, Santa Fe Chamber Music Festival (David Shifrin and the Orion Quartet; and John Bruce Yeh and the Calder Quartet)	
2013	*Dreamsongs*	cello and chamber orchestra	25		ProMusica Chamber Orchestra, Bellingham Festival, San Francisco Chamber Orchestra (Joshua Roman)	

SUGGESTED LISTENING

In addition to the recordings listed here, several live performances are mounted on this book's Web site: http://www.press.uillinois.edu/books/miller/kernis/.

Label/no.	Works included	Performers (Conductors)
Arabesque Z6727	String Quartet no. 1 "musica celestis," String Quartet no. 2, "musica instrumentalis"	Lark Quartet
Argo 289 460 226-2	*Air*, Double Concerto for Violin and Guitar, *Lament and Prayer*	Joshua Bell, Pamela Frank, Cho-Liang Lin, Sharon Isbin, Minnesota Orchestra (Zinman), St. Paul Chamber Orchestra (Wolff)
Argo 444 454-2	*New Era Dance*	Baltimore Symphony (Zinman)
Polygram/Argo 448 174-2	*Colored Field* (English horn version), *Still Movement with Hymn*	Julie Ann Giacobassi, San Francisco Symphony (Neale); Frank, Neubauer, Brey, O'Riley (quartet)
Black Box BBM1107	*Before Sleep and Dreams, 100 Greatest Dance Hits, Superstar Etude no. 1, Air, Meditation (In Memory of John Lennon)*	Andrew Russo, Felix Fan, David Tanenbaum, Kashii String Quartet
Cedille CDR 90000 105	*Newly Drawn Sky, Too Hot Toccata, Symphony in Waves*	Grant Park Orchestra (Kalmar)
CRI CD635	*Brilliant Sky, Infinite Sky; Love Scenes; Morningsongs*	Sanford Sylvan, Carmen Pelton, Jan Opalach, et al.
Delos DE 3423	*Trio in Red*	David Shifrin, Fred Sherry, Anne-Marie McDermott
Dorian Sono Luminus DSL 92142 and 92152	String Quartet no. 1 "musica celestis," String Quartet no. 2, "musica instrumentalis"	Jasper Quartet
Innova 759	*Ecstatic Meditations*	Volti Chamber Choir

Label/no.	Works included	Performers (Conductors)
Koch KIC-CD-7667	*Simple Songs; Valentines; Songs of Innocents, Books 1 and 2*	Susan Narucki, Donald Berman
Naxos 8.559650	*Two Awakenings and a Double Lullaby*	David Tanenbaum, Kernis, et al.
Naxos 8.559662	*Air*	Tim Fain, Pei-Yao Wang
New Albion NA83	*America(n) (Day) Dreams, Mozart En Route, Superstar Etude no. 1, Nocturne*	Chester String Quartet, et al.
Phoenix PHCD142	*Before Sleep and Dreams, Meditation (In Memory of John Lennon), Le quattro stagioni della cucina futurismo*	Eberli Ensemble
Phoenix PHCD160	Second Symphony, *Invisible Mosaic III, Musica Celestis*	City of Birmingham Symphony (Wolff)
Phoenix PHCD165	*Symphony in Waves*, String Quartet "musica celestis"	New York Chamber Symphony (Schwarz), Lark Quartet
Signum SIGCD186	*Goblin Market, Invisible Mosaic II*	New Professionals Orchestra London (Miller), Mary King (narrator)
Stradivarius STR 33898	*Superstar Etude no. 2*	Emanuele Arciuli
Virgin 7243 5 45464 2 6 and 7243 4 82019 2 8	*Colored Field* (cello version), *Musica Celestis, Air*	Truls Mørk, Minnesota Orchestra (Oue)

NOTES

Chapter 1. Introduction

1. The quotation comes from the award's Web site: http://www.music.northwestern.edu/about/prizes/nemmers-prize/ (accessed November 7, 2012).

2. Interviews took place in New York and California in 2011 and 2012 and were supplemented by extensive email correspondence and occasional phone calls.

3. Bernard Holland, "Shades of Brahms and Jerry Lee Lewis," *New York Times*, February 23, 1996, C22. The three pieces on the program were *100 Greatest Dance Hits*, *Superstar Etude no. 1*, and *Still Movement with Hymn.*

4. Bernard Holland, "Sorrowful Soliloquies from a Versatile American Voice," *New York Times*, January 21, 2005, B4.

5. Carlo Boccadoro, "'Non esiste una ricetta per scrivere': Aaron Jay Kernis," *Musica Coelestis* (Torino: Einaudi, 1999), 102–3 (translated by Giacomo Fiore with revisions by Aaron Jay Kernis).

6. Benjamin Ivry, "A Composer of Grand Gestures," *Christian Science Monitor*, January 4, 2002, 20.

7. Ann McCutchan, *The Muse That Sings: Composers Speak about the Creative Process* (New York: Oxford University Press, 1999), 240.

8. Aaron Jay Kernis, interview in *Disney's Millennium Symphonies*, a supplemental booklet issued in conjunction with the performance of *The Garden of Light* (October 1999).

Chapter 2. Learning the Craft

1. Unless otherwise indicated, quotations from Kernis come from my interviews or discussions with him.

2. Aaron Jay Kernis, interview on "The Composer's Voice," Minnesota Public Radio, September 6, 1998 (for Mahler); email message to the author (for Bartók).

3. The date of the move is clarified by Kernis's report cards.

4. Aaron Jay Kernis, report card for 1967–68.

5. The address was 45 West Bort Street, Long Beach.

6. Rebecca Gratz (1781–1896) established the first Jewish Sunday school in the United States in Philadelphia in 1838.

7. I thank Uziel Adini for the information on Gratz College's elementary school program, which no longer exists.

8. Aaron Jay Kernis, report card for 1968–69.

9. The first home was at 744 Mulberry Court, the second at 3117 Addison Court, Cornwells Heights.

10. Joshua Kosman, "String Players' Choice: Why Star Performers Want New Compositions from Aaron Jay Kernis," *Strings* 79 (July 1999): 34.

11. Programs from Bensalem High, November 27, 1974 (Baroque concert); December 17, 1976 (holiday concert); and April 15, 1977 (spring concert). The orchestra had about five first violins and five seconds.

12. This quotation is taken from a biographical statement Kernis submitted as part of his college applications (document in Kernis's personal archive).

13. Ibid.

14. Kosman, "String Players' Choice," 34.

15. Renee P. Connor, "Student Scores Big with Original Works," *Courier Times* (Bucks County), undated clipping (1975).

16. A few of the other students continued in music as well: for example, Sandra Sprecher is now a composer and videographer in New York.

17. This quotation is from the notes accompanying the score.

18. Ev Grimes, interview with Aaron Jay Kernis for the Yale Oral History of American Music Project, November 13, 1986.

19. Alan Rich, *Careers and Opportunities in Music* (New York: Dutton, 1964), 20.

20. Joseph Franklin, *Settling Scores: A Life in the Margins of American Music* (Santa Fe: Sunstone, 2006), 44.

21. Grimes, interview with Kernis.

22. Franklin, *Settling Scores*, 43–44.

23. Ibid., 44.

24. "John Adams: An Interview with Aaron Jay Kernis," *Conjunctions* 19 (1992): 175.

25. "Little Tree" won the Fred Waring Choral Award in the junior division (1976); "Two Sonnets" and "Madrigal" took second prize in the Federation's Cavalcade for Creative Youth Junior Composers Contest (1977).

26. Quotations in this paragraph are taken from interviews with Kernis by Miller, Grimes, and Boccadoro.

27. "Adams: Interview with Kernis," 175.

28. Carlo Boccadoro, "'Non esiste una ricetta per scrivere': Aaron Jay Kernis," *Musica Coelestis* (Torino: Einaudi, 1999), 104 (with addition by Kernis).

29. Paul Celan, *Speech-Grille and Selected Poems*, trans. Joachim Heugroschel (New York: Dutton, 1971).

30. Boccadoro, *Kernis*, 109.

31. This quotation is from the program notes to the score.

Chapter 3. Kernis Meets the New York Philharmonic

1. Quotations in this paragraph (in order) come from Bill Zakariasen, "A Warm Welcome for Newest Music," *New York Daily News*, June 10, 1983; Will Crutchfield, "New Composi-

tions at Yale," *New Haven Register*, February 10, 1983, 21; Andrew Porter, "Tumult of Mighty Harmonies," *New Yorker*, June 20, 1983, 86–89; Tim Page, "Philharmonic: New Music in a Festival Rehearsal," *New York Times*, June 9, 1983, C16; Alan Rich, "Invaders from the New West," *Newsweek*, June 20, 1983, 81; Patrick J. Smith, "'Horizons '83' Via the New York Philharmonic: Does a 'New Romanticism' Really Exist?" *Musical America*, October 1983, 23–24.

2. Samuel Lipman, "The Philharmonic's New Horizons," *New Criterion*, September 1983, 48.

3. Joan La Barbara, "'There's a Hungry Crowd Out There,'" *Musical America*, October 1983, 9.

4. Kernis was the youngest composer; only one was female. The composers whose works were presented included John Adams, Sándor Balassa, Luciano Berio, Marc Antonio Consoli, George Crumb, Peter Maxwell Davies, David Del Tredici, Jacob Druckman, Lukas Foss, John Harbison, Aaron Jay Kernis, Barbara Kolb, Fred Lerdahl, Donald Martino, Bernard Rands, George Rochberg, Leonard Rosenman, Frederic Rzewski, Gunther Schuller, William Schuman, Joseph Schwantner, Tison Street, Morton Subotnick, Toru Takemitsu, Nicholas Thorne, and Charles Wuorinen. Conductors were all male: Jacob Druckman, Lukas Foss, Raymond Leppard, Zubin Mehta, Larry Newland, Gunther Schuller, and Arthur Weisberg.

5. Crutchfield, "New Compositions at Yale."

6. Quotations in this paragraph are taken from the festival's program book.

7. Information about these rehearsals comes from a rehearsal schedule in Kernis's papers.

8. Igor Stravinsky, *The Poetics of Music in the Form of Six Lessons*, trans. Arthur Knodel and Ingolf Dahl (Cambridge: Harvard University Press, 1947), 63, 65.

9. The poem may be found at http://www.poetryfoundation.org/poem/175895 (accessed October 13, 2013).

10. The quotations in this paragraph are from Ev Grimes, interview with Aaron Jay Kernis, Yale Oral History of American Music Project, November 13, 1986.

11. James Rushton, interview with the author, July 13, 2012.

12. "Paris" and "The Blue Animals" first appeared in Anderson's collection *Looking for Jonathan* (Pittsburgh: University of Pittsburgh Press, 1968). "Walking Barefoot" was published in *Death and Friends* (Pittsburgh: University of Pittsburgh Press, 1970). All three poems are found together in Jon Anderson, *The Milky Way: Poems, 1967—1982* (New York: Ecco, 1982).

13. The quotation comes from the program notes to a performance at the Manhattan School.

14. The quotation comes from the notes to the score.

Chapter 4. Coming to Grips with History (1984–1991)

1. As in previous chapters, any quotes from Kernis not referenced by endnotes come from interviews or email correspondence with the author.

2. Ev Grimes, interview with Aaron Jay Kernis, Yale Oral History of American Music Project, November 13, 1986.

3. The quotation is from the notes to the New York Philharmonic New Music Project reading session, June 10, 1987.

4. The quotation is from the notes for performance by the New York Youth Symphony Orchestra, February 24, 1985. (The performances took place on February 17 and 24, 1985.)

5. The quotations in this paragraph are from Grimes, interview with Kernis.

6. The quotations in this paragraph are from the program notes to the performance of *Invisible Mosaic I* by the Andiamo chamber ensemble, February 7, 1989.

7. Ibid.

8. The earliest performances were by the Andiamo chamber ensemble (two of the three movements of *Invisible Mosaic I*), the Ensemble InterContemporaine in Paris, conducted by Kent Nagano (*Invisible Mosaic II*), and the American Composers Orchestra in New York under Stanislaw Skrowaczewski (*Invisible Mosaic III*).

9. Quotations in this paragraph are from the program notes to the performance of February 7, 1989.

10. Gerard Schwarz, interview with the author, October 10, 2012.

11. Carlo Boccadoro, "'Non esiste una ricetta per scrivere': Aaron Jay Kernis," in *Musica Coelestis* (Torino: Einaudi, 1999), 113 (translation by Giacomo Fiore).

12. Hugh Wolff, interview with the author, July 25, 2012.

13. Brett Campbell, "An Interview with Aaron Jay Kernis: Coming to Cabrillo," *Classical Voice*, August 10, 2009. http://www.sfcv.org/events-calendar/artist-spotlight/an-interview-with-aaron-jay-kernis-coming-to-cabrillo.

14. James Rushton, interview with the author, July 13, 2012.

15. Czesław Miłosz, introduction to Anna Swir, *Happy as a Dog's Tail* (New York: Harcourt Brace Jovanovich, 1985), ix.

16. The original proposal included the following composers who did not end up taking part in the project: José Maceda (1917–2004), the Philippines; Gyorgy Ligeti (b. 1923), Austria; Sofia Gubaidulina (b. 1931), USSR; Léo Brouwer (b. 1939), Cuba; Heinz Holliger (b. 1939), Germany; and Coriún Aharonián (b. 1940), Uruguay. Copies of the films are housed in Special Collections at the library of the University of California, Santa Cruz and at the John Cage Archive in New York.

17. Cage texts are quoted courtesy of the John Cage Trust.

18. Funding came from the Jerome Foundation.

19. Letter from John Adams to Aaron Jay Kernis, March 23, 1988.

20. Wolff, interview with the author.

21. Kernis's statements regarding his embrace of the symphonic form come from his program notes to the *Symphony in Waves*.

22. I thank the staff at the St. Paul Chamber Orchestra for providing copies of the program and the reviews.

23. The quotations in this paragraph are taken from two articles by Bernard Holland in the *New York Times*: "Welcome Whiffs of Haydn and Bach during a Year of You-Know-Who," December 29, 1991, H25 (the first quotation); and "New York Chamber Symphony," November 12, 1991, C14 (the remaining quotations).

24. Members of the quartet at this time were Eva Gruesser (violin 1), Robin Mayforth (violin 2), Anna Kruger (viola), and Astrid Schween (cello). The quartet had been founded in 1985 by cellist Laura Sewell. Kay Stern had been the original first violinist (Anna Kruger, email to the author, August 14, 2012).

25. The quotations in this paragraph come from Eva Gruesser, telephone interview with the author, September 24, 2012, and Anna Kruger, telephone interview and email with the author, August 11 and 14, 2012.

26. The quotation is taken from Kernis's own analysis of his score, found among his personal papers.

27. Kernis transposes the modes, a practice that was not characteristic of medieval and Renaissance music. The phrygian section is centered on B, the lydian on B♭.

28. The quotations are from the program notes to the first string quartet.

29. Information in this paragraph comes in part from an email message from Evelyne Luest to the author, May 14, 2013.

30. Linda Hoeschler, interview with the author, July 27, 2012.

31. The quotations in this paragraph come from the program notes to the Chicago Symphony performance in November 2002.

32. Stephen Mitchell, ed., *The Enlightened Heart: An Anthology of Sacred Poetry* (New York: HarperPerennial, 1989).

33. *Mitchell, Enlightened Heart*, 58.

34. The translation by A. Cohen is taken from the Soncino Bible (London: Soncino, 1945).

35. The quotations in this paragraph come from Kernis's notes to the score.

Chapter 5. War, with Interludes (1991–1995)

1. Allan Kozinn, "Cellist Plays Solo and Chamber Pieces," *New York Times*, March 12, 1989, 68; John Rockwell, "Andiamo in Works Old and New," *New York Times*, February 9, 1989, C18.

2. Lou Harrison, interviews with the author and Fredric Lieberman, February 10 and October 21, 1994.

3. The quotations in this paragraph are from Kernis's interviews with the author and with Jenny Raymond, Yale Oral History of American Music Project, August 1, 1998. Quotations in this chapter and elsewhere that are not directly referenced come from the author's interviews with the composer.

4. Lesley Chamberlain, preface to Filippo Tommaso Marinetti, *The Futurist Cookbook*, trans. Suzanne Brill (San Francisco: Bedford Arts, 1989), 7.

5. Filippo Tommaso Marinetti, "Manifesto of Futurist Cooking," *Gazzetta del Popolo* (Turin), December 28, 1930.

6. Filippo Tommaso Marinetti, "Futurist Manifesto," first published in the *Gazzetta dell'Emilia* (Bologna), February 5, 1909. Kernis took his English texts from *The Futurist Cookbook*, trans. Suzanne Brill, preface (unpaginated) and pp. 36, 101, 102, and 105–7.

7. These quotations come from the first movement of Kernis's *Le quattro stagioni dalla cucina futurismo*. For the context in Marinetti's manifesto, see the edition by Suzanne Brill cited in note 6, pp. 36, 101.

8. This assessment by Kernis is found in Carlo Boccadoro, "'Non esiste una ricetta per scrivere': Aaron Jay Kernis," *Musica Coelestis* (Torino: Einaudi, 1999), 110, translated by Giacomo Fiore.

9. *The Complete Poems of Christina Rossetti*, ed. R. W. Crump (Baton Rouge: Louisiana State University Press, 1979), passim. Further quotations from the poem are from this edition.

10. The sources on Rossetti consulted for this discussion include Janet Galligani Casey, "The Potential of Sisterhood: Christina Rossetti's *Goblin Market*," *Victorian Poetry* 29, no. 1 (Spring 1991): 63–78; Ellen Golub, "Untying Goblin Apron Strings: A Psychoanalytic Reading of 'Goblin Market,'" *Literature and Psychology* 25 (1975): 158–65; Kathleen Jones, *Learning Not to Be First: The Life of Christina Rossetti* (Gloucestershire: Windrush, 1991); Katherine Mayberry, *Christina Rossetti and the Poetry of Discovery* (Baton Rouge: Louisiana State University Press, 1989); Dorothy Mermin, "Heroic Sisterhood in 'Goblin Market,'" *Victorian Poetry* 21, no. 2 (Summer 1983): 107–18; Miriam Sagan, "Christina Rossetti's 'Goblin Market' and Feminist Literary Criticism," *Pre-Raphaelite Review* 3 (1980): 66–76; and Sharon Smulders, *Christina Rossetti Revisited* (New York: Twayne, 1996).

11. Aaron Jay Kernis, undated note about *Goblin Market* in his personal archive.

12. Rebecca Miller, pers. comm.

13. Ibid.

14. Alastair Macaulay, "Attitudes in Slow-Motion: Colourful and Decadent," *The Times* (London), January 16, 1995. The form is melodrama in the strict sense of spoken text over music.

15. The Absolut concerto series continued through 1994, when Absolut Vodka switched to Seagram's as its distributor.

16. See, e.g., John Mueller, "The Polls—A Review," *Public Opinion Quarterly* 57 (1993): 80–91. Mueller makes the point that the polls showed different results depending on the way in which the questions were stated. Nevertheless, the results indicate substantial support for military action.

17. For a detailed discussion of this work, see Xi Wang, "An Analysis of the Second Symphony of Aaron Jay Kernis," DMA diss., Cornell University, 2009.

18. Hugh Wolff, interview with the author, July 25, 2012. Wolff notes that for many modern works with loud percussion, players wear special earplugs that reduce decibels without reducing detail.

19. Allan Ulrich, "An Onslaught of Anguish: Symphony Performs Kernis' Potent '91 Work," *San Francisco Chronicle*, March 8, 2002, D17.

20. Pierre Ruhe, "ASO, on War Footing, Captures Fury of Battle," *Atlanta Journal-Constitution*, May 7, 2004.

21. See, e.g., Anthony Tommasini, "Again, a Quest for the Great American Symphony," *New York Times*, August 10, 1997, H27; Joshua Kosman, "Music That Cries Out to Be Heard: Kernis' War Protest Captures a Moment in Time Without Getting Bogged Down in It," *San Francisco Chronicle*, March 3, 2002, Sunday Datebook, 50.

22. This quotation comes from the notes on the title page of the score.

23. The original triumvirate consisted of John Adams, Christopher Hogwood, and Hugh Wolff (see Chapter 4). After two years John Harbison replaced Adams.

24. Wolff conducted the City of Birmingham Symphony Orchestra in this recording, stimulated by Andrew Cornall at Argo Records. See Chapter 6.

25. The award from Meet the Composer was matched by local funding. After the first year, Meet the Composer canceled its support, feeling that Kernis was not engaging in

enough direct outreach (a decision that "created a minor scandal," according to Linda Hoeschler). For the next two years the partner organizations maintained his residency, but Kernis's salary was somewhat reduced. He gave up his apartment in St. Paul and commuted from New York.

26. This information comes from Kernis's letter of agreement for this position and from Andrea Matthews, "Bully Podium: SPCO Composer-in-Residence Aaron Jay Kernis Has Advice for Aspiring Composers and a Warning for Those Who Would Cut Arts Funding," *Minnesota Monthly*, September 1995, 24–25.

27. Information in this paragraph comes from the author's interview with Linda Hoeschler, July 27, 2012.

28. Michael Barone, interview with the author, July 27, 2012.

29. Ibid.

30. American Public Radio, press release, "Saint Paul Sunday Morning to Premiere Aaron Jay Kernis's 'Still Movement with Hymn,' a New Work Commissioned by American Public Radio," December 1, 1993.

31. This quotation is from the notes to the score.

32. Ann McCutchan, *The Muse That Sings: Composers Speak about the Creative Process* (New York: Oxford University Press, 1999), 237.

33. For more details about the commission, see Julie Giacobassi, "Colored Field: Concerto for English Horn," *Double Reed* 19, no. 2 (1996), 69–74.

34. Thanks to David Flachs, director of production at Schirmer, for this information.

35. Quotations in this paragraph from Frank and Pascal come from Joshua Kosman, "String Players' Choice: Why Star Performers Want New Compositions from Aaron Jay Kernis," *Strings* 79 (July 1999): 32–37. For an interview with Isbin about the Double Concerto, see Jim Tosone, "Breaking New Ground: A Conversation with Sharon Isbin," *Guitar Review* 109 (Spring 1997): 12–19.

36. Quotations from Wolff, Alsop, Rushton, and Kernis come from interviews with the author.

Chapter 6. Triumphs and Tribulations

1. This information comes from the award letter of January 20, 1995. Later quotations in the paragraph are taken from the awards ceremony program.

2. Andrew Cornall, interview with the author, July 25, 2012. Argo recordings of Kernis's music include *Symphony in Waves* (New York Chamber Symphony, Gerard Schwarz, conducting) and the first string quartet (Lark Quartet), 1992; *New Era Dance* (Baltimore Symphony, David Zinman, conducting), 1995; *Colored Field* (Julie Giacobassi, English horn, with the San Francisco Symphony, Alasdair Neale, conducting) and *Still Movement with Hymn*, 1996; *Invisible Mosaic III*, *Musica Celestis*, Second Symphony (City of Birmingham Symphony Orchestra, Hugh Wolff, conducting), 1997; and *Air* (Joshua Bell, violin), Double Concerto for guitar and violin (Cho-Liang Lin, violin, Sharon Isbin, guitar), and *Lament and Prayer* (Pamela Frank, violin), 1999.

3. For a database of the festival's programs, see http://cabrillomusic.org/index.php?option=com_festivalhistory (accessed September 27, 2012). The database erroneously lists *Invisible Mosaic II*.

4. Mark Swed, "Danger Ahead! Aaron Jay Kernis, a Profile of a Young Composer on the Fast Track," *NewMuse* (Summer 1995): 2.

5. Jim Tosone, "Aaron Jay Kernis on Concerto for Violin, Guitar and Orchestra," *Guitar Review* 109 (Spring 1997): 20.

6. This quotation comes from the program notes to the Yale performance of 2002.

7. Hugh Wolff, interview with the author, July 25, 2012.

8. Edward Rothstein, "Crying Out to the Heavens with 414 Voices," *New York Times*, May 5, 1995, 13.

9. Johanna Keller, "Well, It All Began When Mahler Got Disney Thinking," *New York Times*, October 3, 1999, "Art and Leisure," 29.

10. Paul Lieberman, "For Eisner's Kingdom, a New World; Disney's Foray into the Realm of Classical Music—the CEO's Idea—Debuts Tonight," *Los Angeles Times*, October 8, 1999, 1.

11. http://www.canalacademie.com/ida3578-Le-Theatre-du-Chatelet-une-tradition-de-l-audace.html (Canal Académie: Magazine francophone des Académies sur Internet, accessed July 10, 2012).

12. Jean-Luc Choplin, interview with the author, August 2, 2012.

13. Aaron Jay Kernis, pers. comm.; Gerard Schwarz, interview with the author, October 10, 2012.

14. As in other chapters, quotations from Kernis come from my interviews or discussions with him unless otherwise noted.

15. Anna Kruger, the original violist, was still with the ensemble for the commission and premiere of the second quartet but left the group in 1998 before the recording was made. (Anna Kruger, telephone interview and email correspondence with the author, August 11 and 14, 2012.) The new personnel consisted of Diane Pascal, Jennifer Orchard, Danielle Farina, and Astrid Schween.

16. *Kaufman Cultural Center News*, Winter 1997, 1.

17. This quotation comes from Kernis's program notes.

18. Quotations in this paragraph come from Xi Wang's interview with Kernis, reproduced in her dissertation ("An Analysis of the Second Symphony of Aaron Jay Kernis," DMA diss., Cornell University, 2009, 49).

19. Choplin interview. The gradual increases in commission fee are documented in a series of preliminary contracts and communications in Kernis's personal archive. A clause in the contract prevents me from disclosing the exact final fee.

20. Allan Kozinn's claim, in a review of the premiere of the Central Park operas, that Kernis had "demanded, received, and rejected" seven versions of the libretto is patently false. Susan Feder, vice president of G. Schirmer (who negotiated Kernis's commissions), corrected the record in a letter to the editor of the *New York Times*. See Allan Kozinn, "Playwrights as Librettists for a Trilogy Set in a Park," *New York Times*, July 26, 1999, E1; Susan Feder, "'Central Park': Counting Librettos," *New York Times* (letter to the editor), August 8, 1999, AR4. See also Anthony Tommasini, "Of Central Park They Sing," *New York Times*, July 18, 1999, AR29. The discussion of this incident is based on documents in Kernis's personal archive, including his letter to McNally, the Schirmer lawyer's letter to Kellogg, and Kellogg's formal statement.

21. Letter, Paul Kellogg to Jac Venza, executive producer of *Great Performances*, WNET, May 5, 1998.

22. Jenny Raymond, interview with Aaron Kernis for the Yale Oral History of American Music Project, August 1, 1998.

23. David Patrick Stearns, "A Premiere Composer," *Philadelphia Inquirer*, November 27, 2001, "Magazine," C1, C8.

24. Karen Campbell, "Harmonic Convergence: Aaron Jay Kernis Connects with the Minnesota Orchestra as His Style Takes an Optimistic Turn," *Symphony Magazine* (November–December 1998): 38–39.

25. James Oestreich, "A Most Audacious Dare Reverberates," *New York Times*, December 17, 2006, A33. The Composer Institute did not take place in 2013 due to an ongoing labor dispute that silenced the Minnesota Orchestra for the entire 2012–13 season.

26. "Roth and Graham Win Arts Pulitzers: Also Honored Was Composer Aaron Jay Kernis." *Philadelphia Inquirer*, April 15, 1998.

27. This quotation comes from a souvenir book issued in conjunction with the Millennium Symphonies performance.

28. Program book for the New York premiere, p. 21.

29. For more information about this project, see Sarah Thomas de Benítez, *What Works in Street Children Programming: The JUCONI Model* (International Youth Foundation), 2001.

30. Jelena Petrovic, "Y2 Composer," *LiveMusic* (Spring 1999): 76.

31. Choplin interview.

32. Johanna Keller, "Well, It All Began When Mahler Got Disney Thinking," *New York Times*, October 3, 1999, "Art and Leisure" 46.

33. Critic Paul Lieberman wrote that Masur wanted to eliminate the boy soprano but that Kernis insisted on retaining him as necessary to prefigure the children's chorus. Kernis does not recall this discussion, however. See Paul Lieberman, "For Eisner's Kingdom, a New World: Disney's Foray into the Realm of Classical Music—the CEO's Idea—Debuts Tonight," *Los Angeles Times*, October 8, 1999, 1.

34. The concerts, held on November 11 and 18, 1999, were called "Messages for the Millennium." The six works were composed by Thomas Adès (England), Hans Werner Henze (Germany), Kaija Saariaho (Finland), Somei Satoh (Japan), John Corigliano (United States), and Giya Kancheli (Republic of Georgia). Thanks to Welz Kauffmann for his insights into the input and efforts of Masur (Welz Kauffman, interview with the author, August 3, 2012).

35. Millennium Symphonies souvenir book.

36. Quotations in this paragraph and the next from Philip Kennicott, "The Night Mahler Met Mickey Mouse," *Washington Post*, October 9, 1999, http://www.highbeam.com/doc/1P2-630025.html; Mark Swed, "Some Beauty in This Strange Beast," *Los Angeles Times*, October 11, 1999, 1; Paul Griffiths, "Disney 'Millennium Symphonies,'" *New York Times*, October11, 1999, E3; and Greg Sandow, "Disney Takes a Cautious Ride Into Classical Music," *Wall Street Journal*, November 1, 1999, A24. Information on the audience response comes from the Choplin and Kauffmann interviews as well as the author's interview with Elizabeth Dworkin (September 25, 2012).

37. David Patrick Stearns, "New York Harvests a Garden of Delights," *USA Today*, October 12, 1999, 5D.

38. Choplin interview.

39. Swed, "Some Beauty" ("effusive lyricism"); Griffiths, "Disney 'Millennium Symphonies'" ("exultant rhythms"). The comments about frequent climaxes and the work being too big to hold together successfully are derived from comments by Sandow, "Disney Takes a Cautious Ride," and Kennicott, "The Night Mahler Met Mickey Mouse."

40. Sandow, "Disney Takes a Cautious Ride." At the time *Garden of Light* was in preparation, Kernis began to feel a need for help with managing his career. He turned to Elizabeth Dworkin, who remains his representative.

41. Michael Anthony, "Kernis' Stirring 'Garden of Light' Premieres in Minneapolis," *Minneapolis Star Tribune*, September 20, 2002.

42. Matt Peiken, "Kernis Succeeds in Giving New Life to Concertos," *St. Paul Pioneer Press*, April 19, 2000, 1E-2E.

43. These directions come from the score.

44. Jane M. Von Bergen, "Kimmel Puts His Money—and Stamp—on Institutions," *Philadelphia Inquirer*, December 14, 2001, A1, A22.

45. From the Grawemeyer Web site http://grawemeyer.org/ (accessed August 15, 2012).

46. Information and quotations in this paragraph come from Marc Satterwhite, email to the author, August 14, 2012.

47. Anthony Tommasini, "In Philadelphia, New Hall's Sound Is in the Ear of the Beholder," *New York Times*, December 17, 2001, E1.

Chapter 7. Family Matters (2002–2009)

1. This information comes from interviews with Aaron Kernis and Evelyne Luest. As in previous chapters, quotations from Kernis come from my interviews or phone conversations with him unless otherwise indicated.

2. Quotations in this paragraph come from "Sonic Mass and Scope," *G. Schirmer News*, February 2004, 1.

3. Quotations in this paragraph come from the program notes to the first performance.

4. This quotation comes from the program notes to the Singapore performance.

5. On this piece, see the article by H. Wiley Hitchcock, "Henry Cowell's Ostinato Pianissimo," *Musical Quarterly* 70 (1984): 23–44.

6. Emanuele Arciuli, email message to the author, May 23, 2013.

7. For information about the concert, see Allan Kozinn, "Many-Faceted Dreams of That Time Round Midnight," *New York Times*, November 21, 2002, E6.

8. This quotation comes from Kernis's program notes.

9. Welz Kauffman, interview with the author, August 3, 2012, and follow-up email messages.

10. http://www.press.uillinois.edu/books/miller/kernis/.

11. On Wise and the Cincinnati temple, see http://www.wisetemple.org/?page=history (accessed August 13, 2012).

12. The first organ in a Reform temple was introduced in 1815 in Berlin. See *Jew-*

ish Encyclopedia, s.v. "Organ," http://www.jewishencyclopedia.com/articles/11761-organ (accessed October 5, 2012).

13. Stephen Mitchell, *A Book of Psalms, Selected and Adapted from the Hebrew* (New York: HarperCollins, 1993).

14. On the tortured history of the auditorium and the political maneuverings that repeatedly blocked its construction, see Leta E. Miller, *Music and Politics in San Francisco: From the 1906 Quake to the Second World War* (Berkeley: University of California Press, 2012), chap. 6. The history of the San Francisco Conservatory is detailed in ibid., chap. 5.

15. It is also possible to perform the work without guitar; Kernis provides additional notes for the pianist in this version. The premiere took place on January 28, 2007.

16. This quotation comes from Kernis's program notes.

17. This information comes from the program notes to the performance at Yale University, November 6, 2009.

18. Ibid.

19. *Selected Poems of Solomon Ibn Gabirol*, trans. Peter Cole (Princeton: Princeton University Press, 2001).

20. Gerard Schwarz, interview with the author, October 10, 2012.

21. In his setting of this text, Kernis omitted one of Ibn Gabirol's four stanzas and one recurrence of the refrain.

22. The Ashamnu text in its present form is already found in the liturgy of Amram Gaon, who died in 875; see Ismar Elbogen, *Jewish Liturgy: A Comprehensive History* (Philadelphia: Jewish Publication Society, 1993), 125. On this prayer see also Macy Nulman, *The Encyclopedia of Jewish Prayer* (Northvale, NJ: Jason Aronson, 1996), 38–39. Thanks to Peter Cole for reading and commenting on this portion of my text.

23. This quotation comes from unpublished comments that Kernis provided to a reporter who was writing about his trumpet concerto. He further revised these comments for the present book. I thank Kernis's agent Elizabeth Dworkin for making these comments available to me.

24. See Anthony Tommasini, "The Tried and the True Step in after the Storm," *New York Times*, December 30, 2010, 3.

25. This quotation is from the program notes.

26. The pitches sounded by the shofar can vary depending on the performer and the instrument. Some shofarot are made from ram's horns; others come from the horns of other animals. Particularly popular today are Yemenite kudu horns. The pitches for the tekiah and shevarim blasts are usually close to a fifth but can sometimes be a fourth. The overtones that speak also depend, of course, on the size of the instrument.

27. Schwarz interview.

Chapter 8. Looking to the Future

1. One place this quotation is found is in Kernis's notes for the first string quartet, 1991.

2. Aaron Jay Kernis, "Composer's Voice," a program aired on Minnesota Public Radio, September 6, 1998.

3. Ibid.

4. As in previous chapters, quotations from Kernis come from interviews with him or from email correspondence unless stated otherwise.

5. These works are, in the order listed in the text, *On Distant Shores* (2011), *L'arte della danssar* (2011), *Perpetual Chaconne* (2012), *Pieces of Winter Sky* (2012), and *Dreamsongs* (2013).

6. *Fifteenth-Century Dance and Music: Twelve Transcribed Italian Treatises and Collections in the Tradition of Domenico da Piacenza*, trans. and annot. A. William Smith (Stuyvesant, NY: Pendragon, 1995).

7. "Dorma ador" (2000) is based on a tune in the Portuguese manner created by Janika Vandervelde.

8. The text quoted here is taken from the introductory material published in Kernis's score. The translation is my own.

9. The Italian text as given here is taken from the introductory material in Kernis's score. The translation is my own.

10. James Rushton, interview with the author, July 13, 2012.

11. Philip Collins, "The Future Is Now: Aaron Jay Kernis Works Futurism, Minimalism, Politics, and the Sounds of the Street into His Unpredictable Musical Compositions," *Metro Santa Cruz*, August 10–16, 1995, 9–10.

12. "Composer's Voice," program on Minnesota Public Radio, May 2, 1993.

13. Email message to the author, July 29, 2012.

14. "Aaron Jay Kernis Awarded $100,000 2012 Nemmers Composition Prize," http://www.music.northwestern.edu/about/prizes/nemmers-prize/2012-press-release.html (accessed November 5, 2012).

15. Andrea Matthews, "Bully Podium: SPCO Composer-in-Residence Aaron Jay Kernis Has Advice for Aspiring Composers and a Warning for Those Who Would Cut Arts Funding," *Minnesota Monthly*, September 1995, 24–25.

16. Gerard Schwarz, interview with the author, October 10, 2012.

17. Peter Occhiogrosso, "Dig the New Breed," *Lingo* 4 (1995): 17.

INDEX

Page references in *italics* refer to illustrations or musical examples; those in **bold** to main discussions of topics

LETA E. MILLER is a professor of music at the University of California, Santa Cruz. She is the author of *Music and Politics in San Francisco: From the 1906 Quake to the Second World War*.

AMERICAN

Composers

Lou Harrison
Leta E. Miller and Fredric Lieberman

John Cage
David Nicholls

Dudley Buck
N. Lee Orr

William Grant Still
Catherine Parsons Smith

Rudolf Friml
William Everett

Elliott Carter
James Wierzbicki

Carla Bley
Amy C. Beal

Christian Wolff
Michael Hicks and Christian Asplund

Robert Ashley
Kyle Gann

Alec Wilder
Philip Lambert

Aaron Jay Kernis
Leta E. Miller

The University of Illinois Press
is a founding member of the
Association of American University Presses.

Composed in 9.5/13 Janson Text
with Meta display
by Lisa Connery
at the University of Illinois Press
Manufactured by Sheridan Books, Inc.

University of Illinois Press
1325 South Oak Street
Champaign, IL 61820-6903
www.press.uillinois.edu